A LONG PATH

THE SEARCH FOR A TENNESSEE BICENTENNIAL LANDMARK

A LONG PATH

THE SEARCH FOR A TENNESSEE BICENTENNIAL LANDMARK

KEM G. HINTON

TUCK·HINTON ARCHITECTS

THE STORY OF THE TENNESSEE BICENTENNIAL CAPITOL MALL

FOREWORD BY DENISE SCOTT BROWN & ROBERT VENTURI

HILLSBORO PRESS

Franklin, Tennessee

TENNESSEE HERITAGE LIBRARY
Bicentennial Collection

Printed in the United States of America

01   00   99   98   97   5   4   3   2   1

Library of Congress Catalog Card Number: 97–73253

ISBN: 1–57736–028–1

Cover layout by Bozeman Design. Book design by the author.
Front cover artwork by Margaret Longmire Butler and the author.
Back cover photograph by Michael Lewis.

Published by
HILLSBORO PRESS
an imprint of
PROVIDENCE HOUSE PUBLISHERS
238 Seaboard Lane • Franklin, Tennessee 37067
800-321-5692

Contents

The Search for the American City

Denise Scott Brown and Robert Venturi

In this fascinating account of the design and building of Nashville's Capitol Mall, a key member of the design team documents the search for a fitting commemoration of Tennessee's Bicentennial. The result is a beautiful volume. Unlike today's condensed planning reports or glossy promotions, *A Long Path* harks back to plans published during the City Beautiful Movement for cities such as Chicago and Minneapolis. These illustrated tomes referred to urban antecedents in ancient Egypt and Greece, Georgian London, or the Paris of Haussmann. History was mined as a source for tools to achieve the ambitions of the growing American city.

A Long Path considers historical antecedents too, but now it's America's history. The earlier classical tradition is revisited as well, but through a study of the new republic's borrowing from tradition, particularly from Greek architecture, to express the values of the nascent United States. In search of elements to celebrate in a public landscape, Kem Hinton scans several generations of American history and considers influential aspects of both precolonial America and today's multiple cultures.

The search links Philadelphia to Nashville and Hinton to us. Philadelphia was William Strickland's home base. In Nashville's Capitol and Philadelphia's Second Bank and Merchants' Exchange, he adapted ancient Greek architecture creatively to the purposes and expressive needs of a new country in a new world. These beginnings, whose strength and excitement are sensed even today, form the base upon which the Capitol Mall designers have built.

Philadelphia and Nashville are both laid out on the classic American grid pattern. Their streets define rectangular blocks with little or no hierarchy and end in open space—metaphorically, the frontier—rather than the vistas of palaces and churches of the European city. The expedient grid has its own virtue. Its juxtaposition of unity and variety suggests an opportunity-laden democracy; the equality of locations within it and its adaptability to change have served Nashville and Philadelphia well over two hundred years.

Hinton studied architecture at the University of Pennsylvania before starting his architectural practice in Nashville. Perhaps for this reason, in taking on the daunting task of the Capitol Mall, he has

lovingly embraced the same elements and memories of the American city as we have. Casting a broad net over the social, political, historical, and architectural dimensions of Nashville in the years between statehood and now, he and his team celebrate creeks, railroad trestles, maps, and markets, as well as the fora, fountains, and amphitheaters of historical precedent. These elements, conjoined in the public sphere, communicate with people as they walk. The Mall becomes a speaking landscape, whose words and forms are intended to be as meaningful to today's citizens as were the symbols of Gothic architecture to the religious in the Middle Ages.

While the story is explicitly about Nashville and its Capitol, it could describe many American design odysseys in search of civic architecture over the last two centuries. Designing in and for the American public environment has always been a complex task. The pressures of the political process, group interests, and changing popular tastes have had their effect on the creation of the Mall in Washington, D.C., Central Park in New York City, and more recently, the Vietnam Memorial in Washington, D.C. The lessons of the successful design processes for the

Tennessee State Capitol and its Mall are, first, the importance of energetic and sophisticated public and private support to gain acceptance for the design and provide resources to implement it. Second, good designers are needed who can, as well, understand and operate within the public polity.

The Tennessee Capitol and Mall have had the benefit of more than their share of tenacious benefactors and gifted and wily designers. To see this, we need only look at the strength of what has been built, preserved, enhanced, and passed on to the future. May the Capitol Mall serve Tennessee well and help the Athens of the South be what it can best be in its third century.

And let us honor another hero of this American tale, the American grid city itself—an invention so flexible, so adaptable, that it has survived the impact of train, automobile, interstate, urban renewal, and some generations of misplaced architectural ego—not always well, but well enough to offer opportunity to those, like Hinton, who love it and draw from within it the hope and promise of its future. Long live the grid plan. May it prosper another two hundred years.

CB

TENNESSEE BICENTENNIAL CAPITOL MALL

Forged to honor the Capitol and exalt all that is Tennessee

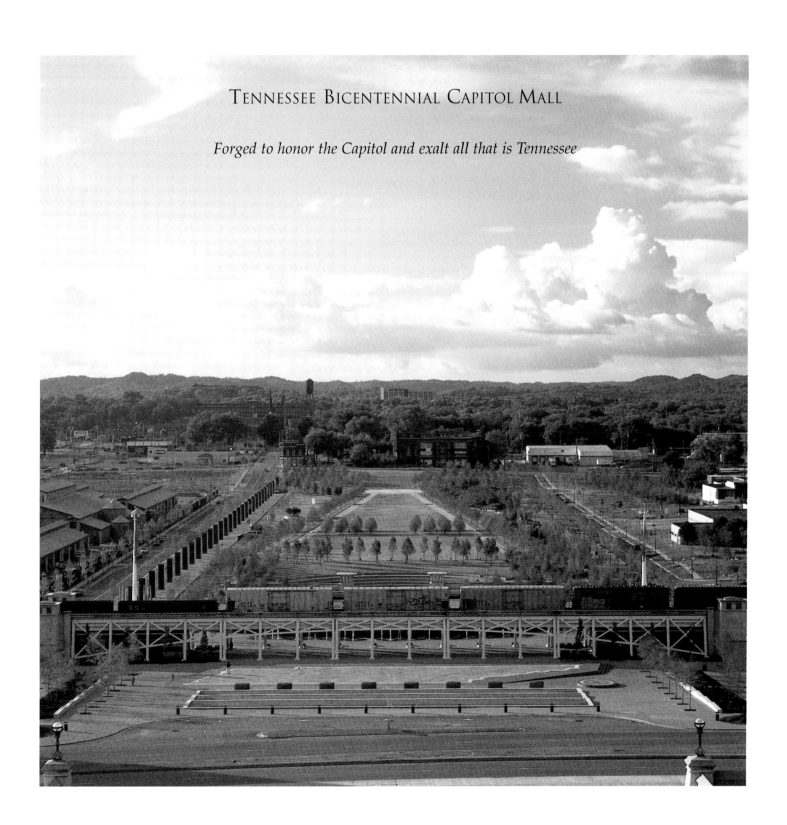

A Centurial Proem

The weary hunter stops at the end of the long path. He has traveled many weeks to reach this place, a destination known for generations to his people. Wiping sweat from his brow, he is immediately captivated by the beauty of the small stream and the open meadow before him. A small herd of bison in the distance shuffles but hardly notices his arrival, and the furry creatures continue to lick the glistening salt oozing from a spring beside the creek. Above to the south is a prominent hill, and although it is late fall, cedar trees covering this landmark provide a rich green to the otherwise gray afternoon. It is his first visit to this sacred place where food and water are plentiful and available for all. He wonders if this is the meadow where his spirit will wander when his time is gone. It is 1696, and he will travel many other trails before his life is through.

A century passes and the spirit of this hunter indeed returns to find a site now occupied by strangers, a different race of pale color from the east. The wildlife and his people have all but vanished, and the smell of civilization now hovers over the once untamed land. The new settlers have erected a spacious wood fort and many log cabins, several near the stream he remembered. The meadow now features crops, and the terrain is changing quickly. This settlement is becoming an established community, a town. The new inhabitants celebrate the news that this land and much more both east and west have become a "state," part of a new nation. The spirit does not understand.

Another century passes, and the spirit again revisits his hunting ground. The lovely creek is gone, the earth leveled. A robust, smoke-filled city inhabits the territory. The once quiet setting is now a bustling neighborhood with carriage paths crisscrossing the landscape. The nearby hill is crowned with a stone temple, a handsome building rising above all others in the vicinity. A loud whistle erupts from a train that rides on tracks lifted by a wooden trestle above the land along the base of the big hill. Baseball is played nearby, directly beside what was once the largest spring in the meadow, and the spirit recognizes the pungent sulphur odor of the spring water. At twilight, he notices dancing reflections on clouds to the west from new electric lights at a festive celebration honoring the state's centennial.

In 1996, the spirit visits yet again. The landscape has changed with even greater force. Automobiles and trucks scurry everywhere at a hectic pace in this foreign land of asphalt and commerce. The stream remains invisible but has been recalled by a winding footpath that leads to a long green park. Here stone features and trees point to the government temple on the nearby hill, the statuesque building now surrounded by many taller structures and its command of the vicinity quite different from when first seen. The spirit longs for the original meadow but knows that time and change offer a different destiny. He notices engravings on stone markers rising from the surface and stops beside one entitled "The First Tennesseans." A curious term. He crouches down and touches water from the small bubbling pool named in honor of a spring from which he drank long ago. The greenery has returned, the creek has been remembered, and the place as once before is again available to all. In this future, the spirit discovers the past.

PREFACE

You can then work from these facts until you learn
everything you wish about the city in the past,
present, and future.
Or else you can say, ". . . now I know this path
is only one of the many that opened before me
on that morning. . . ."

Italo Calvino

For the past five years, I have had the good fortune to participate in the creation of the Tennessee Bicentennial Capitol Mall. The following pages present the story of that endeavor, sharing the intriguing saga of the design of the Mall and the interesting history of the property upon which it stands. This book is a personal perspective with certain limitations of knowledge, understanding, and ability. However, I hope that sparkles of interesting facts and issues will nevertheless fall upon readers as they did upon me during the process of conceiving and designing the new park.

I have always been interested in those ways that the history and meaning of a place might be expressed in new architectonic compositions to derive contemporary forms from an informed observation, acknowledgment, and use of the past. Of particular fascination are those endeavors that seek to uncover hidden or lost associations and characteristics, discovering and exalting the indigenous, the endemic, and the intrinsic. By looking more closely at ourselves, our history, and the places upon which we stand, we will always, I feel, discover valid yet equally fresh relationships for an architecture of today.

Developing a design for the Bicentennial Mall presented a special challenge in this context. The history, significance, and architecture of the State Capitol were readily apparent and available for use in the composition of the new park. Less evident but no less useful was the history of the land of the Lick Branch where the Mall was built. Blanketing the immediacy of place and function was the fascinating opportunity and obligation to create in this park a concise reflection of the polygenetic meanings of an entire state. To bequeath a landscape for future generations, the team of designers simultaneously traveled in many directions and on many inspirational trails, attempting to use the obvious, the forgotten, and the unexpected to help forge the new present.

During the evolution of the Mall, I witnessed every conceivable trait, condition, or situation one might expect in such an undertaking: political leadership, gifted planning, forthright disagreements, odd turf wars, genuine cooperation, contradictory agendas, distinguished research, partisan intrigue, unflappable commitment, thoughtful design, decision overload, coordination nightmares, skillful construction, and, above all, trust. In the early years of the project, I had the honor of explaining the novel concept of a park that would ensure visual prominence of the State Capitol. As the design evolved, I was challenged to defend the expenditures and the forthcoming changes to an area disregarded by many. As the park finally arrived, I have had the pleasure of observing its reception by the citizens of Tennessee and their guests. It has been a most colorful journey.

Entrusted by officials of the Tennessee State Building Commission and joined by talented architects, planners, engineers, landscape architects, historians, consultants, and contractors, the long path has been exciting and rewarding. Without the commitment of these talented and dedicated individuals, the Tennessee Bicentennial Capitol Mall would not have evolved as it has into a meaningful birthday gift for a state two hundred years young. Through the administration of two governors and two general assemblies, a new place for and about the Volunteer State was conceived, built, and dedicated. On behalf of the designers and builders involved in that rare undertaking, I would like to thank the government of the state of Tennessee for its trust in our collective skills and talents.

PROLOGUE

The Classical Code: Maintenance and Revision

Christine Kreyling

I placed a jar in Tennessee,
And round it was, upon a hill.
It made the slovenly wilderness
Surround that hill.

The wilderness rose up to it,
And sprawled around, no longer wild.
The jar was round upon the ground
And tall and of a port in air.

It took dominion everywhere.
The jar was gray and bare.
It did not give of bird or bush,
Like nothing else in Tennessee.

Wallace Stevens, "Anecdote of the Jar," 1923

To understand the Tennessee Bicentennial Capitol Mall, it is best to stand on the crest of Capitol Hill and gaze north. At our backs is William Strickland's temple of Tennessee democracy, the State Capitol. At the Belvedere, a spacious overlook area halfway down the slope, lie the relics of the Capitol's original columns and capitals. Straight ahead is the Mall itself. Taken in conjunction, the Capitol, old columns, and new Mall articulate in three dimensions the past, present, and future of the classical

spirit in Tennessee and in the nation beyond.

That classical spirit is a way of perceiving the world and using the arts to persuade others to see it similarly. Like Wallace Stevens's jar, classicism extends clarity and order, stability and permanence into a wilderness—making the wilderness seem to rise to the human authority rather than engulf it. Strickland crossed the mountains between Philadelphia and Nashville to prove what the country's founding fathers firmly believed: the classical style with its attendant ideology could be infinitely unfolded in place and time.

Strickland's Greek Revival temple to state government stands at the back of every Tennessean, as well as all the Americans who moved through the state on their way south and west. "Like nothing else in Tennessee" or on the frontier beyond, the Capitol is a tribute to Strickland's belief that the Greek temple represented eternal principles of wisdom, strength, and beauty. It was a belief shared by the Tennesseans who had hired the architect to carve from local limestone a symbol of a new golden age for the state's acropolis.

The fragments of columns, capitals, and cornice that lie in a memorial garden on the hill's northern flank convey a different oracular message. Pulled down in 1955 because the Tennessee limestone had weathered poorly, these pieces of our past prophesy the inevitable ruin of all that is man-made, whether on the Attic Peninsula or in Tennessee, in Athens or in Nashville. They lay in a field near the Tennessee State Penitentiary until the Mall's planners brought them to public view. That Tennessee at two hundred has created from these remains a memorial to the Capitol's original stone carvers establishes a classical continuity that reaches beyond the America of the nineteenth century to the ancient ruins of the Aegean.

The Bicentennial Mall expands the classical spirit, not only to the north, but into the state's present and future as well. Tradition requires reinterpretation to remain alive; the Bicentennial Mall takes a tradition and turns it inside out.

The Mall in Washington, D.C., is a lawn stretching from the U.S. Capitol to the Lincoln Memorial. Its perimeter is lined with buildings that form a sculptural edge to the grassy expanse. The lawn and trees offer welcome relief to what would otherwise be an overwhelming display of government as monument.

The Bicentennial Mall could not afford to be a passive open space. An act of piety to Tennessee's classical past, the Mall's large plain of land to the north was the means to preserve the only remaining sight line to Strickland's Capitol, a view now obstructed to the south and east by modern skyscrapers. North of the Capitol, however, there is no Washington Monument, no Smithsonian complex—no reason for people to assemble. Our Mall had to stand as a destination on its own.

The Bicentennial Mall's Tennessee history walk and the topographical representation of the state as it climbs from the Mississippi flood plains to the mountains in the east supply the content that in Washington is housed inside the surrounding buildings. The Bicentennial Mall embodies the classical principles of order, symmetry, and clarity by means of a ground plan that filters these ideals through the practices of Baroque and subsequent Beaux-Arts planning. Within its nineteen-acre rectangle, paths laid out in diagonals of diminishing perspective worthy of a Quattrocento painting lead to a carillon enclosing 280 degrees of a circle that relays the focus back to the Capitol.

Focus on the Capitol is concentrated by a literal revival of an ancient motif. An open-air theater is slung into a partially excavated site that recalls the earthen compass of a Greek theater, with the Capitol rising as backdrop to the south. In ancient Athens, the Theater of Dionysos was comparably situated on the slopes of the Acropolis beneath a colonnaded temple.

As a massive public-works project undertaken for the education and edification of its citizens, the Bicentennial Mall is a revival of the American City Beautiful Movement, which brought classically inspired civic purpose to the planning of our public spaces in the years before World War I. As a memorial to the heritage and physical character of Tennessee, the Mall recalls the Acropolis of Athens, the Forum of Rome, and other ancient sites that used civic monies to sanctify places of collective gathering, commemoration, and ceremony.

Reaching beyond these obvious classical parallels, the Bicentennial Mall heads to the north and into the future, extending Athenian civic ideals into a new version of wilderness. Unlike the times of William Strickland, the wilderness of the late twentieth century is no longer one of trees to be felled for fields to be plowed. Today our American wilderness is a man-made one of strip malls and interstates, of asphalt and automobiles.

The Tennessee Bicentennial Mall carves out of this wasteland a space in which Tennesseans and visitors can pause and reflect on the longevity of civic identity, on democracy's reliance on an educated citizenry, and on the need to carry a vital understanding of the past into the future. Pericles would have been proud. More importantly, every Athenian would have understood.

A LONG PATH

THE SEARCH FOR A TENNESSEE BICENTENNIAL LANDMARK

INTRODUCTION

THE TENNESSEE CENTENNIAL EXPOSITION: A HARD ACT TO FOLLOW

THE TENNESSEE CENTENNIAL EXPOSITION
A HARD ACT TO FOLLOW

When state planning officials began years ago to ponder appropriate ways to recognize and celebrate the upcoming 1996 Tennessee Statehood Bicentennial, they wisely started with a review of what had occurred a century earlier. Tennessee achieved its first one hundred years of statehood in 1896. For many reasons, economical and political, the official celebration did not take place until one year later in Nashville with the Tennessee Centennial and International Exposition of 1897. This fabulous temporary fair opened on May 1, 1897, on the grounds of a former racetrack in the western section of the city near Vanderbilt University. Before the exposition closed just six months later, almost 1.8 million visitors had paraded through the gates, an astonishing attendance especially in the days before transportation was forever changed by the automobile.

The second half of the nineteenth century was the age of expositions, a trend that had prospered in Europe and spread to the United States in 1876 with the national Centennial Exposition in Philadelphia. This movement to display industrial inventions and cultural advancements included many distin-

guished examples, among them the 1889 Universal Exposition in Paris, an event permanently marked by the construction of the originally hated but now beloved Eiffel Tower. Additional precedents in America included expositions in Louisville in 1883, New Orleans in 1885, and, most influentially, the spectacular World Columbian Exposition of 1893 in Chicago. Nashville held a successful exposition in honor of the city's Centennial in 1880, and rival Atlanta sponsored expositions in 1881, 1887, and 1895. Such events were particularly important in the South to showcase the rebirth of a region that had been ravaged by a divisive war only a generation earlier. It was the time of what historian Don Doyle called the "New South dream," where a glorious future of prosperity and racial harmony lay ahead. Tennessee's place in the emerging South needed to be recognized, and the Centennial Exposition firmly accomplished this goal.

The theme of the exposition was "Tennessee! Her Illustrious History, Marvelous Resources, and Wonderful Capabilities." A concerted effort was made to glorify the achievements of industry, commerce, and agriculture while carefully

avoiding emphasis on the Civil War. The view was forward to the new century with exhibits clothed in sparkling neoclassical buildings not unlike those of the great Beaux-Arts "White City" created in Chicago four years earlier. Names of four of the major buildings at the six-month extravaganza—Commerce, Agriculture, Machinery, and Transportation—reflected the progressive, technological emphasis of the exposition. Visitors were shown the promise of the dawn of the twentieth century, the *new* Tennessee, albeit one wrapped in the images of antiquity. Governor Robert Taylor's words at the arrival of President William McKinley to the exposition were indicative of what must have been the emotions of many who came to tour the impressive collection of buildings and exhibits: "Our honored guests shall see today . . . the triumphs of our brain and brawn and the tangible evidences of our activity. And some of them who saw our ruined country thirty years ago will certainly appreciate the fact that we have wrought miracles."

Although the twenty exposition buildings, constructed of wood and stucco, were demolished after the fair, one remained. Nashvillians could not bring themselves to

View of neoclassical exhibition halls   TSLA

Parthenon with tightrope walker "Arion"   TSLA

Advertisement of the exposition   DD

Pallas Athena by Enid Yandell   TSLA

Rialto Bridge and Auditorium building   TSLA

destroy their own representative structure, an exact replica of the Parthenon in Greece. Centerpiece of the exposition, this temporary building remained on the site until a permanent replacement of concrete was built from 1920 to 1931. The Parthenon had served as a fine-arts gallery during the exposition, showcasing a cultural interest to balance the other more pragmatic exhibits, and preserving it signaled a commitment by Nashville, the state, and, by implication, the entire South to the ideals of art. Ann Reynolds, executive director of the Metro Historical Commission, writes: "In contrast to the manufacturing, industrial, and utilitarian character of the North, the South had long seen itself romantically as the heir to the classical legacy of fine arts, even as it sought the wealth of capitalism." The rebuilt Parthenon also ensured physical evidence to fortify the growing image of Nashville as the "Athens of the South." It continues to this day as the architectural emblem of the city and, with the surrounding Centennial Park, serves as an amenity in honor of the successful but forever vanished exposition.

Planning officials responsible for the 1996 Tennessee Bicentennial recognized

The Negro Building   TSLA

Electric lights create a stunning evening display   TSLA

Ribbon cutting for *Tennessee Treasures*   TSM

Bicentennial train *Spirit of Tennessee*   TN200

that the obligations to commemorate a statehood anniversary at the end of the twentieth century were quite different than those of a century earlier. In the present age of overwhelming media coverage, the Internet, and virtual reality, the concept of an exhibition at a single location seemed perhaps inappropriate. In lieu of a centralized exposition, planners instead considered a cross-state approach for the Bicentennial. With the establishment of the Tennessee Bicentennial Commission in 1992, plans would be developed for community-based Bicentennial activities in all ninety-five counties. In addition, over forty special statewide projects would be planned and coordinated by Tennessee 200, the nonprofit organization created to facilitate and manage programs of the 1996 celebration.

Instead of inviting Tennesseans to travel to a central location, planning officials decided that the exhibits would journey to see the citizens. In that vein, two projects would evolve to share the heritage and opportunities of Tennessee. As a prelude to the Bicentennial, the Tennessee State Museum would launch a unique, three-trailer mobile exhibition entitled *Tennessee Treasures*. This traveling museum, featuring

many of the most cherished artifacts from the museum's extensive collection, would begin in Jonesboro, the first town in Tennessee, and journey to every county in the state from September 1993 until December 1994, a cultural-outreach event unprecedented in state history. In 1996, another outreach endeavor would also occur, the *Spirit of Tennessee* Bicentennial train. Developed jointly by the Tennessee State Museum and Tennessee 200, the eight-car, six-hundred-foot-long exhibit train would visit thirty-nine communities across the state in 1996 from July 4 through mid-November. Not unlike the Centennial Exposition, emphasis would be directed to the promises of a new century. The train would also feature information on transportation and trade—the trails, rivers, railroads, highways, interstates, and the information superhighway— elements shaping the commercial and cultural identity and future of the Volunteer State. The major cultural event of 1996 would be the Tennessee Bicentennial Arts and Entertainment Festival, an ambitious multiple-performance extravaganza during May. Although this event would take place in Nashville, it would involve performers and cultural organizations from

across the state to showcase the talents of Tennessee. And on June 1, the actual anniversary date of statehood, a grand one-day party would take place.

Yet it was recognized that the outreach exhibitions and events, similar to the festivities and temporary structures of 1897, would be ephemeral, providing rich memories but leaving no permanent physical gift. The planners for the Bicentennial therefore began to consider an appropriate permanent civic gesture, one that would outlive the numerous cultural events planned for 1996. The desire for a lasting Bicentennial project would eventually focus on the State Capitol. It would be here that the goal for an appropriate gift would ultimately congeal, a way to recognize the future while paying homage to the state's statuesque centerpiece building.

For almost a century after it was built, the Tennessee State Capitol was the tallest and most prominent structure in the city. Yet since the Life & Casualty Tower arrived on the skyline in 1957, Nashville has witnessed the arrival of more skyscrapers, each helping to slowly diminish—if not completely obscure—the presence of the Capitol. This trend had advanced to the point that a clear view of the statehouse

State Capitol by 1990 is surrounded by skyscrapers

was possible from few directions. With the impending arrival of a celebration for the state's two-hundredth birthday, an idea was adopted for an urban park that would establish and preserve a permanent visual corridor to the Capitol. The notion of a significant green space in a historic vicinity of the capital city had been suggested several times in the previous decades, yet now it would receive a once-in-a-century endorsement and therefore tremendous forward inertia. This park would come to be known as the Tennessee Bicentennial Capitol Mall. It would be the location for public events held during the 1996 Tennessee Bicentennial and afterward become a lasting civic gift. Initiated in spirit and planning by the administration of Governor Ned McWherter, authorized by the Tennessee State Building Commission, and endorsed by both the Tennessee Bicentennial Commission and the Tennessee Capitol Commission, the proposed park would be built on relatively flat, previously underdeveloped property extending from the base of Capitol Hill at James Robertson Parkway north to Jefferson Street. The Mall would form a linear connection between the active area around the Capitol and the less-utilized yet convenient and potentially valuable property directly north. Following the model of the well-known National Mall in Washington, D.C., the new park in Nashville would be a flexible environment, providing an appropriate location for statehood anniversary celebrations while improving a once important but now neglected part of Nashville.

It was intended that when the festivities of 1996 were concluded, the Bicentennial Mall would remain as something more than a pretty lawn. Rather, the park would serve as a special permanent destination, a place containing both scenic and educational qualities not duplicated elsewhere in the state nor anywhere in the nation. It would be a spirited outdoor museum that would preserve views of the magnificent Capitol and symbolically convey the accessibility of state government. The park would arrive at a certain time, and it would honor that time, but it would also attempt to eclipse time, simultaneously recognizing the Bicentennial while becoming an enduring amenity bestowed to the future generations of Tennessee.

The ambitious projects outlined in the adopted master plan, including revisions to Capitol Hill, completion of a new Farmers' Market, and construction of the Bicentennial Mall, were completed under the administration of Governor Don Sundquist. Now that the Mall is open, the focus shifts from initial expectations and anxieties to present and future concerns over maintenance, security, and management, and how best this new urban ingredient might influence nearby growth during the next century. Will this special gift from government become an effective catalyst or will the opportunity be misinterpreted and fumbled? New challenges, new prospects, new obligations. From a cherished resource to a dumping ground to now the site of a park of spacious proportions, the historic land of the Lick Branch has come full circle. The dynamics will hopefully continue.

CW

PART ONE

A TENNESSEE ACROPOLIS

EARLY HISTORY OF THE BICENTENNIAL MALL SITE
TEMPLE OF DEMOCRACY
THE GROUNDS OF THE CAPITOL
EVOLUTION OF A CAPITOL AND A CITY
URBAN RENEWAL AND BEYOND

EARLY HISTORY OF THE BICENTENNIAL MALL SITE

To settle in a territory is, in the last analysis, equivalent to consecrating it.

Mircea Eliade

Maps from the early half of the nineteenth century show the property of the young community of Nashville already divided and organized by a grid of streets. These documents also illustrate an unusual area that was essential to the early founding of the city, a part of Nashville now vanished. Flowing across the established street grid in a meandering course just north of the new town is a stream, the Lick Branch. Also known as French Lick Creek, this brook, which had its origins several miles west, followed the area terrain and eventually flowed east into the Cumberland River. Along its banks were several prominent freshwater springs and salt deposits. Because of the abundant water and mineral outcroppings, large herds of wildlife inhabited the vicinity and surrounding region. Bison, deer, turkey, bear, and other game flourished in the area. Buffalo trails to the site from many directions formed paths later used as roads by settlers, a transformation memorialized in 1995 by the topiary wireframe buffalo at Bison Meadows Park on Hillsboro Road nearly seven miles away. Many Indian tribes hunted the land; the Cherokee, Chickasaw, and Shawnee Indian tribes all made use of the area. Because of fighting between the tribes over rights to

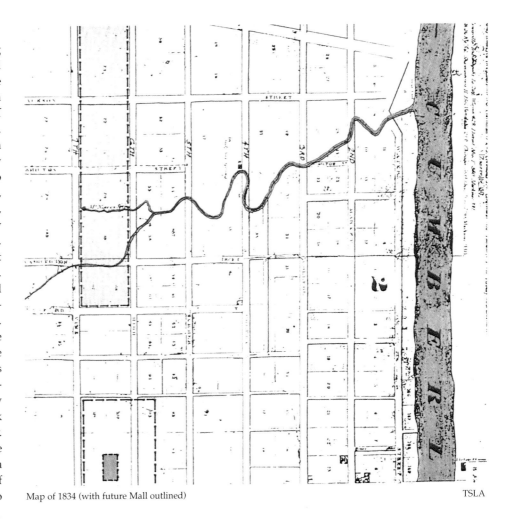

Map of 1834 (with future Mall outlined)   TSLA

Painting of McNairy Spring   TSLA

11

Wildlife in Middle Tennessee ABC

Bison Meadows Park PCD/*TN*

James Robertson ABC

the land, however, it was held by no single group when traders and later settlers arrived from the east. The vicinity around the beautiful stream and nearby areas of cane and open fields composed an authentic "sacred hunting ground." This natural area and the creek within, which were later to be abused and ultimately erased, were crucial in the early settlement of Nashville and primarily responsible for its specific location on the 680-mile-long Cumberland River in Middle Tennessee.

French traders ventured into the area of what is now Middle Tennessee in the very early part of the eighteenth century to establish trading operations with the Indian tribes that inhabited or traveled through the region. With plentiful game, minerals, and fresh water, the creek outlet on the big river was an excellent location to establish a trading operation. Charles Charleville established a fur-trading post in 1714 less than a mile north of the Lick Branch near the banks of the river that the French called "Chauvenon" (a corruption of Shawnee), a waterway later renamed "the Cumberland." Another French trader, Jacques Timothé Boucher de Montbrun, came to the area and settled in 1769 near what was then known, due to his predecessors, as the French Lick.

His fur-trading operation was substantial and lucrative, and he constructed a storage cabin near the creek, a well-known outpost on the frequently traveled river. Later this gutsy trader came to be known as Timothy Demonbreun, and since he remained in the area as a permanent resident for the rest of his days, he is considered Nashville's first nonnative settler.

Having learned of the beautiful land, abundant game, and absence of Indian settlements in this area of the wilderness, a party of settlers on the Watauga River in East Tennessee decided to venture west to establish a new community. James Robertson led the first of two groups three hundred miles overland to the site and arrived in late 1779. He was joined the next spring by a flotilla of settlers who were led by John Donelson. This second party had journeyed one thousand miles down the Tennessee River and up the Cumberland to the location of the French Lick. Here they established a new settlement, Fort Nashborough, in honor of General Francis Nash of North Carolina, and the town had its first true beginnings.

Due to their sizable distance from any recognized government, the settlers quickly established their own civil government

with the signing of the Cumberland Compact on May 13, 1780. When the North Carolina legislature created Davidson County in 1784, the town name was changed to Nashville, the French influence of *ville* replacing the British *borough*. Now an established settlement, newcomers of great skill and ambition came to the area, including Andrew Jackson in 1788 and John Overton in 1789.

The new settlers made quick use of the area around the creek. Crops were planted and harvested in the rich soil. For most of the early history of Nashville, the creek and the surrounding area remained a valuable natural resource. Along the banks of this stream were several large springs, including Sulphur Spring near what is now Fourth Avenue and McNairy Spring near Seventh Avenue, later also known as City Spring. McNairy Spring is depicted in a mid-nineteenth-century painting as an idyllic water source, an amenity cherished by local citizens. The sulphur water that flowed from the springs was valued for its supposed healing properties, and many entrepreneurs would later sell both the water and the salt that was present in the vicinity. This salt and the other mineral deposits in the wilderness of the new country were so important that a

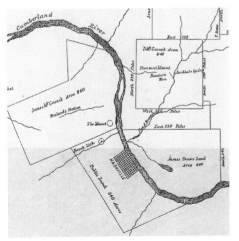

Survey by David McGavock, 1786   TSLA

View of Nashville in 1830   TSLA

North Carolina law required these natural resources to be available to all citizens. The law stipulated that a minimum of 640 acres be provided around an identified mineral source or salt spring, and consequently one of the first maps of the frontier settlement in 1786 indicated that 640 acres north, south, and west of the small riverside community of Nashville, including the creek and its springs, be "public land," available to all. The noble egalitarian attitude toward this part of the city vanished in less than fifty years and would not return for more than two centuries. Overlooking the creek that James Robertson and his settlers cherished was Nashville's first cemetery, and many of its original citizens found final rest in this quiet setting.

Already an important point in the overland travel paths of the region, Nashville continued to prosper with most of its growth centered on the river, the principal transportation artery in the area. The first steamship, the *General Jackson*, arrived in 1816, and thereafter river commerce to Nashville increased dramatically. As the city grew, the original grid of streets expanded with little acknowledgment of the actual topography of the vicinity. Nashville was anything but flat, yet the rigid street grid was superimposed like a branding from above.

The area north of the town remained essentially undeveloped until the mid-1830s when a residential community began to replace the agricultural nature around the Lick Branch. Settled by skilled European immigrants and later renamed Germantown, this community grew quickly in the late 1850s. The neighborhood was peppered with butcher shops, packing houses, and agricultural operations. It was also the home of many talented craftsmen who had brought their abilities and trades from overseas. One of the city's early architectural treasures, the Church of the Assumption, was erected in 1859 by German Catholics from the thriving neighborhood. Lick Branch separated Nashville proper from this and other settlements north. The low-lying area of the creek was prone to frequent flooding when the Cumberland River filled to capacity, and several bridges were eventually erected to span the wide floodplain.

During the 1850s, railroad construction established Nashville as a prominent city in the growing South. The new rail service complemented the already brisk steamship commerce on the Cumberland River and augmented the numerous turnpikes that had been built in the 1830s and 1840s from the growing town to other important destinations in the region. When the railroad came to Nashville from Louisville, a bridge was built across the Cumberland River, and because of the change in elevation and the frequent flooding, the rail line built in the late 1850s was elevated on a wood trestle as it crossed the area between the prominent landform called Cedar Knob and the wide, shallow plain near the creek. The railroad curved around the northern bottom of the dramatic hillside, remaining on the trestle as it turned west and then south to connect with the main train depot near what is now Church Street and the Gulch. Yet even these important infrastructure projects would pale in comparison to the decisive fact that Nashville, in 1843, had advanced beyond being the most vibrant commercial centerpoint of the state to also become the acknowledged permanent headquarters of Tennessee, the state capital city. And with the establishment of Nashville as the capital, another indelible phenomenon would take place with the construction of a spectacular architectural masterpiece, the State Capitol, on Cedar Knob overlooking the Lick Branch.

13

TEMPLE OF DEMOCRACY

*The two great truths in the world are the
Bible and Grecian architecture.*

Nicholas Biddle

The State Capitol is arguably the most cherished single building in Tennessee. Completed prior to the outbreak of the Civil War, this masterpiece of Greek Revival architecture established a new identity for antebellum Tennessee. The Capitol was once the most dominant structure on the skyline and the political and symbolic center of the state, but its visual prominence has been slowly eroded by the continued growth of Nashville. A great struggle achieved this superb structure, and a brief overview reveals the architectural and political significance of not only William Strickland's masterpiece, but also of the entire vicinity surrounding this beloved building.

The Tennessee General Assembly declared Nashville as the Tennessee capital city on October 7, 1843. Previously the location of the government and the meeting place for the legislature had traveled around in a frustrating series of moves from Knoxville to Kingston to Nashville to Murfreesboro and then back to Nashville. After nearly fifty years as a sovereign entity, the state was ready to stop its hopscotch pattern and erect a permanent home—a capitol building. City officials in Nashville helped make the decision easier for their state counterparts by offering Campbell's

Hill, the growing town's highest landform, as the site for a new statehouse. Owned by Judge G. W. Campbell and formerly known as Cedar Knob because of its thick covering of these indigenous trees, the prominent hill rose west of the town square almost two hundred feet above the city and overlooked the picturesque stream immediately north. A commission was appointed by the legislature to oversee the design and construction of a new statehouse. This new Capitol Board of Commissioners was composed of former Governor William Carroll as chairman, John M. Bass, Morgan W. Brown, William Nichol, and Samuel D. Morgan. The commissioners faced one immediate decision: to select an architect capable of undertaking the great challenge of designing a statehouse for the still relatively young state. Holding an architectural design competition was much discussed, but the board instead decided to review plans and choose an architect directly. In 1844, they made a decision to request the prominent architect William Strickland of Philadelphia to come to Nashville and present a concept for their review.

William Strickland was born in November 1788 in Navesink, New Jersey. His family settled in Philadelphia, and his

William Strickland   TSM

father worked on several buildings designed by the famed architect, Benjamin H. Latrobe. Latrobe had designed the Bank of Pennsylvania in 1798, the first Greek Revival building erected in the United States, and he was responsible for rebuilding the U.S. Capitol after the War of 1812. He was an associate of Thomas Jefferson and worked with Jefferson on several of his architectural endeavors. The talent of young William caught the eye of Latrobe, and at age fourteen, Strickland became an apprentice to one of the most gifted architects in the nation. Strickland was an impetuous youngster, and he served Latrobe for only two years. Afterward he

View of Capitol in late 1850s   TSLA

15

Second Bank of the United States

Tower of Independence Hall

The Hermitage in 1831   TSLA

worked at several different professions, including scenery design and engineering, but his fondness and talent for architecture was always apparent. His first important commission came in 1818 when he entered and won a design competition over other distinguished architects, including his mentor Latrobe, for the Second Bank of the United States in Philadelphia. Strickland's winning Greek Revival design for the bank was a Doric temple almost identical to the Parthenon in Athens. His structure still stands in the eastern section of the city near Independence Hall.

At this point in history, Greek Revival was taking firm hold as a prominent style for civic buildings in the new country. The United States had inherited the dream of democracy, and not only did the country intend to use a form of government inspired by the Greeks, but also to use Greek architecture to reinforce a commitment to the spirit of democracy. By using Greek models, architects in the United States were establishing a separate architectural identity, distancing themselves from the influence of Britain. Philadelphia became the center of the Greek Revival movement, and Strickland one of its best advocates. Others adopted the style with great zeal, and before

long, Strickland was in the company of other East Coast architects, including Charles Bulfinch and Robert Mills, who had embraced Greek Revival as the proper style for the new United States. The style later spread to Nashville in 1831, when architect David Morrison gave permanence to the gospel of Greek Revival with his work for Andrew Jackson at The Hermitage. Strickland's 1818 Second Bank in Philadelphia would be somewhat duplicated by Morrison in 1835 for the State of Tennessee Union Bank in Nashville.

Strickland had excelled in other fields. He was an inventive engineer and had traveled to Europe several times, though he never visited Greece. He had been persuaded to follow the Greek Revival style primarily by his early teacher Latrobe, but he was capable of adopting other historic styles depending on the client and circumstances. He had also been influenced, as most architects of the time, by James Stuart and Nicholas Revett's study of Greek temples and monuments published in 1762 entitled *Antiquities of Athens*. With the success of the Second Bank, Strickland's reputation was secured as one of the most capable Grecophiles of his day. Due to his engineering expertise, he was called upon

in 1828 to design and engineer the reconstruction of the tower above Independence Hall, a confirmation of his diverse skills. He was also well-known in Philadelphia society and helped entertain Lafayette during his celebrated visit of 1825.

Strickland's most inventive architectural achievement was the Philadelphia Merchants' Exchange, a commercial building designed in 1832 for an unusual corner site near the Second Bank. Here Strickland introduced a composition never before used, placing one Greek structure atop another. Above a building that featured a beautiful semicircular portico of Corinthian columns against the odd street corner, Strickland placed a tall slender tower, an oversized copy of a previously insignificant Greek structure, the Choragic Monument of Lysicrates. The idea was brilliant, a tour de force of Greek Revival architecture. Thomas Jefferson had suggested a similar design concept to Robert Mills, one of the architects of the U.S. Capitol and designer of the Washington Monument. But Strickland was the first to use it. Towers had never been used in Greek architecture, but domes, towers, and cupolas were all used in Georgian architecture, and the use of

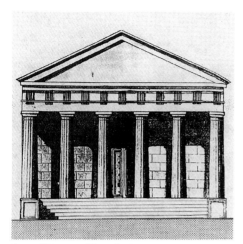

State of Tennessee Union Bank, 1835   TSLA

Merchants' Exchange   DJ

Robert Mills's Washington Monument, 1836   KWC

these vertical forms helped make a city skyline more interesting while calling attention to individual buildings. The big Greek building with the little Greek monument on top was a hit, and it elevated Strickland to new prominence. Not only could he accurately replicate the glory of Greece, but more importantly, he could transcend it, providing a definitive American interpretation of the Greek Revival. Like the Constitution of the United States, Strickland's work was an inventive enhancement of Greek ideals. It was also equally American.

The Merchants' Exchange opened in March 1834. It was one of Strickland's favorite buildings, and his office was located there until he left Philadelphia. Important commissions continued to flow to this popular individual, and his fame and wealth continued to grow. He was called upon in 1837 to design a new replacement sarcophagus for George Washington, clear evidence of his stature among other well-known architects of the day. He also dabbled in civil-engineering projects.

But Strickland's fortunes changed. He lost money in several investments, and design commissions in his hometown dried up. Financial panic in 1837 caused uncer-

tainty in the entire Northeast, especially in Philadelphia. Strickland had established friendships in Europe, and the slow arrival of new projects found him visiting England, where he helped edit a book about public architecture in the United States. Commissions were few, and when he returned home, Strickland turned his attention from Philadelphia to Washington. He was already well-known in the nation's capital city, not only for his achievements in Philadelphia, but also for his work as a consultant on the U.S. Capitol Building with Latrobe and later with Charles Bulfinch and Robert Mills. Continuously commuting from Philadelphia, he worked on various projects in Washington from 1842 to 1844.

While in Washington, Strickland received from Nashville the inquiry, authorized on June 16, 1844, regarding his availability to come to the new Tennessee capital city and submit his ideas for a statehouse. Earlier in April of the same year, however, he had received a request to work on the planned renovation and ambitious expansion of the U.S. Capitol, perhaps the most prized of all commissions at that time. His plans for this celebrated endeavor were submitted for review on April 21, 1844. One month later, his alternative scheme for the

Strickland's Washington Monument, 1844   BUL

17

Louisville Jefferson County Courthouse   AAS

Strickland's drawing for Tennessee statehouse   TSLA

First Presbyterian Church of 1851

Washington Monument—which had been originally designed in 1836 by Mills but not yet started—was presented to Congress and seriously considered. Strickland did not respond immediately at the chance to come to Nashville perhaps due to the U.S. Capitol and Washington Monument prospects and other expected commissions evolving at the time. The considerable distance to the wilderness of Tennessee and the small town of Nashville and the strain that such a commitment would make on his family created a very difficult decision. It would be a great challenge to leave the comfort and sophistication of the Northeast and move to a city where his reputation as an accomplished architect was known only to a few. Strickland's plans for the U.S. Capitol and Washington Monument were not accepted. Ironically, one of Strickland's pupils, Thomas Ustick Walter, would later receive the cherished U.S. Capitol commission to enlarge the building and design the massive white dome that caps it today.

Although Strickland had not accepted the original offer to travel to Tennessee, he later sent a drawing. Pleased with this preliminary sketch, the board wrote him again on April 2, 1845. Their determination to confirm his services had also been the result of reviewing ideas submitted for the new statehouse by other individuals interested in the prestigious commission, including talented local architect Adolphus Heiman, James H. Dakin of New Orleans, and Gideon Shryock of Louisville. Shryock, a native of Kentucky, had tutored under Strickland in Philadelphia for three years before returning to his home state in 1827. Such was Shryock's admiration for his teacher that he named his firstborn son William Strickland. Shryock had designed the nation's first Greek Revival statehouse, completed in Frankfort in 1830. He had also designed the Louisville Jefferson County Courthouse of 1835, a building illustrated in an 1845 engraving, bearing a striking resemblance to Strickland's design for the Tennessee Capitol. The Louisville architect was so angry with the Tennessee Capitol board's decision not to utilize his services or pay him for his time that he eventually filed a formal protest on May 12, 1846, almost a year after their final choice of his mentor.

Strickland remained the commission's prime choice. The members were most certainly aware of his talent from their visits to Philadelphia and Washington or from the impression his work had on local architect David Morrison and many others, including Shryock. Board members also knew the immense importance of selecting the right person for the task, and Strickland's past accomplishments were sufficient to erase any doubts regarding his ability. This time Strickland accepted the offer, traveled the considerable distance, and arrived in the new capital city on April 29, 1845. Strickland would plan other projects in Nashville, most notably the Egyptian Revival First Presbyterian Church completed in 1851, but the Capitol he was now to design would become the undisputed capstone of his distinguished career.

Strickland visited Campbell's Hill and then quickly prepared a design. Less than one month after his arrival, he presented plans for the building, including specifications and an estimate, to the commission on May 20, 1845. He thought that the building would take about three years to complete and would cost $340,000. If convict laborers were used, as required by the legislature, he estimated that the cost would drop by almost a third. The contract for Strickland's services was signed on June 18, 1845, and after a parade and appropriate Masonic ritual, the cornerstone was laid on Independence Day, 1845. How ironic that the one individual who had completely

Detail of column and entablature   BS

First floor hallway   BS

House of Representatives chamber   BS

revised the national image and reputation of Tennessee, Andrew Jackson, died less than a month before this great statehouse would begin its progression upward.

The Capitol is rectangular in shape, an Ionic temple in plan, measuring 238 feet long, 109 feet wide, and more than 206 feet tall. The building has two main stories, or floors. The first level is the stone base with pronounced horizontal rustication, a floor that contains the governor's office, the original Supreme Court chambers, and offices for the constitutional officers. Above is the second floor, the main level of the structure containing the great halls for the House of Representatives, the Senate, and the State Library. Two levels of window openings appear on the upper facade, but this main level is primarily a gracious open space with a soaring reception hall, one of the greatest indoor spaces in the state. The stone stairway that leads up to this main level is a spectacular master work and offers a sense of dignity and pomp appropriate for both occupants and visitors. A vaulted crypt level beneath raises the entire composition, and a surrounding exterior stone terrace anchors the massive temple to the ground.

The facade features dramatic porticos at each of the four principal facades. The

The Capitol, circa 1859   TSLA

dignified Greek porticos create, with the symmetry of the plan, the distinct impression that the statehouse is available and welcoming in all four directions. These porticos endow the building's classic appearance and stature. The Ionic columns are based on those found at the Erectheum on the Acropolis in Athens and emphasize

the four porticos. Strickland intentionally configured the interior so that the east facade, facing the Cumberland River (and Nashville's visitors arriving by boat), would serve as the main ceremonial entrance. The classic Ionic pediments at the north and south gable ends recall Strickland's earlier work at the Merchants' Exchange. The side

Choragic Monument of Lysicrates   DT

Tower at Merchants' Exchange

Tower at State Capitol

porticos on the east and west sides have flat pediments, but all four facades possess the massive thirty-three-foot-tall Ionic columns and, above the entablature of architrave, unadorned frieze and cornice. From the center of the rectangular temple-like building rises the tower that gives the building its unique appearance and lasting identity. Similar to the Merchants' Exchange, Strickland again employed the compositional technique he had originated thirteen years earlier, that of placing one Greek form atop another. He again used the Choragic Monument of Lysicrates, enlarged even more than the version in Philadelphia.

The Choragic Monument of Lysicrates is a small structure in Athens originally known as the Lantern of Demosthenes and is one of many small monuments erected on the Street of Tripods. Just over six feet in diameter and only thirty-four feet tall, it is composed of a circular form with six engaged Corinthian columns and a radial entablature and is supported by a rusticated stone base, nine feet square. Curving stone-wall panels connect the delicate columns and give the impression of a solid form, although the structure is hollow. The monument, dated 334 B.C., is the first known in which the Corinthian Order was

used externally and as the sole system. The beautiful acanthus leaves of the columns and the delicate acroteria of the cornice made this a favorite of Greek Revivalists. Karl Friedrich von Schinkel in Germany, Shryock in Kentucky, and many others incorporated or reconfigured the elegant monument in their own interpretations. Strickland would use it yet a third time as the tower above his design for Tennessee's Wilson County Courthouse of 1848.

At the Merchants' Exchange, Strickland had used primarily only the upper part of the Choragic Monument, adding slender vertical window openings on the curved wall between the six columns. The windows gave the form transparency, and when illuminated, the tower became a spectacular lantern on the skyline of Philadelphia. In a large wood model of the Nashville version prepared by Strickland to show to the commissioners, he proposed to add a tall rusticated base proportionally larger than the model of antiquity to support the round upper part of the monument. A revision of some consequence occurred before the eighty-foot tower was actually built. Eight columns, not six, were used, perhaps to correspond with the large four-sided, temple-like building beneath. Instead of

Model of tower   TSM

windows between each of the eight columns, only four are provided, and the remaining four are implied only as depressions in the curved stone face. Further reinforcing the four principal axes of the design, these depressions reduce the effect of an open lantern yet provide more solidity

West facade

BS

The Acropolis in Athens

to the form. How ironic that from all available Greek models, Strickland would choose this monument to tower above his masterpiece that continues to grace the downtown profile of Music City, a city now known worldwide for its music traditions. The ancient Choragic Monument honored Lysicrates, a great choral leader. The tower above the Tennessee State Capitol, a beacon on the skyline of Nashville for nearly a century and a half, is a monument to *music!*

During construction, which involved not only convict but also slave labor, as many as 233 individuals worked on the project at the same time. Though first used by the legislature on October 3, 1853, the building proper, including the tower, was not completed until 1855. Final work, including the stone terraces, would not be finished until four years later.

Strickland and commission board members quarreled throughout the project, and there was continuous criticism of the slow pace of the work. Strickland complained about the ineptitude of unskilled labor and legislative funding delays. The stress on the architect and his family was immense. Strickland died unexpectedly on April 7, 1854, at the City Hotel, where he had lived with his family in somewhat temporary

conditions. As he had requested, Strickland was buried in a tomb on the northeast corner of the building. Having been involved in the project for several years, Strickland's oldest son, Francis, succeeded his father to supervise completion of the building. Francis was dismissed by Commission Chairman Samuel D. Morgan in May of 1857. In 1858, Harvey M. Akeroyd was hired and remained in a position of authority until the building was finished. The last stone on the terraces was laid on Saturday, March 19, 1859. The total cost of the building had almost quadrupled from the original estimate.

When the Capitol was finally completed, it was a spectacular success. It was the largest and tallest building in the state, and with the exception of minor criticisms about the acoustic qualities of some of the larger chambers, the building was hailed as a masterpiece throughout the nation. It transformed the image of both city and state. Nashville was already known as the "Athens of the South," and now a great temple of government was perched above the city to confirm the reputation. The comparison to the ancient mentor was complete.

Of the commission members, only Samuel D. Morgan remained on the board throughout the entire time of the stormy and

controversial construction. Were it not for his tenacity and insistence that the building be completed as originally designed, pressure from skeptics and disgruntled legislators might have caused the building to be altered or abandoned. On Christmas Eve 1881, eighteen months after his death, the remains of this determined individual were buried in the southeast corner of the Capitol, on the other side of the building from the tomb of the talented designer whose statehouse Morgan had guided to completion.

Unfortunately, before the turn of the century, the Capitol building showed signs of severe deterioration, and stone replacement appeared inevitable. The building had been built of fossilized Bigby limestone, quarried less than a mile west of the Capitol from a site selected prior to Strickland's arrival from Philadelphia. Although Strickland and the commission members were convinced that the limestone would create a beautiful temple of enduring quality and permanence, this material and the manner by which it was installed proved to have significantly less durability than anticipated, and it weathered poorly. Not until the statehouse was a full century old would it receive the attention and caring restoration that it deserved.

The Grounds of the Capitol

It has been an effort to preserve the State Capitol free from injury . . .
It is again in the hands of the state, and no effort should be spared
to preserve its beauties.

Joseph S. Fowler, State Comptroller, 1865

As the Capitol neared completion in the early 1850s and its astonishing form continued to rise, the commission and state-government officials wrestled with the question of what to do with the property surrounding their beautiful new achievement. After the long years of construction, the site was a wreck. According to an early description by one of the commissioners, R. J. Meigs, writing for the *Nashville City Directory*, "The grounds, which are unenclosed, are in a most chaotic state, a mere mass of huge broken rocks, together with various dilapidated outhouses, altogether a disgrace to the state and city." In 1857, the state purchased the remaining land on the hilltop, the northeast corner of Campbell's Hill, which had been the site of the small Holy Rosary Cathedral. The state now possessed a full rectangular plot of land, a summit around the majestic new temple of Tennessee government. In the spring of 1860, the commission hired J. P. Hayden, a local civil engineer, to perform a survey and determine appropriate ways to stabilize the prominent yet messy hillside parcel. Hayden developed a plan that included a proposal to surround the property with a wall-like stone fence. The plans were further enhanced when the commission

View of Market Street from College Hill   TSM

View of Capitol, circa 1864   USNA

Fort Andrew Johnson   TSLA

Andrew Johnson   ABC

Cannons on east terrace of statehouse   TSLA

next hired prominent Nashville landscape gardener William Pritchard to design a scheme for the full development of the grounds. Pritchard's ideas were controversial and included the use of cedar trees. The species was indigenous to the site, and Pritchard expected they would again prosper in the rocky soil. Although heated debate arose regarding the layout, his plans were accepted by October 1860.

Little was immediately accomplished, perhaps due to the strenuous political events of the day. The Civil War erupted in April of 1861, and for several months, citizens of Nashville waited to see if the war would be finished quickly as some had predicted. Such optimism quickly dissolved, and on February 16, 1862, much of Nashville's population vacated the city in mass panic, fearful of an invading Union army that was descending in haste to capture the city. The Union troops arrived on February 25 and seized control of the undefended city, the first Confederate state capital to fall. Thousands of Union soldiers immediately poured into town. When Nashville was captured—or liberated, depending on one's political persuasion—Nashville resident and Union-loyalist Captain William Driver retrieved his beloved ship flag from hiding,

hustled from his house on what is now Fifth Avenue South at Peabody Street to the Capitol, and watched as the giant seventeen-foot-long "Old Glory" was hoisted up the flagpole above the main east entrance portico. This historic flag, flown all over the world before its trip up this inland mast, is now displayed in the Smithsonian's National Museum of American History.

Just a few days after the Union troops arrived, former Governor Andrew Johnson was appointed military governor of Tennessee. Since Nashville was located on a navigable riverway, was the junction of many major roads, and was served by five railroads, it was obviously important for the Union to maintain control over the city. Working with Fort Negley directly south, the lofty location of the new statehouse provided an ideal watchtower for Johnson and his Union forces, and the Capitol building served as his headquarters until the end of the war.

"Fort Andrew Johnson" became the local term for the Capitol, an unflattering nickname given in reprisal of the military governor who was hated by loyalists of the Confederacy. From a strategic standpoint, the name was well deserved, for the small amount of landscaping that had been

installed was quickly removed for clear views in all directions from the elevated building. Soldiers camped around the statehouse, several of them writing home to tell of the majestic building. A cedar stockade was built across the stone terraces, and heavy guns and other fortifications were added in anticipation of an attempt by the Confederacy to recapture the city. The concern was valid, for Nashville represented a tactical target of great importance, and the Capitol itself had become a political prize.

The Tennessee Capitol was featured on the twenty-dollar bill of the new Confederate currency. An engraving of the statehouse on the currency confirmed the structure's status as one of the key accomplishments of the southern states—one of only three buildings featured on southern money. Nashville had lost to Richmond as the capital of the Confederacy, but the powerful image of this magnificent Tennessee building was unquestionable. The Capitol continued to appear on the twenty-dollar note through 1864, even though it remained under Union occupancy from 1862 until the war ended. It was the power of the image, the power of the achievement that remained so valuable and essential for the South.

Photograph by George N. Barnard of Nashville skyline from Fort Negley, 1864 (Capitol at left in the distance)   USMA

Capitol Hill in the late 1870s   TSLA

The statehouse was used as a hospital after the Battle of Stones River in early 1863 and remained as a valuable observation point until Federal occupation of the city ended on July 1, 1865. Because no major battle occurred in the immediate vicinity, the building remained essentially undamaged during the tumultuous years of the divisive conflict.

Five years after the war, the General Assembly in 1870 finally authorized improvements to the Capitol grounds based on the original plans. The majority of the official documents had been misplaced or destroyed during the war, and a new landscape architect, John Bogart of New York, was hired. Bogart had worked with nationally recognized landscape architects Frederick Law Olmsted and Calvert Vaux, and he was a knowledgeable practitioner of the picturesque landscape design popular in the second half of the nineteenth century. Bogart's plans apparently pleased the commissioners, and they were satisfied that he had tried to follow the basics of the original scheme as recalled through the memories of Chairman Morgan, Pritchard, and others.

The property around the Capitol was to be a pleasure ground for the public, a civic gift, created by an abundant number of gracefully ascending and descending walkways proposed by Bogart. His scheme, completed in 1877, featured a winding carriage route, many meandering paths and stairs, and a small pond on the north side. The main entrance by carriage was from Park Place, the beautiful residential street that stretched only one block along the east side of the Capitol property. A narrow carriage road wound around the north and west sides to arrive at the top. As intended by Strickland, guests would arrive and enter through the east entrance. Elaborate gatepost entrances for pedestrians were created at the four corners of the massive stone fence, the main one at the southeast side at the corner of Park Place and Cedar Street (now Charlotte Avenue). The nine-acre parcel was transformed into a beautiful strolling park and garden for Tennesseans. Major W. F. Foster, an engineer and the ancestor of several generations of Nashville builders, was in charge of construction. As the project was built and finished, original participant William Pritchard remained in charge of the grounds.

The main revision to Capitol Hill during the last two decades of the nineteenth century was construction of a large terrace on the eastern slope. This flat area overlooking the city became the location of the famous equestrian statue of

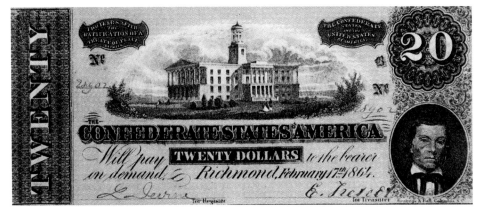

Confederate twenty dollar note

Andrew Jackson, one of three by Clark Mills (the others at prominent locations in Washington, D.C., and New Orleans). The statue was unveiled as part of Nashville's Centennial Celebration on May 20, 1880. The beautiful terrace was thereafter named Jackson Plaza, and articulate Victorian townhomes were built surrounding the property on Park Place, Gay Street, and Seventh Avenue. Little changed on the lovely grounds until the arrival of a new century, with the only significant revision being the replacement of most of the original cedars with deciduous shade trees.

Mills's statue of Andrew Jackson

Dedication of Jackson statue on May 20, 1880   TSLA

27

Evolution of a Capitol and a City

*Those who look down from the heights conjecture about what is happening
in the city; they wonder if it would be pleasant or unpleasant to be in
[the city] that evening. Not that they have any intention of going there,
but [the city] is a magnet for the eyes and thoughts of those who stay above.*

Italo Calvino

The arrival of the twentieth century
would continue the trend of incremental
yet continuous change to the area around
the Tennessee Capitol. In 1902, a new
pedestrian approach was created directly
south of the statehouse possessing an elaborate fountain and a series of winding
stone steps that connected directly to
Charlotte Avenue. A statue of Civil War
hero Sam Davis by Julian Zolnay was
placed near the southwest entrance in 1909.
At the time, state government was
growing and the Capitol building was
becoming very crowded. The neighborhood surrounding the Capitol grounds was
also changing. Various ethnic minorities
settled between the statehouse and the railroad tracks below, including descendants
of slaves, Russian and Hungarian Jews,
and even a Japanese family. The culturally
diverse neighborhood was unique to the
city, but one not without turmoil or
strife. Many of these poorer minorities also
occupied older residential structures,
several of which had been changed into
rental boarding houses. The adjacency of
these residents very close to the white-
dominated inhabitants of the Capitol was
tenuous at best. Many of the lovely nineteenth-century townhomes that had once

View of Jackson Plaza, circa 1930

TSLA

Aerial view on May 21, 1940   WW/TSLA

29

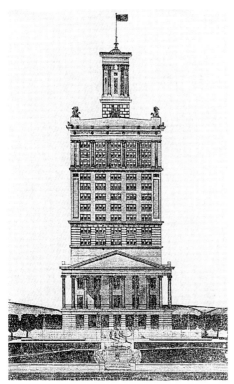

Frahn's 1917 expansion proposal   TSLA

graced the peripheral streets fell into disre-
pair, and original residents fled, perhaps
one of the first examples in Nashville of
"white flight." The run-down vicinity was
slowly becoming a civic embarrassment.

Rescuers appeared in the form of two
determined women interested in the civic
good. In 1916, Elizabeth A. Eakin and
Margaret J. Weakley, both members of
Nashville's Centennial Club, formed the
Tennessee Capitol Association, a non-
partisan association of concerned women
who urged the state to acquire property
and preserve all of the land around the
statehouse. Their mission statement
explained that they were determined to
preserve "the natural beauty upon the hill
from which the Capitol would command
majestic sketches of vistas on every side"
and to protect it from "the encroachment of
anything that would tend to lower the
dignity of the building, and therefore the
state." Through the strenuous efforts of
Eakin, Weakley, and their newly formed
association, the area immediately around
the Capitol was to be preserved as the
location of any future expansion of state
offices. Local architect Russell Hart, fresh
from education in New York and Paris and
impressed with the vast classical beauty of
those cities, offered to help. He developed
conceptual plans that included a broad
plaza on the south side of the Capitol and
an open-air Greek amphitheater on the
north slope of Capitol Hill.

In 1916, the YMCA announced plans to
erect a boarding house at the corner of Park
Place and Charlotte Avenue, and an out-of-
town publishing company announced
plans to build a large office building at the
corner of Seventh and Charlotte. Eakin
advanced the funds necessary to prevent
both sales and retain the sites until each
could be sold to the state. She and Weakley
continued to press officials to purchase
other land around the Capitol building,
and the prime sites at both the east- and
west-corner gates of the grounds were
finally acquired by the government.

The growth of state government and
the crowded conditions in the once
spacious Capitol caused several individuals and legislators to seriously consider
an expansion or an annex to the statehouse. Early in 1917, local architect Harry
Frahn suggested an unbelievable Capitol
expansion, a ten-story addition directly
atop the historic building. Though little
thought was given to his scheme, it reinforced the pressing need to find additional
room for state-government offices. The
situation was becoming intolerable, but
World War I held the state's attention, and
no decisive action took place until the
conflict overseas ended.

Electric lights transform statehouse   TSLA

Capitol park from northeast   TSLA

Capitol Hill, 1940   WW

In 1919 the General Assembly authorized the construction of Victory Square (also known as War Memorial Park), a landscaped plaza in honor of the veterans of the Great War. In addition, the War Memorial Building was erected in 1925, the first new state building containing not only offices, but a much-needed auditorium. This neoclassical building, designed by Edward Dougherty, forever changed the orientation of the civic entrance to the Capitol. Although the east side of the statehouse had originally served as the ceremonial entrance, with its carriage entry drive on Park Place and its broadside facing the Cumberland River, access was more direct and less arduous on the south side, a condition already confirmed by the 1902 fountain and steps. With the construction of the War Memorial Building and the adjacent park, the grand vision of Russell Hart to extend the Capitol grounds directly south was finally realized, though in more modest proportions. Fortunately, the location of the new War Memorial Building maintained an open view of the Capitol from the south. Plans developed by architect Hart and endorsed by Eakin had also alluded to a grand promenade that might be added in the future to continue south for a considerable distance,

perhaps to Fort Negley. This concept, not unlike the great parks and boulevards Hart had seen and studied in Europe, was one of the earliest mentions of an urban plan that

would direct an entire section of the city to the Capitol. Eighty years would pass before an interpretation of this bold idea for a linear promenade would again be considered.

War Memorial Building and Victory Square   TSLA

31

Looking north from Capitol, 1864   TSLA

While downtown Nashville grew from the time of the Civil War into the early part of the twentieth century, the area in and around the once cherished Lick Branch would forever change. The prosperity of Nashville after the war created increasing demands on the picturesque area of the small stream, its resources now being tested to their limits. Horsedrawn streetcar services provided local public transportation and connected the city with the expanding residential areas north of the brook in 1866, but by this time, the once beautiful brook was becoming an eyesore—filled with garbage and raw sewage that flowed slowly into the Cumberland River. The original city cemetery had already been moved away from this area to its present location near Rutledge Hill, and the vicinity was now becoming known as Sulphur Spring Bottoms, an uncomplimentary description for this low-lying, flood-prone area.

Nashville was without an effective sewer system, and several cholera epidemics were blamed on the lack of adequate sanitary facilities. An open sewer, Lick Branch was a prime example of a sani-

The creek is buried in 1892   TSLA

tation problem. The worst cholera epidemic in 1873 killed more than a thousand people, causing a public outcry for prevention of future sanitation-related disasters. In 1889, the stream was channelized, making it more straight and deep. But the sanitation problem became so severe that in 1892 the creek was again channelized. This time the stream was buried in a massive eighteen-foot diameter brick sewer twenty-five feet below the ground. The Lick Branch completely vanished from sight. The trench excavated for the sewer was quickly filled with cinders, rubble, and dirt. Now that the path and sloped banks of the creek were gone, additional fill material was brought into the area to further raise the surrounding grade above hazardous flood level and to make it flat and more useful. Archaeological studies of the site in 1994

Drawing of Nashville published in 1888 (Lick Branch outlined)   NPL

and 1995 discovered that this entire area remained popular for waste disposal, especially from local hotels and restaurants, with broken plates and bottles abundant in the research digs.

The vicinity directly above the now vanished stream never became popular for residential use, but it was nevertheless valuable for many other purposes with its revised flat terrain and proximity to downtown, the river, and the railroad. Fresh mineral water was still available at area springs, especially from wells at Sulphur Spring and also from Morgan Park Spring several blocks north. Entrepreneurs erected one- and two-level warehouses and small manufacturing facilities, and the area became a popular location for industries serving the city, including laundries, coal yards, salt works, ammunitions, manufacturing facilities, gas works, stock yards, food supplies, feed companies, and others. What was once ideal for grazing wildlife proved a tad messy for the civilized folks of the city but fine for the necessities of an emerging metropolitan culture.

Nashville Gas Company, founded in 1851, operated several gas-production facilities on Second Avenue and built several large above-ground tanks in the area. Noel

Skyline view looking northwest (trestle and flooded creek in the distance), circa 1900   TSLA

and Company Ice Manufacturers, founded in 1914, was built on Tenth Avenue. The Nashville Union Stock Yards, a thriving consolidation by entrepreneur James E. Caldwell of several smaller stockyards, opened in 1919 on Second Avenue directly above the Lick Branch sewer line. Other similar facilities were located in the vicinity, including feed stores, slaughterhouses, packing plants, fertilizer manufacturers, and produce operations—a continuation of the area uses that had begun before the Civil War. In addition, warehousing and light industries prospered in the area since the railroad could offer direct spurs off the active main line.

33

Lick Branch floods in 1912   TSLA

Germantown had prospered as one of the better residential neighborhoods in the city, but after World War I, anti-German sentiments bruised this community, and many original landowners moved away. The pressure of economic and social change continued into the mid-part of the twentieth century, yet the general use of property in this area remained residential.

Of all the many businesses and activities in this part of Nashville, perhaps the one most remembered is the famous baseball park known as Sulphur Dell. When Union soldiers came to Nashville in 1862, they brought a new pastime to the area: baseball. The game was played by these temporary residents in an open field just north of Sulphur Spring. Home plate faced southwest to the beautiful new Capitol in the distance. After the war, baseball increased in popularity in Nashville. The first professional baseball team was established at the ballpark in 1885, and by the turn of the century, the game had become a favorite sport in the city. Nashville's team, the Volunteers, played to sellout crowds for many years. The only perfect no-hit game was played just over eighty years ago on July 11, 1916, when the Vols beat rival Chattanooga, 2-0. In 1927, a new grandstand

Sulphur Dell Ballpark, circa 1930   TSLA

was erected to accommodate the growing popularity. The orientation was flipped, with home plate now facing northeast. The grandstand was built just above Sulphur Spring and severely affected the flow of water. Because the ballpark was crunched between Jackson Street and Fourth and Fifth Avenues, it had a short right-field fence, a curse for pitchers but a delight for hitters. The field was below street level, and the outfield was twenty-five feet higher than home plate. Grantland Rice had tagged the field "Sulphur Dell" in 1909, but disgruntled visiting teams called it "Suffer Hell." Worried over possible contamination from the adjacent underground Lick Branch sewer, city health officials eventually closed the spring at the edge of the ballpark to the public. When the team played its last game on September 8, 1963, baseball had been played at this site longer than any other place in the nation. Later, the grandstands were demolished and the site was flattened to become a parking lot.

Boys enjoy last game at Sulphur Dell on September 8, 1963   JE/TN

URBAN RENEWAL AND BEYOND

Nature is often hidden; sometimes overcome;
seldom extinguished.

Francis Bacon

Construction of the War Memorial Building with its abundant office space relieved the pressure on the Capitol, but it was only a matter of time before additional government office space would again be required. The result of Eakin and Weakley's Tennessee Capitol Association was the preservation of properties later to be used for the Tennessee Supreme Court Building of 1936 designed by Marr & Holman and the State Office Building of 1940 designed by Emmons Woolwine and later renamed in honor of the first governor, John Sevier. Although the state had erected these two buildings and continued to use the adjacent residences for office space, the vicinity around the Capitol continued to decline. The area directly northwest had become so detestable that it was known as "Hell's Half Acre," an area of prostitution and gambling that annoyed both city and state officials. It was not until the end of the Second World War, however, that substantial federal funds would join with local and state efforts to allow the removal of the unsightly clutter around the Capitol. This time forces from the North showed up not as soldiers but as dollars.

Just one week after the U.S. Congress passed the Congressional Housing Act of

1949, Nashville applied for and became the first city in the nation to receive federal funds for a brand new, post–World War II concept called urban renewal. The generous dollars from Washington allowed implementation of ambitious plans that had already been developed by the Nashville Housing Authority and the City Planning Commission to transform the northern side of the Capitol grounds and an entire section of Nashville bordered by the railroad embankment directly north. Designed by the firm Clarke, Rapuano and Holleran of New York, this mammoth undertaking was the first large-scale urban-renewal project in the United States.

The impact of the urban-renewal project on Nashville was incredible. The concept of urban renewal was the planning equivalent of the atomic weapon. It was big and simple: the removal of anything seedy with one giant sweep of a bulldozer. The project had a modernist approach with the eradication of almost all historic buildings in the process, with older structures considered, rightly in some instances, to be dirty, outdated, and valueless. But making it happen was anything but simple and required enormous cooperation between state and city officials and their different

Hell's Half Acre   TSLA

agendas. Governor Gordon Browning and Mayor Tom Cummings, their advisors, and constituents all struggled with the process, the politics, and the possibilities. Their successors dealt with the challenges of final implementation.

The plan required the demolition of hundreds of shacks, outdoor privies, and the dilapidated nineteenth-century town houses that surrounded the Capitol grounds. More than 600 families and 140 businesses were relocated, but not everyone agreed to leave. Lawsuits were

Skyline view, 1953 CW

Targets of demolition   MDHA

filed by many companies and minority churches. In the end, the hill and nearby area were swept clean, a dramatic accomplishment given the numerous political and construction obstacles. The result was a fresh new start for the vicinity.

The Capitol Hill redevelopment revolved around one major element, a large new road. The existing rectangular street grid was replaced by a wide radial boulevard. This roadway, later named James Robertson Parkway, addressed the hillside topography of Capitol Hill in grand fashion with a sweeping turnpike that provided easy and convenient vehicular access all the way around the base of the great landform.

Not since the construction of the railroad at the time the Civil War had a transportation medium so closely followed the main topographic feature in this part of the city. The pristine James Robertson Parkway made a gigantic loop connecting Main Street in east Nashville across the Victory Memorial Bridge to Church Street and Eighth Avenue on the west side of downtown. New road lanes were separated by a gracious grass median, rare even today, and motorists could now cruise around the base of the big hill. For most of its path, the road remained at grade level, but at its west side, the parkway plummeted both physically and aesthetically with the construction of elaborate ramps and submerged roadways—features acceptable at the time but now seen for their inhospitable urban-planning liabilities.

The development of James Robertson Parkway was fairly rapid. New buildings arrived over the course of two decades, the first few being on the east end of the parkway close to the Metro Nashville Davidson County Courthouse. Motels were

Changes underway in 1952   TSLA

built on the parkway, including a fresh new Holiday Inn at the corner of Eighth Avenue directly below the Capitol. The largest new facility was the Municipal Auditorium, a domed enclosure designed by the firm of Marr & Holman and completed in 1962, serving the city for more than three decades. Taylor & Crabtree Architects designed the Tennessee Education Association building, a modest yet crisp four-level building finished the same year at the corner of the boulevard and Sixth Avenue. WLAC-Channel Five television

Dedication ceremony, November 6, 1953　　MDHA

Hillside revisions continue　　TSLA

James Robertson Parkway, 1958　　BG/NB

station added an expressive structure by Earl Swensson Associates to the parkway in 1968, and a new facility designed by Quincy Jackson for one of the city's strongest black congregations, First Baptist Church Capitol Hill, arrived in 1971 on the west end where the boulevard split into side connectors and the depressed roadway trough. Nearby, the University of Tennessee erected a large classroom building in the same year. Also designed by Earl Swensson Associates, this exuberant horizontal, concrete composition would later become the downtown campus of Tennessee State University. Most of the buildings on the parkway were isolated structures corresponding to the planning ideals of the time: individual buildings on individuals plots with parking all around.

The arrival of the parkway brought many new businesses to the vicinity, but the railroad berm remained an adjacent impediment to development north. The original wood trestle had been revised during the early part of the century, and instead of the wood timbers being replaced, earth was simply piled beneath the forms—creating perhaps the most dramatic urban barrier in this part of Nashville. Penetrated only by streets that

originally crossed under the trestle tracks, this curving mound of dirt had become an impenetrable edge, a dramatic, lumpy scar across the city. It perplexed both property owners and city and state planners. Property on the south side of the berm was relatively valuable, property on the north side much less so. Being on the wrong side of the tracks held meaning here perhaps like nowhere else.

The major changes to the city were complemented by an unbelievable transformation of the area near the Capitol. A massive parking plateau was created on the north and west sides of Capitol Hill in the early 1950s. This wide parking lot, midway down the hill, required the removal of Gay Street, replaced with a one-way connector that skirted down the now very steep topography to connect to the parkway below. The sections of Seventh and Eighth Avenues down the sloped topography of Capitol Hill were completely removed and transformed into middle- and upper-level loop roads, facilitating increased parking for employees of the state but removing the connections north. The new parking spaces immediately west of the Supreme Court building connected directly into Charlotte Avenue.

State government continued to grow, and the massive, eleven-story Cordell Hull Office Building by Hart and McBryde was begun in 1952 on the east side of Park Place, fortunately leaving an open view of the Capitol's east facade. The same year, the State Library and Archives building by Clinton Parrent was dedicated on the other side of the hill on Seventh Avenue.

As the terrain around the Capitol was transformed, so too was the statehouse, inside and out. The massive urban-renewal work and the changes to Capitol Hill were complemented by long-overdue replacement of the deteriorating limestone on the exterior of the statehouse. The General Assembly appropriated funds in 1953 to begin the slow repair and restoration of the structure. Limestone from Indiana was used in lieu of the original Bigby stone. In addition, the basement crypt level was excavated and transformed from a storage basement into much-needed offices. A few restoration tragedies occurred, most sad being the removal of delicate lampposts at the exterior steps beneath the four porticos. To provide more convenient access for pedestrians and governmental officials, the Motlow Tunnel was excavated in 1958. A boxy, new granite entrance on Charlotte

Capitol restoration underway, April 9, 1957   MDHA

Restoration architect Charles Warterfield Jr.   CW

Opening between Sevier and Hull buildings

Avenue led to elevators installed directly beneath the Capitol structure.

To further accommodate the need for additional automobile parking around the statehouse, a new plateau was created, increasing dramatically the area of pavement and parking adjacent to the stone terraces that surrounded the Greek Revival structure. This plateau required regrading and the installation of a granite wall at the outer edges, expanding the paved area outward from the terraced base of the statehouse. A stone-edged, precipice-like condition resulted all around, and a flat, asphalt park for cars was created within. The original carriage drive off Park Avenue was replaced with a grand stair, and vehicular access to the statehouse was moved to a new radial road that connected to Seventh Avenue. The beautiful gateposts and stone fence on the north side of Capitol Hill were destroyed, and due to the extensive landform transformations, much of the hillside was stripped of the trees that had been planted long ago. The beautiful rectangular park surrounding the statehouse and the once lovely neighborhood nearby were almost completely eviscerated by both the urban-renewal scheme and the changes closer to the Capitol. What

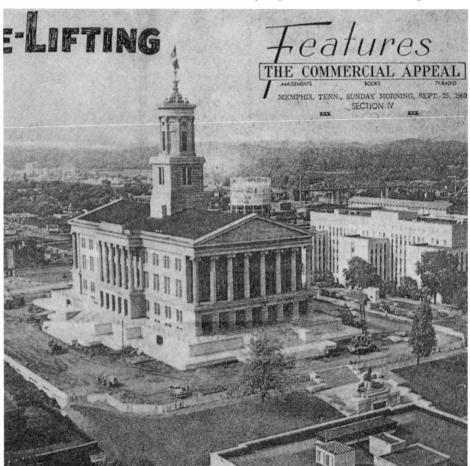
Creation of a new acropolis   CA

Motlow Tunnel entrance

A new Capitol Hill   BG/*NB*

Hillside erosion by the 1980s

little remained was less useful because it was now too steep. Strickland had designed his building to sit nicely on the gentle hill of Cedar Knob. His statehouse now stood on a much more prominent platform. The site was barren, but it was also strong. The thematic connection to Greece continued; the Tennessee temple of democracy now stood on an acropolis.

Instead of moving to a different location, as had been the choice of many other state legislatures across the country, state government remained at the Capitol. This was an important accomplishment, especially given the inclination of the era to demolish or abandon anything historic or old and replace it with a clean new "modern" facility. To oversee future projects involving not only the Capitol and surrounding grounds, but all other state construction endeavors, the Tennessee Building Commission was created in 1955. (Later, the Capitol Commission would be established to protect the integrity of the statehouse and grounds alone.) The mammoth restoration project coordinated by Victor Stromquist with Woolwine, Harwood and Clarke Architects was completed in 1960. A photograph of a Civil Rights march in September 1961 indicates

Civil Rights march, September 1961   HGL/*TN*

the dramatically cleansed hillside while also conveying the preserved visual power of the Capitol as the final destination of any complaint or cause—the summit of state government. Later that same year more than six hundred new trees would be planted on Capitol Hill.

According to *Nashville Banner* columnist and historian Kay Beasley, the massive urban-renewal project had a startling, almost inconceivable impact on Nashville:

The results of the $9.6 million project were staggering: north of Capitol Hill filled and

41

Capitol Towers

Polk tomb

Statue of Alvin C. York

reshaped with mountains of dirt and stone; the broad James Robertson Parkway; twenty-five new structures, including the State Library and Archives, Cordell Hull Building, and Municipal Auditorium; new businesses and vastly increased tax revenues, allowing the city to recover its investment.

The urban-renewal scheme was finished in 1966 when the last parcel was sold to private interests. New buildings were erected under the plan well into the 1970s.

Urban renewal had completely transformed Nashville and the land immediately adjacent to the Capitol building, yet the opportunity to enhance the grounds and create a place inviting and useful for all Tennesseans had been missed. The state now possessed a refurbished Capitol on a dramatic plateau, but massive regrading and removal of existing vegetation and walkways had created a statehouse that was almost completely removed from the average citizen. James Robertson Parkway, once a promising green corridor defining the lower edge of Capitol Hill, also never fully developed to its potential. Instead, trees on the boulevard were only marginally maintained, street lighting was subsequently changed, and the sidewalks

were rarely used, especially on the north and west sections of the radial road. The parkway became simply a rapid way to get from one side of the city to another by car. Were it not for the unfortunate sale of land at the southwest corner of James Robertson Parkway and Fifth Avenue, users and visitors would still have a chance to see the Capitol from this very important street intersection. Unfortunately, a boxy apartment house was built on this spot in 1961, a local example of modernist rhetoric in the form of Capitol Towers Apartments. This wide, lean form was built too close to the boulevard and obscured a prominent view from the busy intersection to the statehouse above on the pronounced hill. Since Fifth Avenue was the easiest way for pedestrians to traverse into and out of downtown, the bulky building blocked the scene from citizens both on foot and in cars.

Regardless of these shortcomings, the historic significance of the Capitol grounds endured. The dramatic statue of Andrew Jackson remained a prized sculptural destination, although rarely visited because of its mid-hill location and the overly steep stairway from Park Place. The tomb of President and Mrs. James K. Polk, designed by Strickland and moved to the Capitol

grounds in 1891, was now hard to find in a secluded location on the northeast corner. The pathway system that had originally connected the corner stone gates with the statehouse had been removed. Few sidewalks remained, not even one to Polk's tomb. Yet organizations still desired to give significance to important events by erecting markers and monuments in a haphazard manner through the latter half of the twentieth century on the almost inaccessible grounds of the Capitol. A statue of World War I hero Alvin C. York was unveiled in 1968 above the once dramatic southeast entrance to the grounds. Other less visible ingredients were also added, including a time capsule by Governor Ray Blanton, a tree for Martin Luther King Jr., a plaque for the Daughters of the Confederacy, six cedar trees to recognize the Holocaust, and a replica of the Liberty Bell, many in areas difficult or impossible to reach. The east side of the hill had become, as landscape architect Joe Hodgson described, the *"dumping ground of good intentions."*

State and city officials had invested tremendous resources in the 1950s to improve this area of Nashville. But other forces would soon impact the stature and prominence of the Capitol. The influence of

Replica of Liberty Bell

Philadelphia Savings Fund Society Building

Life and Casualty Tower, 1957   FG

Philadelphia and its impact on the Capitol returned as Strickland's ownership of the Nashville skyline would finally be challenged in 1957 by the completion of Edwin Keeble's striking thirty-one-story Life & Casualty Tower. Although several large buildings had risen by the middle part of the twentieth century, Keeble's soaring tower several blocks southeast of the statehouse surprised everyone with its dynamic modern profile. When finished, it was the tallest building in the Southeast. In the late 1920s, Keeble had studied at the University of Pennsylvania when architect George Howe was introducing the gospel of the new International Style to eager pupils. As Strickland had benefitted from his days in Philadelphia with Latrobe, so too had Keeble learned from Howe and others, and the L&C Tower owed its fundamental composition of curved base, linear shaft, and big-lettered top to Howe and Lescaze's 1932 landmark Philadelphia Savings Fund Society Building in Philadelphia. An unbuilt plaza designed by Keeble was to have created a friendly outdoor space between his new tower and Strickland's 1851 Presbyterian Church next door—an ironic gesture given the unusual connection the architects of different centuries shared.

New tower nears completion in 1955   CW

Soon after, other towers would rise as downtown Nashville continued to grow in the 1960s and 1970s, and with each passing year, newer and taller skyscrapers diminished the visual dominance of the Capitol.

Like the statehouse, the L&C Tower would soon be overshadowed by larger neighbors, but with its vertical power and urban sensitivity, it would remain the finest skyscraper in the city.

National Life and Accident Insurance Company added the Windy City twist to the skyline in 1966 when it commissioned Skidmore, Owings and Merrill Architects of Chicago to design its new corporate palace. The result was a square-form travertine tower rising above a spacious but barren plaza reminiscent of a De Chirico painting. The quintessential isolated modern statement was being furiously duplicated across the country at that time. Greek Revival architecture had been the messenger of democracy, yet this new style, a century later, was one of corporate ambition, and it captured the city's taste almost as easily as Union troops had one hundred years earlier. Although later criticized by postmodern critics as too austere, too bombastic, and too sterile, this robust building, finished in 1970, remains perhaps the finest example of the pure modernist genre in Nashville, with articulate, but often overlooked details and appointments.

The National Life Tower, later purchased and renamed American General Center by

43

L&C Tower rises above skyline in 1960   BG/*NB*

Legislative Plaza

its new owners in 1982, had been erected directly behind the neoclassical War Memorial Building, creating a striking composition when seen from Deaderick Street and Legislative Plaza. But at over thirty stories in height, its close adjacency, only one block away, dwarfed the Capitol. The die was cast; it was now permissible to build a very tall building close to the state-house. Within two decades, more than seven tall structures would rise within the immediate vicinity, further depriving the Capitol of breathing room. Several of these would be erected not by nearby corporate boards but by the state itself, including the Andrew Jackson State Office Building in 1969, the massive James K. Polk Center in 1981, and the Rachel Jackson Building in 1985, thus creating a towering state government campus immediately south of Charlotte Avenue. Once a statuesque achievement on a prominent hilltop, the Capitol had become a rather delicate figure surrounded by numerous larger siblings. Fortunately, the elevated location of the statehouse still provided visual prominence at the northern edge of the downtown skyline. The building's unique temple-like form atop the dramatic green hill remained a distinctive composition, yet it was now easily and

National Life Tower

clearly seen only from the north and west parts of Nashville.

The most dramatic recent change to the visual presence of the Capitol occurred in 1974 with the completion of Legislative Plaza. Similar to Victory Square Park, which it replaced, Legislative Plaza preserved a generous and enhanced view of the Capitol.

Designed by the firm of Steinbaugh, Harwood and Rogers, this urban oasis changed the underused park surrounded by cars and city buses to a spacious pedestrian forecourt, delivering new visual stamina to the south facade of the Capitol directly across the street. Like the park it replaced, the center axis of the plaza was again fortunately left unobscured, and the flat granite surface has become one of the great civic spaces in the Southeast. Offices for state officials and a parking structure were built beneath the tree-lined plaza and connected to the Capitol under Charlotte Avenue into the bunker-like Motlow Tunnel entrance. With the creation of convenient indoor access to the statehouse, the need for pleasant immediate outdoor surroundings on the steep hill around the Capitol was certainly no longer a high priority. Seen now as an inviting and active extension of Capitol Hill, Legislative Plaza became the preferred location for newer state monuments, including the Vietnam and Korean War Memorials. It is used year-round for political rallies, festivals, and outdoor performances, perhaps the only true outdoor "civic room" in the city.

With its broad steps down to the edge of Sixth Avenue, Legislative Plaza established

Festival on Legislative Plaza

Capitol Boulevard

Farmers' Market sheds

Germantown housing   ME

an excellent pedestrian connection with Deaderick Street, a juxtaposition emphasized by the dramatic skyline alignment of the War Memorial and American General buildings. However, the potential axial impact of the new plaza to the downtown in a southward direction was immediately snuffed out by the lackluster evolution of Capitol Boulevard, a short street with a great name but in reality neither a boulevard nor a friend of the statehouse. Stretching only one block from the south edge of the plaza on Union Street to nearby Church Street, this street was an important path from the once vibrant commercial shopping district to the state-government campus. But the arrival of the Hyatt Regency Hotel in the mid-1970s turned the entire west side of the street into a barren facade that featured an unattractive loading dock. The other side of the road did not prosper due in part to the construction of an oddly conceived street revision, featuring zigzag lanes, few parking spaces, raised planters, and misplaced flower beds. Regardless of the arrival of the Church Street Centre shopping mall, Capitol Boulevard became another missed opportunity, a street requiring perhaps only minor revisions to return as a connector of

important sections within the city and meet its potential as a valuable and unique link to the statehouse.

While there was astonishing change and growth in the downtown near the Capitol, the evolution of the land above the vanished Lick Branch continued at a slow ebb during the latter half of the twentieth century. The area remained a mixture of light commercial, warehouse, and wholesale agriculture activities, with Eighth Avenue the vicinity's main vehicular corridor. Farmers' Market moved from the city courthouse area to this section of Nashville in October 1954. Located at the corner of Eighth and Jefferson and opening onto Jackson Street, the new market featured metal sheds that would provide coverings for the farmers who came to sell their produce. This new location also included a grocery store at the west side, at that time one of the largest in the city. For the next four decades, the open-air market remained a unique Nashville destination, a centralized place where a past retail tradition survived.

Further north of Germantown, the northwest section of Nashville had been severed in the late 1960s by the arrival of the interstate highway system. The impact

of the freeway on the black community was tremendous as the roadway slashed through the fabric of the city, providing much-needed transportation enhancement but at a tremendous cost. Separated by the industrial and commercial uses along the edge of the river and the new interstate canyon on the north and west, the fragile neighborhoods of Germantown and Buena Vista fought for survival. Enhancement of Jefferson Street and Eighth Avenue would be key factors in any rebirth of this surrounded mixed-use vicinity.

Substandard housing and areas of gambling and prostitution had been eradicated on Capitol Hill in the 1950s, but the undesirable activities did not simply vanish. Although public-housing units were built to accommodate the forced move and provide much-improved conditions, the weakened areas north of Jefferson Street and west of Eighth Avenue continued to decline as the inner-city decay pattern prevalent in other cities also spread to Nashville. An intense effort to preserve the Germantown community began in the 1980s by preservationists, urban pioneers, and stubborn land owners. Due to their tenacity, this small community slowly evolved into a protected and now

Werthan Bag complex   ME

Eighth Avenue and Jefferson Street

Charlotte Avenue

cherished enclave of historic structures, including restaurants, churches, offices, and homes.

Eighth Avenue, the primary vehicular approach road from the north, slowly evolved into a suburban strip highway ruled by the automobile, even though many nearby residents traveled by foot or by public transportation. Isolated businesses dotted the corridor, including branch banks, fast-food outlets, and car dealerships, mixing with the historic structures of Werthan Bag Corporation and the well-designed Cheatham Place public-housing structures directly across the street. The evolution of Charlotte Avenue, approaching from the west, was no different, and by the late 1980s it also exhibited the same major problems found in many areas of Nashville and across the country: chaotic signage, utility pole congestion, lack of vegetation buffers or trees, and vehicle-intensive suburban development. These streets suffered from the lack of any enhanced planning, possessing instead brutal roadway blight, a contemporary visual equivalent to the slums that once surrounded Capitol Hill.

Other area facilities continued the trend of industrial, warehousing, and wholesale

operations. Service companies, shops, beverage wholesalers, and small offices also moved into the area. U.S. Tobacco Company enlarged its already sizable presence on the west side of Eighth Avenue in 1981 with a new office-warehouse addition designed by Burkhalter-Hickerson Architects. This long building with its entrance on Harrison Street did little to enhance pedestrian activity on Eighth, but its strong presence and stunning newness helped signal the important possibilities that remained in the vicinity.

While the areas west and north of the future Mall site evolved, so too did the area east near the river. The original Nashville Union Stock Yards had closed in 1974, but the central brick building fortunately survived demolition and reopened in 1980 as the Stock-Yard Restaurant. Feed and seed stores and distribution operations remained in this general vicinity north of the railroad berm, including Hardison Seeds, Wiles Feeds, Davidson County Farmers' Co-op, and numerous Formosa Brothers wholesale fruit and vegetable centers.

Riverfront Apartments was a daring attempt built in 1986 by entrepreneurs Nelson Andrews and Miles Warfield to bring residential activity into the convenient

U.S. Tobacco Company

Stock-Yard Restaurant

47

Kerrigan Ironworks shed on Cumberland River

Shed and railroad tracks

Developer Nelson Andrews

Interior street beneath refurbished shed

REH

Riverfront Apartments

area between Germantown and the downtown. Located on a slender parcel of property on First Avenue overlooking the Cumberland River, this development entailed the rehabilitation of the existing nine-hundred-foot-long Kerrigan Ironworks shed. Spearheaded in design by architect Seab Tuck, the industrial structure became a linear carport for occupants of a new three-story apartment complex. Additional apartments were also built north of the shed near an old smokestack, just beyond the outlet where the historic Lick Branch once flowed into the river.

The value of the flat area between the railroad tracks and Jefferson Street was slowly being recognized and reconsidered by entrepreneurs, local companies, city planners, and state officials. But without a creative plan, a big project (such as a stadium), or a massive civic jolt, the full evolution of this historic terrain from an industrial service environment to an active, integral part of the city would probably take several decades, and the land that once separated the city due to a depressed stream might continue to separate downtown from a slowly reviving Germantown due to a depressed objectivity.

The Capitol dominates the Nashville skyline in the 1860s

Similar view in early 1990s

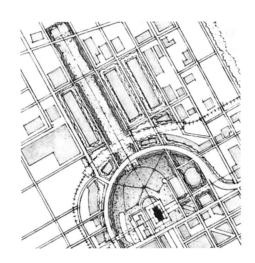

PART TWO

THE SEARCH FOR A LANDMARK

PREVIOUS IDEAS

THE CHARRETTE

PARKS OF INSPIRATION

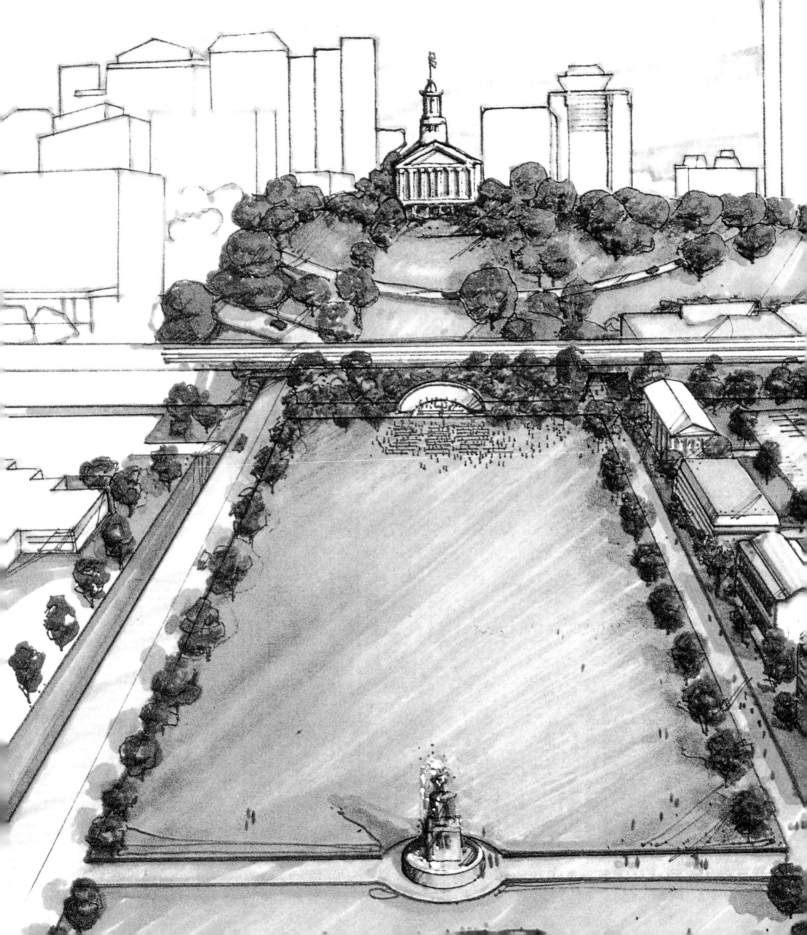

PREVIOUS IDEAS

Nothing that was worthy in the past departs.

Thomas Carlyle

Precisely who first authored the concept for the Bicentennial Mall is not known. Over the course of nearly three decades, ideas surfaced from many individuals that ultimately led to the creation of the park. When the urban-planning firm of Clarke, Rapuano and Holleran of New York was asked by city officials to return to Nashville in 1968 and prepare a master plan for the area north of the railroad berm, they delivered an ambitious redevelopment scheme that included a large sports stadium near Jefferson Street. No attempt was made to link the greenery of Capitol Hill with this vicinity immediately north, a prospect understandable and predictable given the rough nature of the barren property and the industrial zoning of this quadrant of the city. The city and state had worked together during the massive 1950 urban-renewal process, but no similar future collaborative effort was on the horizon. The state focused its attention around the Capitol, while the city studied ways to maximize the industrial and commercial property between James Robertson Parkway and Jefferson Street. Sulphur Dell Ballpark had closed in 1963, and the area needed help.

Not until a talented architect from East Tennessee pondered both the land of

Sketch by Don Booten for John Bridges, 1989

Capitol Hill and the abundant property north would the first seeds be planted for a park linking formerly unconnected urban districts. The idea for the park would occur as a quick sketch, part of a larger endeavor in 1969 when architect Robert Church of Knoxville provided a clever plan to quench the growing thirst for state-employee parking around the Capitol. His concept was to transform the entire north and west sides of Capitol Hill into a multi-level parking garage for two thousand cars. Conceivably a brutal prospect, Church's garage scheme was quite elegant, a monumental composition that saddled into the sloped topography and gracefully curved around the hill, reinforcing the majestic landform. The stunning proposal received national recognition in the 1970 *Progressive Architecture* Awards Program, a rare occurrence for a parking structure. As Strickland had been influenced by Latrobe, Church had studied under another architect from Philadelphia, the influential late-modernist Louis Kahn. With its clear geometric order and layered concrete elements, the monumental garage design clearly reflected Kahn's impact on young Church. Construction of the sophisticated garage was ultimately vetoed by the governor, but the

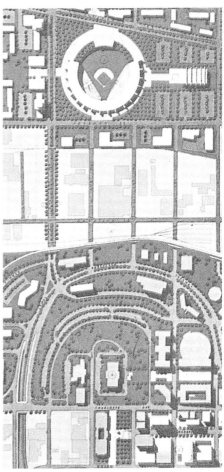

Stadium concept of 1968   MDHA

53

Model of Robert Church's Capitol Hill Garage MHMA

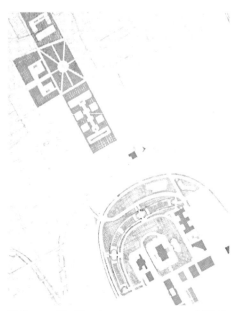

Mall concept by Church MHMA

exercise to develop the plan left one special seed. Church and state architect Clayton Dekle apparently discussed the possible aspect of ultimately extending the greenery of Capitol Hill north sometime in the future to reinforce the impact of the new garage. As early as 1965, Dekle had considered the possibility of moving the primary north-south vehicular access to the Capitol from Eighth Avenue over to a stately, wide boulevard replacing Sixth and Seventh Avenues, and Church prepared a rough diagram to indicate a new hybrid based on Dekle's earlier ideas. Instead of a vehicular concept, his 1969 sketch illustrated the plan of a linear park between Sixth and Seventh Avenues, a mall extending north from the railroad berm well into Germantown. It is the first known illustration of the simple yet powerful idea that would not materialize until a quarter of a century later.

State government continued to grow in the 1970s, and as programs and departments expanded, the state erected several new office buildings. In addition, the state leased space in many buildings and became one of the largest tenants in downtown Nashville. But expansion options were important, and it slowly dawned on state officials to

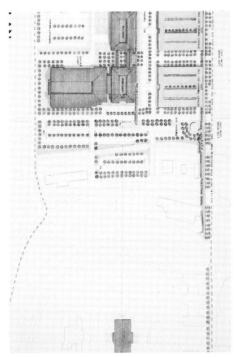

Land-use study by Bruce McCarty   MHMA

consider the relatively inexpensive flat land that lay immediately north of the Capitol. Architects Roy Harrover of Memphis and Bruce McCarty of Knoxville were called in 1984 to study the land north of the railroad berm. Seasoned designers with distinguished projects to their credits (Harrover for

Mud Island and McCarty for the 1982 World's Fair), both submitted separate conceptual arrangements focusing on development of this land for state offices. The state would benefit from the abundant inventory of underdeveloped property, and future growth in this direction would be far cheaper than in downtown. Their rough conceptual ideas further convinced the state to begin and continue acquisitioning this property.

By 1985, things became more serious. Construction on the land that the state had purchased and assembled north of the railroad berm became imminent to fulfill programmed needs, and Gresham, Smith and Partners prepared a preliminary land-use master plan as a guideline for purchasing, phasing, and construction. A new computer-data center and other state operations were planned, all of these north of the train-track earthform. Landscape architect Joe Hodgson helped convince state officials of the possibilities of developing the barren terrain into a decent precinct by preparing an illustration of a linear park, not unlike Church's, in the middle of a state office park development. Hodgson's scheme was more developed, with a series of informal paths complementing the rectilinear park border that

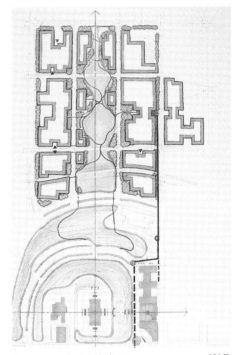

Park concept by Joe Hodgson   H&D

extended to Farmers' Market on Jackson Street.

Assured of the overall long-range possibilities, the state finally began to make use of the property with the erection of new structures. The State Data Center by Gresham, Smith and Partners between Fifth

State Data Center

and Sixth Avenues was finished in 1987. A brisk precast-concrete, one-story building that nevertheless met its fortress-like program objective, it was the first new state building north of the railroad berm. Meanwhile, the state made use of existing buildings and warehouses in the area for other less-sensitive operations: the motor pool, printing center, and supply warehouses. Leftover land, often lumpy, was paved with asphalt or gravel creating an unending sea of parking for state employees. Where buildings did not exist, cars would. At quitting time each day, activity evaporated as employees drove away, and the area became a flat desert with no occupants, no life. The park illustrated by Hodgson remained a misty possibility.

In 1989, Governor McWherter received a call from area businessman Victor Johnson. A prominent civic leader and past president of Aladdin Industries known for his foresight, Johnson wanted to share an idea with the state's top gun. Johnson's associate at Aladdin, John Bridges, had conceived the notion of a linear park north of the Capitol that would be similar to the National Mall in Washington, D.C. Bridges was part owner of the abandoned and dilapidated Elliott School at the corner of

Sixth and Jefferson in Germantown, and a new park would help enhance the wasteland between the downtown and the historic community directly north. Most importantly, it would preserve a stunning view of the Capitol. He had prepared not only a plan view, but also a bird's-eye perspective illustration. Although it was not the first concept for a mall-like park, Bridges's depiction and accompanying written description was convincing and caught the imagination of Johnson, McWherter, and shortly thereafter the governor's staff, particularly Jim Hall, who had been appointed to conceive and direct the initial planning of the Tennessee Bicentennial Celebration. The concept of a green lawn facing the statehouse seemed very appropriate, and with 1996 only seven years away, the new park idea might just work as the signature endeavor for the once-in-a-century occasion. Bridges's sketch even appeared on television, the first mention of the possibility that state officials might enhance their already known office-building agenda north of James Robertson Parkway with a civic gift, a Bicentennial mall. With thanks to Bridges and Johnson, the basic concept linking the park to the upcoming Bicentennial took hold.

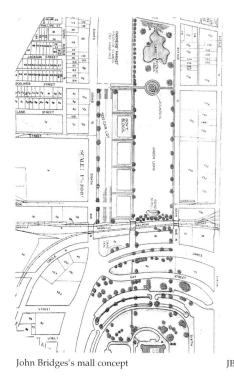
John Bridges's mall concept   JB

Johnson asked New York architect Robert Lamb Hart to help enrich the basic idea. Bridges's rough sketch was for a flat, open yard with a fountain, but Hart's revised scheme was more refined with more fountains and a map of the state stretching across the length of the long

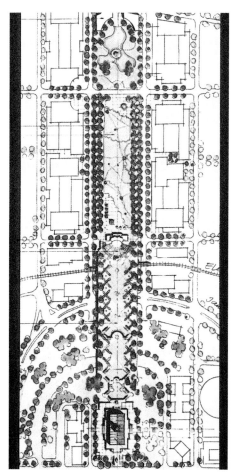

Robert Lamb Hart's proposal   RLH

lawn. However, this creative mall concept got tangled into the pressing need for still more state office space, and Hart added buildings at the south end of his plan against Capitol Hill to satisfy the request. A cluster of office structures was proposed to stairstep down the hill's north slope and bridge over both James Robertson Parkway and the railroad berm with a large parking structure and a levitated pedestrian plaza. Though it provided office space immediately adjacent to the statehouse, the plan had a significant visual expense. After quietly reviewing the scheme (and several derivative plans devised by the state's own staff) with consulting architects, trusted friends, and a citizens advisory group working on the redesign of the downtown, state officials by the middle of 1991 found that crowding the hill with more office structures was not going to be very popular. The sloped terrain and limited access would probably also make such a project rather expensive. The linear park idea was fine, but more buildings clustered on the already crowded hill and a massive structure over the parkway would be a hard sell and perhaps not the proper approach for the city or for the Bicentennial.

Buildings stairstep down Capitol Hill   RLH

State officials quickly turned to less heroic office-building solutions, including the eventual completion of two large office towers on the parkway straddling the block between Sixth and Seventh Avenues that remained reserved for the future park. Although too tall, the twin forms of precast concrete and reflective glass fortunately receded somewhat when seen against the backdrop of Capitol Hill and Strickland's architectural jewel on top. The mall idea, for the moment, went on hold. It was during this pivotal intermission that a new team was assembled to review the past and ponder the future, benefiting from the knowledge and energy of previous schemes yet without the obligation to follow some of their questionable aspects.

THE CHARRETTE

*Men are never so likely to settle a question rightly
as when they discuss it freely.*

Lord Macaulay

To maximize the impending arrival of the Bicentennial Celebration and capitalize on the opportunity to honor this rare event with a permanent civic gesture, state officials under the guidance of Jerry Preston, assistant commissioner of the Department of Finance and Administration, assembled a statewide team of independent design professionals in September of 1991 to advise on an alternative course of action. Wisely, a group of diverse individuals was formed that brought many distinct viewpoints to the table, combining urban-planning, architecture, engineering, and historic-preservation expertise and sensitivity. The team consisted of architect and teacher Jon Coddington of the University of Tennessee College of Architecture and Planning, noted historic restoration architect Charles Warterfield Jr., urban planner and teacher David Johnson also from the University of Tennessee, engineer Bob McKinney of SSOE Engineers, and me, with Tuck Hinton Architects as managing firm. We were asked to study the situation and suggest a solution, if any, to the mall dilemma. A quick and intensive design session followed, a "charrette."

The design team met in September 1991 to evaluate the numerous concepts developed in the past decade for the use of the state land north of the Capitol. These included both public- and private-development schemes, as well as designs conceived in-house by the state. For the most part, the proposals were extensions of the urban-renewal scheme implemented in the 1950s with plans for individual new state office buildings and large parking lots for state employees. Only a few of the proposals emphasized the Capitol or its grounds or acknowledged connections to the city and the surrounding fragile neighborhoods. Many were dependent on spatial programs that were constantly changing or still unknown. Several even suggested the placement of new buildings on the north slope of historic Capitol Hill, a very expensive proposition that might further hide the beautiful statehouse from view by the public. Each had pondered growth through an agenda that perhaps had not yet made use of the inertia of the Bicentennial—the inertia to create something not only practical but also very unique.

After an abbreviated analysis of existing conditions and a critique of these past ideas, an intense discussion concerning the possibilities associated with the approaching Bicentennial Celebration emerged with the

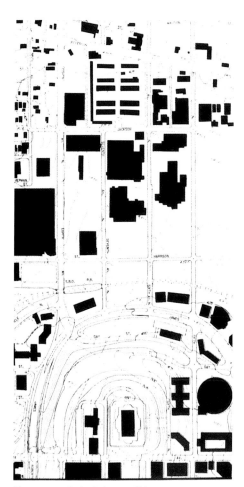

Figure-ground of existing conditions

Land north of the Capitol, 1991   AG

59

Buildings blocking view of Capitol

call for an alternative approach. Messy sketches, hurriedly prepared, were shown to members of the governor's staff and constitutional officers. Though rough, these early diagrams sought to convey the straightforward manner by which a

memorable civic project might be achieved. As much as anything, the charrette provided a quick acknowledgment of both existing conditions and obvious objectives, foremost the preservation and exaltation of the Capitol and Capitol Hill as the single collective centerpiece of any future building endeavor. James Robertson Parkway was seen as possessing tremendous potential that could supersede its existing character and current use as a radial freeway. The railroad berm was seen not as an impenetrable lump but perhaps as a long-hidden opportunity. And the vicinity immediately north—where the long, green lawn would land—was contemplated for its unmistakable linear compositional power. The recommended course would be to allow the charrette team to thoroughly analyze the existing conditions, develop a comprehensive master plan, and then proceed promptly with design phases and construction to meet the deadline of June 1, 1996, less than five years away at the time.

Officials with the state accepted the basic direction proposed in the charrette but only with guarded reservations to

review a more thorough development of the initial ideas presented. It was one of the first occasions in the history of state construction where the expertise and experience of both professionals and academics had been sought at the early stages of project conception to ensure that a rich mixture of thematic visions would be considered. Master plan team member Jon Coddington placed the significance of the moment so clearly:

Because of this singular opportunity and concomitant responsibilities associated with the project type, it became clear to the team and its clients that ends and means had to be closely linked. This meant that each line—whether written or drawn—needed to have not only a technical dimension to it, but an ethical dimension as well. This set the tone of both the process and the product.

With a deep respect for the diverse history of the Capitol and understanding of the design possibilities inherent in the fragile and heretofore underappreciated district directly north, the new course began.

60

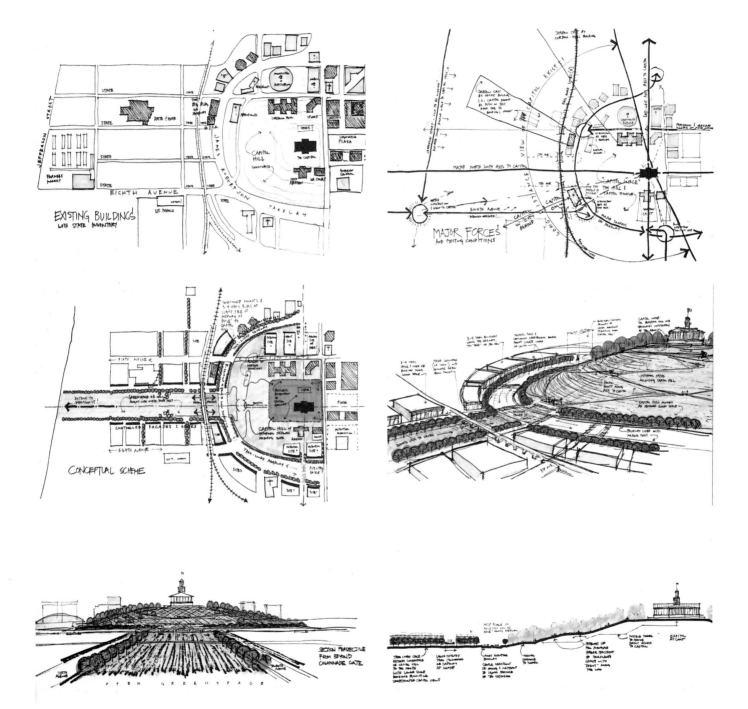

Charrette sketches, 1991

61

PARKS OF INSPIRATION

Example is always more efficacious than precept.

Samuel Johnson

The master plan team pondered to formulate a process to accomplish the immense design opportunity now at hand. Landscape architect Ritchie Smith of Memphis was added to the group to complete the spectrum of design professionals, and our reinforced team next prepared a specific program for the project, a list of objectives that would unite the possibilities of the site with the reality of the site.

First we took time to carefully study other sources of inspiration. It had been suggested that the concept for the new park in Nashville be based on the National Mall in Washington, D.C., one of the greatest outdoor spaces in the world. State officials were certainly comfortable with this most famous precedent, and the idea to create a linear expression that would honor the event of the Bicentennial while also preserving at least one good distant view of the Capitol had become a given objective. Similar to the basic objective of the Tennessee endeavor, the National Mall is an excellent civic gesture, a public yard that provides a cherished natural setting while highlighting important cultural and government buildings. Much could be learned from this well-known model.

Vaux le Vicomte

National Mall in Washington, D.C.   USDI

But there were also many other pertinent examples of memorable outdoor civic spaces, gardens, parks, and malls that we wanted to consider before we began the actual design process. History is filled with dramatic outdoor places, from the formal gardens of the French landscape genius André Le Nôtre at Vaux le Vicomte and Versailles to the more sweeping and intriguing projects of Frederick Olmsted at New York's Central Park and Prospect Park. The success of each has depended on a tremendous variety of factors, from sheer size and location to nearby activities and functional objectives. The design team reviewed examples of situations that, in basic form, seemed very similar to the linear configuration of the proposed

63

View of U.S. Capitol area in 1900   USNA

Bicentennial Mall. These included both formal and informal public spaces in the United States and abroad. Examples of public areas near other state capitol buildings were also investigated.

THE NATIONAL MALL
WASHINGTON, D.C.

By general definition, a mall is a narrow and long, relatively flat, open, green space with prominent structures located along each side. The term *mall* in this context originates from Pall Mall in England and now describes an area where movement is encouraged, a promenade. Particularly important buildings or monuments are normally reserved for each axial end. The term was revised—some feel poisoned—by developers of the 1960s and 1970s who used the phrase to instead refer to their newest retail invention, the enclosed shopping center. The National Mall in Washington, D.C., is perhaps the most recognized example, initially suggested by the gifted French planner Pierre Charles L'Enfant in 1791 and later confirmed and enlarged by the 1901 McMillan Plan. Prominent cultural buildings including those of the Smithsonian Institution, perhaps the greatest collection of adjacent museums in the world, define the long edges of each side of the Mall. The U.S. Capitol and Lincoln Memorial anchor the opposite ends of the dramatic lawn, while the striking vertical form of the Washington Monument highlights the midsection.

Washington is a very large, dense city, and open, green spaces of any significant size are cherished amenities. The valued open space of the National Mall, more than just a park, provides an organizational structure for location of the peripheral buildings and activities while also delivering an unforgettable orientation of the landscape. The bustling tourists from the Smithsonian, the Capitol, and from other landmarks and attractions in this district supply activity and occupancy of the outdoor space with constant movement into and through the long park. This Mall is unarticulated and

Buildings of the Smithsonian Institution and National Gallery flank the National Mall

RC

does not possess any structured activity or strong educational content. Essentially an open lawn with shady trees at the edges, it reinforces the educational, cultural, and governmental activities of the surrounding destinations. The valuable green space is used throughout the year for informal gatherings, demonstrations, and symbolic rallies. Historic markers or monuments, most recently the Vietnam and Korean War Memorials, are located off the central axial lawn. When the museums are closed in the evenings and on holidays, the area becomes void of substantial activity.

The National Mall also establishes an enduring indication of the hierarchy of government buildings. The elevated Capitol, positioned at the east end as the most important single structure, is always visible and available. This marvelous achievement of combining buildings and landscape within the city required enormous planning, not only to develop the concept, but to also establish a framework of

65

Vietnam Veterans Memorial   GTB

Eiffel Tower and Champ de Mars   WL

Minnesota Capitol Mall   TCP

guidelines so that the buildings added in the past century have not compromised the composition. Despite numerous new museums added since World War II, the Mall remains oriented toward the seat of national government and the battleground of our nation's democratic form of government, the magnificent white-domed Capitol.

CHAMP DE MARS, PARIS

Similar to Nashville's own Centennial Park, the Champ de Mars in Paris was originally built for an important but temporary event. When the Universal Exposition was held in Paris in 1889, many inventive structures and buildings were erected for this fair. The most significant was the Eiffel Tower, a monumental structure that has become one of the world's most celebrated landmarks. When the temporary exposition halls near the tower were demolished, a grand linear park remained, the Champ de Mars. This dramatic Parisian park contains a long, open lawn lined with groupings of high-canopy trees, not unlike the model in Washington. The lawn is centered on the axis of the overwhelming nine-hundred-foot tower, making the total composition breathtaking, and it is used as a park by

occupants of the surrounding dense residential areas and for marching drills by the adjacent military institute. Directly across the nearby Seine River is the Trocadero area of the city containing several cultural facilities and a spectacular collection of fountains. Because of the extensive variety of attractions—green space, tower, fountains, museums, river, and park—tourists flock to this part of Paris. However, most come to see the tower and fountains. Few venture across the dramatic length of the beautiful long lawn.

MINNESOTA CAPITOL MALL

Perhaps the most intriguing example of a large outdoor civic space in the United States similar to the one contemplated for Tennessee was the Capitol Mall in St. Paul, Minnesota. Immediately adjacent to Minnesota's beautiful Capitol building designed by Cass Gilbert in 1902, this park has been in place for many years, with roadway and axial paths radiating out in a fan-like pattern from the statehouse to other government office buildings. The Capitol Mall is attractive and provides an impressive foreground to the Capitol, but with the exception of the statehouse, there are few significant

cultural activities around the open park. Void of activity generators, this pretty American lawn remains unused except for occasional outdoor festivals. A design competition in 1986 had resulted in plans to create more outdoor "rooms," more attractions such as a larger fountain and more memorials, and these improvements may eventually enhance the scenic experience and encourage yearlong use of the spacious park.

Other state capitol grounds were also studied, but only a few proved to be overwhelmingly inspirational. Most were simply green spaces or parks around the respective statehouse. This was not to belittle such environments, for many worked quite well. Several had programmed activities to bring visitors— other than politicians and lobbyists—to the sites, and many of the grounds were used with great frequency. Yet few had rich, symbolic, or educational content. Most featured scattered historic markers or memorials to wars or significant past elected officials, a condition very similar to the grounds of the Tennessee State Capitol. We were impressed mostly with these efforts to preserve and promote the environment around each statehouse.

Parc Villette and science and technology museum   DF

Lawn and pavilion at Parc André Citroën

Water feature at Parc André Citroën   TEH

PARC VILLETTE AND PARC ANDRÉ CITROËN, PARIS

In the past decade, two fascinating contemporary parks have been completed in Paris to continue the city's long tradition of providing splendid outdoor spaces for its citizens and guests. The first, Parc Villette, is a stirring eighty-one-acre piece of outdoor architectural theory made physical in the northern part of the city, a strikingly inventive composition designed by Bernard Tschumi and completed in 1989. It was part of the government's effort to resurrect the industrial area surrounding the abandoned central slaughterhouse while preserving adjacent historic structures, including a large nineteenth-century metal shed by Victor Baltard. The park plan is sprinkled with a rigid grid pattern of red follies, small structures that animate the layout and counterbalance the natural features and cultural facilities also woven into the scheme. The sizable slaughterhouse was converted into a science and technology museum, and the vicinity is now quite active because of this new attraction. Full use and appreciation of the unusual park itself has yet to occur.

A second thirty-five-acre urban garden, Parc André Citroën, opened in 1993 in the western section of Paris, the result of a forced marriage of two French design teams. Distinctly different from its complement on the other side of town, Parc André Citroën is a commentary on the landscape, from formal lawns and rigid placement to informal, almost wild, natural plots. Similar to Parc Villette, water is a key component, but here it is used with more concentrated virtuosity: a canal, waterfalls, jet-like vertical fountains, misters, and the Seine River itself. Cubic glass greenhouses and austere granite forms provide a stout architectural balance to the lush plantings and serial gardens. The park is a superb mixture of nature and architecture, one of the finest new outdoor places in the world.

FREEDOM PLAZA

Education was a primary goal on our agenda. One outdoor place that delivers a civic message at civic scale is Freedom Plaza in Washington, D.C., designed in 1977 by the Philadelphia firm of Venturi, Rauch and Scott Brown. Located at the western end of Pennsylvania Avenue where this Main Street of all main streets turns to dogleg around Robert Mills's 1836 Treasury Building, the plaza is a most ingenious teaching destination. A rectangular central platform is elevated slightly above the surrounding streets, and upon the flat surface is a gigantic map of Washington as originally proposed by L'Enfant. The flatness of the large parterre map was to have been enhanced by miniature-scale marble models of both the Capitol and the White House, and the entire plaza was given the design firm's signature complexity by two very tall but thin pylons. The models and the pylons, which would have added enormously to the urban effect by framing views of the Treasury Building, were never built, but the plaza is still quite fascinating because of the richness of the map. Here the majesty of the city is captured and taught at a scale easier to understand. It is symbolic and sculptural yet equally educational.

Other outdoor places in Washington were also visited and analyzed, including the emotive black wall of the Vietnam Veterans Memorial by Maya Lin, the watery Navy Memorial, the popular Pershing Park, and various plazas surrounding important cultural facilities, including the National Gallery East Wing by I. M. Pei and the Holocaust Museum by James Freed.

TENNESSEE EXAMPLES

The design team also found inspiration much closer to home. As might be

Freedom Plaza   VSBA

most cherished structures in the city, the Parthenon. What appealed to us most about this very popular city park were its variety of outdoor spaces and activities, its somewhat informal arrangement, and its orientation to the central Greek structure.

Mud Island Park in Memphis, designed by Roy Harrover and completed in 1982, possesses an extremely interesting water feature, a miniature scale model of the Mississippi River. This active, shallow path wiggles across the park and creates a treasured tactile experience for visitors who walk over and through the creek. Here one learns of the enormous scale and path of the river from its headwaters to the Gulf of Mexico. Children wade through the course of the waterway while adults study engraved outlines of the cities and towns that hug the banks of this most American of all rivers. The river path ingredient of the park is active and fun, and it teaches.

Equally intriguing was Ross's Landing, a new park that surrounds the Tennessee Aquarium in Chattanooga. James Wines of the New York firm SITE conceived this park near the Tennessee River as a series of parallel bands that represent the history of the city and nearby region. Under the leadership of city planner Stroud Watson,

Centennial Park

Wines developed the scheme with the Washington, D.C., firm of EDAW and Robert Seals of Chattanooga. The bands are layered across the site and transform from rigid paths to contorted, flexed borders—a physical commentary on the transition of the city from its street grid to its natural river-edge boundary. The park also integrates a meandering water path similar to Mud Island, yet here it is an abstract representation with a beginning "spring" that symbolically pushes up the concrete pavement. Free-form concrete bridges nearby provide overlooks quite unlike any others in the Southeast. Here

expected, the predecessor Centennial Park in Nashville was evaluated, not only for its original grandeur at the time of the Tennessee Centennial Exposition of 1897, but for its various stages of evolution. From the site of a great exposition and collection of temporary neoclassical structures, it is now an open lawn with peripheral shady zones, a lake, a band shell, gardens and scattered monuments, art and recreation facilities, and one of the

Model of Mississippi River at Mud Island   RPH

compositions, parks, and memorials. Though not formally trained as landscape architects, we have nonetheless been fascinated in the ways that architecture can infuse the public realm. We have therefore participated in several design endeavors related to exterior settings. Most of these projects have been in the form of open competitions, where the boundaries between architecture, sculpture, and landscape architecture can become quite fuzzy. In 1989, our firm submitted a scheme for the National Peace Garden, an outdoor park to be built at Point Park, an interesting peninsula in Washington, D.C., directly across the Potomac River from busy National Airport. Our proposal was for a park filled with sound and music, a mixture of sculptural elements and musical devices to counterbalance the constant noise from the nearby jet runways.

A second unique outdoor composition opportunity occurred in 1990 when our firm developed an idea for an entry to the Minnesota Vietnam War Memorial design competition. This memorial was to be located on the grounds of the State Capitol building in St. Paul, Minnesota. Our concept was to stamp a physical impression of the country of Vietnam onto the

Ross's Landing Plaza   EDAW

landscape of Minnesota in much the same manner that the war had made a lasting emotional impression on the people of the state. The proposed map of Vietnam was to have been against a small open area of water symbolic of the South China Sea,

one learns about Chattanooga, Hamilton County, and the nearby region in a delightful, inventive setting.

Since the formation of our firm in 1984, my partner Seab Tuck and I have been interested in the creation of outdoor

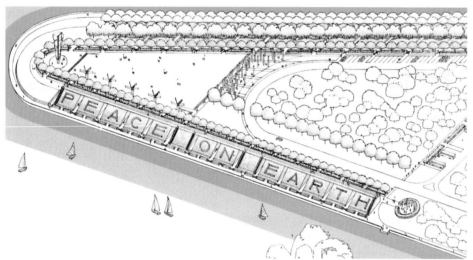

Proposal for Peace Garden in Washington, D.C.

with vertical reed-like elements scattered within the pool. In the land of ten thousand lakes, this single body of water would recall tears and bloodshed abroad years ago. Ironically, from our experience in this second design competition, we had become familiar with the seldomly used land around Minnesota's Capitol.

SUMMARY

Our team considered the urban design impact of each of the unique examples we had studied. From these we had learned much that could be used in our new assignment. This study also allowed us to question preconceptions about duplicating the National Mall and, with the knowledge of other successful places, to seek a solution appropriate for Tennessee.

Construction of an open, green space similar to the National Mall in Washington, D.C., would, of course, be a memorable Bicentennial gift. However, the conditions around the Mall in Washington and those

at the anticipated location of the Tennessee Mall differed greatly. A monumental grass lawn similar to this famous example would be appropriate in Nashville only if a considerable density of people, buildings, and activities surrounded the area. In such a situation, the open space would provide civic, spatial, and ecological relief to otherwise crowded conditions. The Champ de Mars was also an important example because it illustrated a visually dramatic linear space. But without the Eiffel Tower and nearby Trocadero fountains, this space would probably attract and benefit only the residents of the neighborhood, as do many of the lovely parks scattered across Paris. Similarly, the example of the Minnesota Capitol Mall in St. Paul illustrated the risk of simply providing a wide, open park without nearby cultural institutions.

The area in Nashville planned as the location for a new park was distinctly different, an underutilized, quasi-industrial and commercial-service area with no significant activity generators except, perhaps, Farmers' Market. In addition, Nashville is not a crowded city, but rather a medium-sized urban area with relatively low density and a substantial amount of open space. Given the conditions of the site, the Mall in

Tennessee would have to be an activity generator itself. To do this, it could not be simply an unarticulated lawn with a few cute fountains. Rather, it would need to contain elements that would create a unique experience for visitors, young and old. The Mall would need to become a destination point, a place where citizens and their guests would gravitate to learn about the state and its vast diversity and distinct qualities. In Washington, the Mall relieves; in Tennessee, it would need to inspire.

From Washington, Paris, and St. Paul, we had learned of the monumental opportunity where civic space emphasized civic obligation. From Le Nôtre, we had learned of the need to create not only grandeur but intrigue. From the new parks of Paris, we learned of other unique compositional arrangements that inspire. From

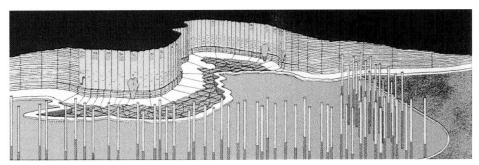

Proposal for Minnesota Vietnam War Memorial

Venturi and Scott Brown, we had learned that a monumental civic destination can teach on a variety of levels and scales, and from Harrover and Wines, we had learned that such an experience could exist in the landscape of Tennessee as easily as it had in more famous locations. From our own proposals for park designs and memorials, we had developed a yearning to creatively contribute to the public realm. And, finally, we knew of the potential power of our own local acropolis and its powerful thematic connection to the ideals of democracy born in Greece centuries ago. The opportunity to use this collected information and inspiration was quickly to arrive as we began to assemble our thoughts and ideas for the task now at hand.

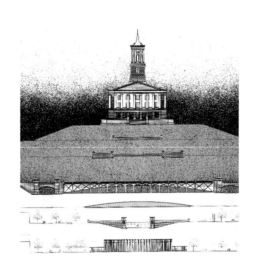

PART THREE

THE MASTER PLAN

RECOMMENDATIONS FOR A BICENTENNIAL DESTINATION
DESIGN FOR A NEW PARK
THE MALL ARRIVES

RECOMMENDATIONS FOR A BICENTENNIAL DESTINATION

*Make no little plans; they have no magic
to stir men's blood.*

Daniel Hudson Burnham

The Bicentennial Commission was formed in 1992, composed of a diverse group of Tennesseans from across the state, and chaired by noted civic leader Martha Ingram. This new commission met for the first time at the Capitol on August 12, 1992. A brief presentation was made regarding the McWherter administration's commitment to construct a Bicentennial Mall as a permanent civic gift in honor of the upcoming state birthday. Because the design was still in the very early stages of development, few details were discussed. A green swath of some form and character would arrive by 1996—in just four years. Much was left to be done.

Having presented a basic concept for the new park, our team next initiated a process to derive an appropriate master plan with a mixture of great expectations and trepidations. This was a unique situation, a unique challenge. We had a wealth of resources to work with, much from which to draw inspiration and direction. Research of the Capitol had revealed its origins, its form, its meaning. Investigation of the French Lick site where wildlife once roamed, traders had traded, and baseballs had been hit brought an appreciation for soil soon to be disturbed. Analysis of other

Aerial view of Capitol and future Mall   PAP

Looking south at Sixth Avenue

75

Master plan team

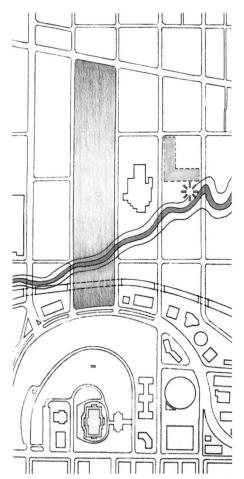

Initial sketch of historic features

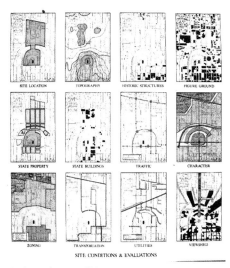

Analysis of site conditions

parks simultaneously brought design courage and caution. Material about Tennessee and the Mall's site from historians, authors, poets, artists, archaeologists, and even state public-relations entities formed a diverse inventory of historic and thematic depth. We had rediscovered a state of immense natural beauty and tremendous diversity. And from interviews across the state with members of the Bicentennial Commission and other state officials, we received input on how the park might reflect this diversity and express ownership by all Tennesseans. Using these research tools, our team conceived a master plan that we hoped would be fitting for the Volunteer State's two hundredth birthday.

RECOMMENDATION ONE
CAPITOL HILL RESHAPED

We began with Capitol Hill, for the Bicentennial Mall could not enhance this adjacent mammoth landform unless the hill itself was first changed. The primary design objective for this summit of land and government was to simply recapture this dramatic site and transform it into an accessible and usable civic park commensurate with both the beauty of the Capitol building and the drama of the unique landform upon which it rests. From a hill covered with cars it would become a hill again available to people.

The team agreed that the recommendations in the 1986 *Historic Structure Report* by John Mesick of New York should continue to be used as the general guide for restoration of the statehouse and nearby grounds. An earlier 1985 master plan for Capitol Hill by Hodgson & Douglas and Gresham, Smith and Partners also proved valuable. These studies had noted the lack

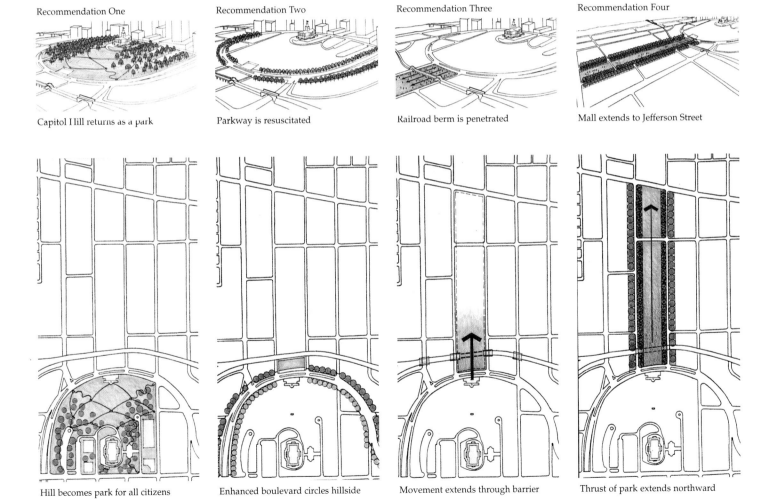

Recommendation One

Capitol Hill returns as a park

Recommendation Two

Parkway is resuscitated

Recommendation Three

Railroad berm is penetrated

Recommendation Four

Mall extends to Jefferson Street

Hill becomes park for all citizens

Enhanced boulevard circles hillside

Movement extends through barrier

Thrust of park extends northward

77

Parking on north slope

Steep slope and retaining wall at Gay Street

A park reserved for cars   JL

of access to the numerous state "treasures" on the hill, including the statues of Andrew Jackson, Sam Davis, and Sergeant Alvin C. York, as well as other small but nonetheless interesting markers and memorials. Both studies suggested realistic adjustments to the hill that would improve circulation and use while boosting the now almost hidden ambiance of the site.

Since the property was originally designed to be an informal "stroll garden," we recommended that the winding paths and original pedestrian entrances should be restored where possible, encouraging more activity and providing improved access to the numerous historic monuments and markers found on the grounds. Walkways would connect from Jackson Plaza to the tomb of President and Mrs. James K. Polk, and a new statue would be erected to honor Tennessee's third president, Andrew Johnson. New planting would be installed throughout the hill to provide seasonal color and additional shade. We also agreed that at some point in the future, the bunker-like Motlow Tunnel entrance at Charlotte Avenue should be demolished and rebuilt, altered to create a more inviting and attractive pedestrian entrance from both the street and nearby Legislative Plaza.

Because the north slope was the largest open space adjacent to the Capitol, this area was proposed to be the key link between the Capitol and the Mall. The unattractive state-employee parking lot on the north slope would be removed, and new lots adjacent to the Mall and in other areas in the immediate downtown vicinity would be added. The prominent land captured by this action would become a pedestrian esplanade overlooking James Robertson Parkway, the Mall, and the entire northern section of the city. A scenic drive with limited short-term parking would connect existing roadways on the east and west sides of the Capitol and provide vehicular access to this new overlook, called the "Belvedere." The overly steep hill would be regraded, and the existing one-way Gay Street connection, built during the urban-renewal project, would also be eliminated, its unsightly scar across the hillside sewn up and forever healed. Trees at the new terrace and Belvedere would be added to frame and reinforce views of Strickland's masterpiece above. The existing trek from top to bottom was steep, descending 120 vertical feet, very little was paved, and adequate stairs were almost nonexistent. From the

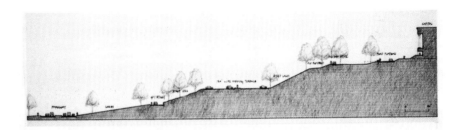

Existing slope of Capitol Hill

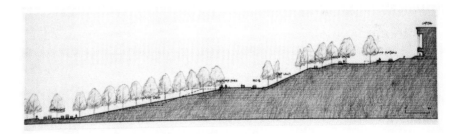

Proposed topographic revisions

proposed Belvedere, new walks would wind up to the Capitol and down to James Robertson Parkway and beyond to the Mall.

Our team proposed two new systems of pathways. A pair of sweeping stairways was proposed from the Belvedere on the midpoint plateau of the steep hill—radial forms that would embrace and define a generous, unobstructed tilted yard. This spacious, elliptical lawn would remain completely open to permanently ensure unobstructed views from the parkway to the Capitol above. It would also result in a spacious amphitheater-like setting for very large gatherings, not unlike that suggested by architect Russell Hart nearly eighty years earlier.

View of Capitol from parkway

A boulevard in need of help

A second pathway system would connect the entire hillside, from the Capitol all the way down to James Robertson Parkway at the busy Fifth Avenue intersection. This system would not be in the middle, but rather on the northeast corner side of Capitol Hill. Views of the Capitol building are quite spectacular from this angled position and correspond to the Greek preference of oblique perspectives. A series of gracious stairways and ramps would crisscross down the steep hill, flaring out in an angle as the distance from the statehouse increased and providing handicap accessibility coupled with monumental visibility. The zigzag pattern would feature additional information on markers, creating rewards along the way to celebrate the accomplishments of individual Tennesseans. The path would become a spirited quest up and a unique promenade down—an ambitious journey either way and a long-overdue final connection of the Capitol to the parkway. Demolition of the boxy Capitol Towers structure—now a condominium—would be required to accomplish this paramount walkway necessity and to return the one remaining large slice of the entire dominant landform back to the citizens of the state, altogether not unlike the acquisition of the

northeast corner of the original Capitol grounds in 1857.

RECOMMENDATION TWO
RETURN OF THE BOULEVARD

Our primary recommendation for James Robertson Parkway was to establish this road as a more appropriate, attractive, functional base for Capitol Hill, the prominent landform around which the boulevard flows. With the existing character of the street and its edges revised, the sweeping crescent-shaped boulevard might be transformed into a definitive corridor, a radial zone uniting the Capitol, hill, and Mall with the existing neighborhood of activities along the parkway.

To improve the identity and spatial definition of the parkway, a continuous colonnade treatment was recommended. This would be achieved by rows of street trees on each side of the parkway reinforced by new sidewalks, improved lighting, outdoor furniture, carefully composed building facades, and signage. The intent would be to enhance the impression of this vehicular path as a grand boulevard, much as had been intended forty years earlier when it was first built. Coordination between city and state agencies would be required since the city

controlled the majority of the maintenance and upkeep of the busy street. We knew that this intention to upgrade the entire boulevard might take many years to accomplish; the initial work would probably be limited only to the section near the Mall.

With increased pedestrian activity north of the Capitol grounds, all the crosswalks on James Robertson Parkway between Fifth and Eighth Avenues would have to be substantially upgraded. This would be especially critical at Sixth and Seventh Avenues, the transition area between Capitol Hill and the site of the proposed Mall. The crossing at Fifth Avenue would still remain perhaps the busiest due to its use as the primary pedestrian connection with downtown. At each crosswalk, asphalt paving would be replaced with cobblestone-like pavers to signal the presence of pedestrian crossing points to often oblivious motorists.

A tunnel allowing access from the north base of the hill to the Capitol was also considered as a potential element in the future. The master plan would need to accommodate this possibility of a direct indoor connection from the parkway and its numerous state office buildings to the Capitol in a manner not unlike the existing Motlow Tunnel on the Capitol's south side. But it was felt that such

Railroad berm

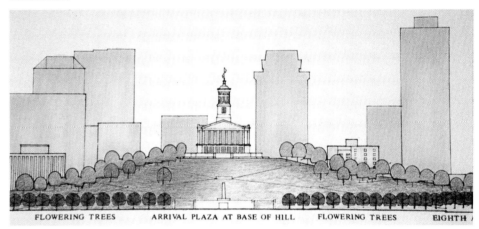
FLOWERING TREES   ARRIVAL PLAZA AT BASE OF HILL   FLOWERING TREES   EIGHTH
Initial concept for enhanced hillside

an undertaking should be delayed until proven absolutely necessary because of the great depth on this side of the hill and the probable exorbitant expense.

RECOMMENDATION THREE
RAILROAD AS AMENITY

For years, the existing CSX railroad berm had proven to be the major physical and psychological barrier to the redevelopment of the area immediately north of James Robertson Parkway. The berm was a formidable barricade, a curving earthform that had effectively divided the city for generations. Once a conduit for passenger service, its tracks now carried mostly noisy freight.

The railroad had been heretofore seen as a liability, an urban obstruction of the most stubborn kind. Earlier schemes either ignored the tracks, accepted them with reluctance, or tried to hide them. Concepts of burying the tracks were impractical due to the awesome expense and enormous travel distance necessary to submerge and then resurface rail lines. Ideas of erecting structures directly above the rail lines were equally questionable with the resulting image of rumbling locomotives tunneling through buildings or parking structures, an all-too-industrial prospect. And the concept

of elevated plazas over the railroad would levitate such pedestrian areas from the surrounding streets, an urban-design concept that usually failed. Our team instead attempted to see the railroad as an amenity requiring only subtle adjustments to work with the overall agenda. The concept of using these train tracks was bolstered by studying the major feature appearing on Tennessee maps in encyclopedias as late as the 1940s and 1950s: railroads. Nashville still remains the crossing point of several important rail lines, valuable right-of-ways that will probably not vanish in the

foreseeable future. We speculated that, as many experts predict, our country would eventually develop passenger transportation systems that utilize these corridors, such as high-speed magnetic trains or simple commuter lines. The path of such trains would cut right across the site of the new park. Commuters of the future might someday overlook the terrain as their ancestors did from the time of the Civil War.

The railroad berm would be conquered by changing it into an open bridge between Sixth and Seventh Avenues. Instead of burying the train tracks or going over the

81

Barrier of bridge and berm

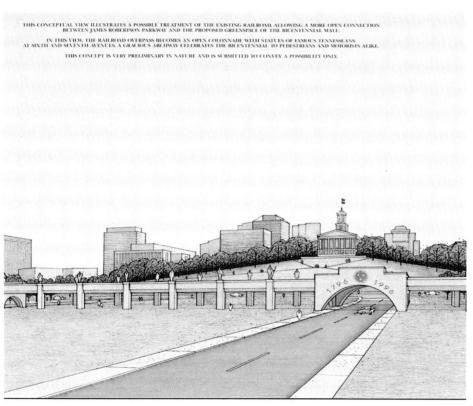

THIS CONCEPTUAL VIEW ILLUSTRATES A POSSIBLE TREATMENT OF THE EXISTING RAILROAD, ALLOWING A MORE OPEN CONNECTION BETWEEN JAMES ROBERTSON PARKWAY AND THE PROPOSED GREENSPACE OF THE BICENTENNIAL MALL.

IN THIS VIEW, THE RAILROAD OVERPASS BECOMES AN OPEN COLONNADE WITH STATUES OF FAMOUS TENNESSEANS. AT SIXTH AND SEVENTH AVENUES, A GRACIOUS ARCHWAY CELEBRATES THE BICENTENNIAL TO PEDESTRIANS AND MOTORISTS ALIKE.

THIS CONCEPT IS VERY PRELIMINARY IN NATURE AND IS SUBMITTED TO CONVEY A POSSIBILITY ONLY.

Early concept for open viaduct

mound of dirt, we proposed to simply go through. By the earthwork being removed and the site between the two streets opened up, the lawn of Capitol Hill could now unroll north like a great green carpet. And though this concept was originally proposed as a simple bridge similar to what one would expect in these days of purely utilitarian structures, we would later revise it to be a more fitting piece of urban design. Historic precedent suggested the form for the new bridge, and the solution that had once conquered the natural constraints of the site returned: a trestle!

Walking north, pedestrians would pass under and through the new railroad trestle viaduct. Rebuilt as an attractive, light, and airy structure, the trestle would need to be less of a barrier and more of a gateway. The viaduct would be elevated slightly for a more spacious area beneath. To minimize rail traffic downtime, it would have to be constructed slightly north of the current berm. Unlike the existing, somewhat skewed path, the new trestle and improved rail line would cross the Mall at a ninety-degree angle, fully perpendicular to the streets and new park.

New railroad bridges, long overdue, would be built at Fifth, Sixth, Seventh, and Eighth Avenues. As part of this transportation enhancement, other infrastructure projects would need to take place. Several utilities would have to be relocated and upgraded. A large Nashville Electric Service overhead power line would have to be placed underground. If all of this were accomplished, the messy image of a cluttered industrial yard and parking wasteland would be transformed to an enhanced rail corridor and an available field ready for future development.

RECOMMENDATION FOUR
EXTENDING THE GREEN SPACE

The Mall would be the centerpiece project, the permanent civic gift by the governor and the General Assembly in honor of the Bicentennial. We advocated early that it should be an urban park whose purpose would be to educate Tennesseans about their rich past and inspire them to think about their future.

We thoroughly agreed with one facet that had already been suggested earlier: to extend the Mall to Jefferson Street. For many reasons this was absolutely essential for the success of the entire endeavor. First, Jefferson Street was being widened and

Looking north down Sixth Avenue

83

Shed roof at Jefferson Street

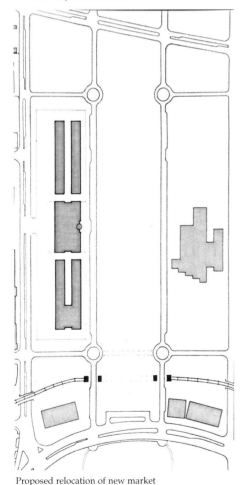
Proposed relocation of new market

Farmers' Market

Seal of Tennessee   TDTD

repaved to become a major vehicular artery into the city from the interstate highway directly east—the traffic strategy including construction of a bland but important new bridge over the Cumberland River. Second, this street was the next major road north of James Robertson Parkway, a busy thoroughfare that bordered Germantown and connected to the nearby community of Buena Vista and beyond to the historic campuses of Fisk and Tennessee State Universities. Finally, the Mall had to reach Jefferson Street to make the necessary civic impact of providing a stunning view of the Capitol from a considerable distance and from a busy main road.

Several earlier schemes had terminated at the gates of the existing Farmers' Market at Jackson Street, accepting as a foregone conclusion that nothing could evict this quirky yet authentic neighborhood and regional amenity. Jackson Street was important to the immediate vicinity but did not connect outside the neighborhood. To accomplish the concept of extending the green space to Jefferson, the call would have to be made from state to city officials to see if the market would agree to relocate slightly south to a new site on Eighth Avenue. Whether they would agree to the

concept no one knew. But Farmers' Market—the authentic open-shed operation —was ready to move. In the past decade, officials of this unique entity had considered several other locations, including East Nashville. The proposition to stay near their existing address made sense and seemed attractive to them if the inevitable relocation challenges and political snags could be resolved.

Much would be gained by the seemingly unachievable move of the market. The adjacent, now dilapidated grocery store would be demolished and perhaps rebuilt some distance from the site where it might still serve the neighborhood without diluting the stringent agenda for special facilities on the periphery of the new park. The grungy liquor store at the southeast corner of Jefferson Street and Eighth Avenue, a thorn in almost everyone's side, would also meet the wrecking ball. The old sheds would be replaced, and an enclosed, conditioned building would be erected to allow year-round operation and minimize the limited seasonal peaks of sales and activity at the market. Erection of new structures nearby on Eighth Avenue would allow the existing market to remain open until the replacement facility was complete.

84

East facade of proposed market

Early concept for Capitol Hill and lawn

The uniqueness of a rejuvenated Farmers' Market would help ensure visitation of the new park next door. We were also enticed by the thematic connection to agriculture, recalling that although this was to be an urban park, its theme of Tennessee must still respond to the state's predominant agricultural image. With "agriculture" stamped prominently across its middle, even the official Tennessee state seal seemed to endorse the proposed relationship.

Moving the market and changing it to a much more useful facility would require complicated negotiations involving the state, city, and the Farmers' Market board of directors to accomplish everyone's objectives. The market would thrive as a unique destination, and the Mall would be populated by at least one active retail neighbor with hopes for other nearby cultural facilities to follow in the future. Most importantly, with the market moved out of the way, citizens would forever have

a grand view of Strickland's masterpiece in the distance.

The Mall would extend the boundaries of the Capitol grounds 2,200 feet north from James Robertson Parkway to Jefferson Street. The nineteen-acre Mall would become permanent open space, much like the Champ de Mars and Centennial Park after their respective expositions. It would be very risky, and the whispers of skeptics critical of the concept, its location, and of the expenditures necessary to accomplish the dream would constantly be heard.

The project would assist as a stimulus for revitalizing nearby existing residential neighborhoods. City officials would hopefully use the arrival of the new park as an incentive to create a new redevelopment district, encouraging entrepreneurs to reconsider the value and opportunities of this often neglected part of Nashville. We proposed that the underdeveloped area immediately around the Mall be revitalized

into a mixed-use district of cultural facilities and museums, state and private offices, and retail space. Residential areas would also need to be incorporated nearby to create a twenty-four-hour occupancy within the new district, and ample parking would need to be provided for all of these uses. The initial development, however, would probably involve only the Mall, parking for state employees, and the new Farmers' Market. Subsequent development would occur over a period of decades, hopefully guided by the original vision of the master plan. Throughout this evolution, the park would probably remain as the centerpiece amenity of the district. Someone or some group would have to push for proper development implementation, much like Samuel Morgan did for the Capitol almost a century and a half ago.

A basic concept was now in place. It was time to conceive the park, the Bicentennial destination itself.

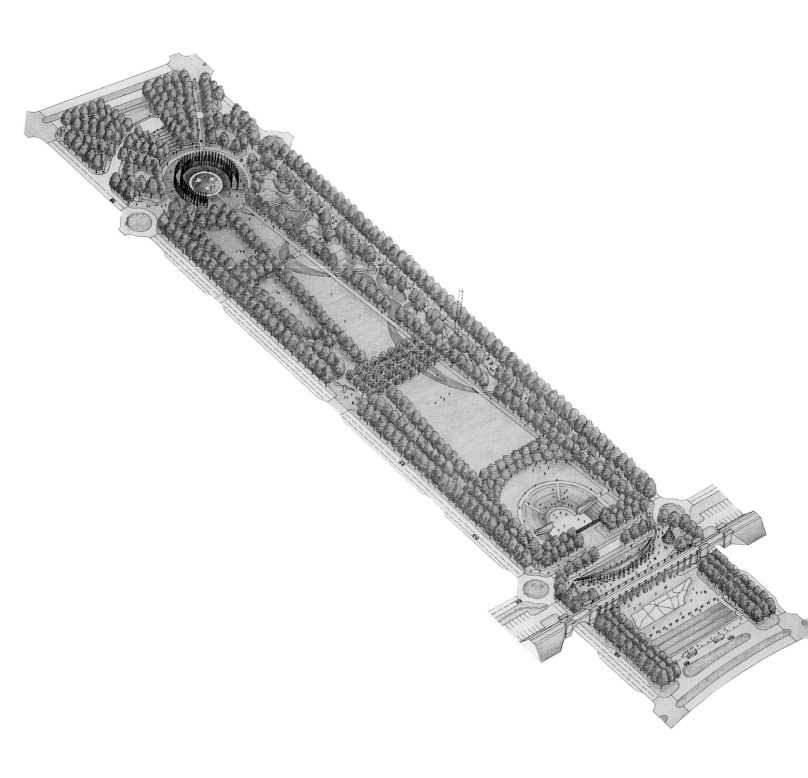

Design for a New Park

*Inspiration descends only in flashes,
to clothe circumstances.*

Patrick White

With the expected relocation of the Farmers' Market and the resulting clean slate of property, the most difficult questions remained regarding the proposed Mall. What should actually be contained within the new park? What should this place do, what should it say? How should it extend and reinforce the greenery and ambiance of the nearby hill? By what manner would it best energize the immediate vicinity? What could it most appropriately say about Tennessee on the occasion of its two-hundredth birthday? Herein was found the ultimate question that we had to attempt to answer in order to formulate the landmark park: What is Tennessee?

A THEME FOR 200 YEARS

We studied many sources for the answer to this question, from James Crutchfield's *Tennessee Almanac* to Wilma Dykeman's *Tennessee*, from the *Tennessee Bluebook* to Charles Crawford's elementary-school textbook on the state. We also poured through marketing material about Tennessee published by the Department of Tourist Development. Older sources were also utilized, and it was stimulating to review older textbooks and encyclopedias to discover what others had written in the past

"Tennessee rock"

about the Volunteer State. Maps of all kinds were contemplated. My son, four years old at the time, proudly announced one day that he had found, in his words, a "Tennessee rock," and we were reminded of the unique forty-two-thousand-square-mile parallelogram, a form easily recognized by even our youngest citizens. Poetry and literature also ignited our creativity and bolstered our concepts, especially the works of Agee, Davidson, Warren, and Twain. The heritage and worldwide reputation of Tennessee music suggested an acoustic element, a sonic feature that would complement the planned visual and historic elements. It would all come together with an almost obvious theme for the design of the park: the land, the people, the music.

After months of careful study, the master plan team presented a proposal for the park itself. This was the program for

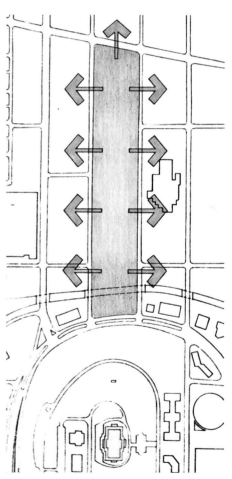
Park as generator of activity

Symbols

The State Seal

The Roman numerals XVI signify that Tennessee was the sixteenth state to enter the Union. The plow, the sheaf of wheat and a cotton stalk symbolize the importance of agriculture, while the riverboat attests to the importance of river traffic to commerce.

The State Bird

The mockingbird (genus *Mimus polyglottos*) was selected as the state bird in 1933. One of the finest singers among North American birds, it possesses a melodious song of its own, and is especially noted for its skill in mimicking the songs of other birds.

The State Insects

Tennessee has two official state insects... the firefly and the ladybug. The firefly emits a luminescent light easily seen on summer evenings. The light is a natural form of incandescent light which man has never completely duplicated.

The reddish-orange ladybug has distinctive black spots on each wing cover. It helps farmers by controlling insect pests, especially aphids. In folk medicine, ladybugs were believed to cure various diseases such as colic and measles.

The State Gem

Tennessee River pearls are taken from mussels in the fresh water rivers and come in various shapes and colors. Unlike cultured pearls, which are partially man-made, these pearls are totally made by the mussel. They are 100% natural pearl all the way through.

The State Capitol

In Tennessee's early history, four different towns served as the seat of government: Knoxville, Kingston, Murfreesboro, and Nashville. Nashville was chosen as the permanent capital city in 1843. The capitol building was designed by noted architect William Strickland, who died during its construction and is buried within its walls. Marble quarried in Tennessee was used for the primary building material. A magnificent example of Grecian architecture, the building was begun in 1845 and completed in 1859.

The State Flag

Adopted in 1905, the flag features three stars representing the grand divisions of the state: East, Middle and West. The stars are bound together in indissoluble unity by an unending white band.

The State Tree

The tulip poplar (*Liriodendron Tulipifera*) was adopted as the state tree by the State Legislature in 1947. The tulip poplar was chosen because it was used extensively by the Tennessee pioneers to construct their houses, barns and other buildings. The tree sometimes reaches a height of 200 feet and frequently shows 50-100 feet of trunk without a branch. The bark is smooth and brownish gray. The leaves are very smooth with a broad notch at the tip. The flowers are tuliplike, green-orange in color, and are 1-3 inches deep.

The State Rocks

Limestone, found just about everywhere in Tennessee, was declared the official state rock in 1979. Tennessee marble, as the metamorphic version of limestone is known, is widely used in public and private buildings. In 1969 the General

Assembly had given similar status to agate, a cryptocrystalline quartz. This semiprecious gemstone is found only in a few areas of the state.

The State Wildflower

The passion flower (genus *Passiflora*) was declared the state wildflower in 1973. It received its name from early Christian missionaries to South America, who saw in the flower's various parts symbols of the crucifixion of Jesus Christ.

The State Flower

The iris (genus *Iridaceae*) was designated as the state cultivated flower by the Legislature in 1933. While there are several different colors among the iris, the purple iris is commonly accepted as the state flower.

The State Songs

Music is such an integral part of Tennessee's heritage that there are not one, but five official state songs: *My Homeland Tennessee...When It's Iris Time In Tennessee...My Tennessee, Tennessee Waltz...and Rocky Top.*

The State Animal

The raccoon (*Procyon lotor*) is a furry mammal with a bushy, ringed tail and a mask-like band of black hair around its eyes. Raccoons eat fish and frogs that they catch in rivers and streams. They measure from 30 to 38 inches long, and weigh from 12 to 25 pounds.

Symbols of the Volunteer State

TDTD

Mural in John Sevier State Office Building by Dean Cornwell, 1941

TSM/TSPS

Resource material

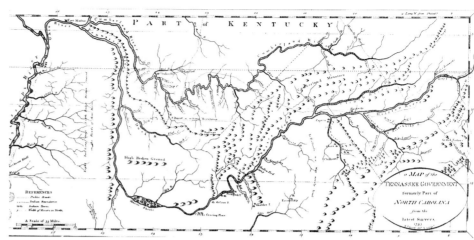

Early 1795 map of "Tennasee"

Historic portrayal of topography

Tennessee State Parks   TDEC

Original inhabitants   TDEC

Beneath the surface   TDEC

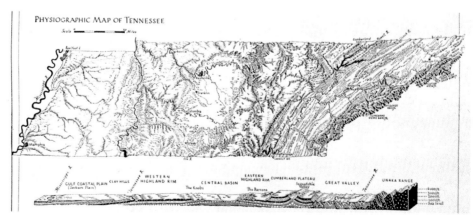

Physiographic map from *Geography of Tennessee*   GCU

Topographical map of Tennessee

the landmark, an outline for the structure of the park. Based on this document, the Mall would embody the principal themes of Tennessee history and its people, the beautiful and varied landscape, and the musical expressions unique to this state.

More importantly, the specifics of the layout would be the fundamental obligation that this new park be a place for learning. Elements within the Mall would need to be not only attractive and inviting but equally educational, conveying pertinent information to children of all ages. Learning from the successes and shortcomings of other outdoor projects, we knew it would be vital that the elements convey information in a delightful, intriguing manner, surprising visitors who otherwise might have expected a picturesque but otherwise dull park. Such elements would need to also be participatory, drawing their strength from issues or histories that would be meaningful to guests from across the entire state. Visitors would ideally journey to the site and discover different levels of meaning, from smaller identifiable items (towns) to medium-sized elements (counties) to larger, more impressive compositions (the total state). These would need to recognize the opportunity to provide meaning through all the human senses,

accommodating citizens of differing abilities while creating a memorable experience.

PLAN FOR THE MALL

The original functional program for the Mall had been divided into three major sections: an arrival area at the south end, a performance area at the center, and a focal area at the north end—this third part intended to pull attention and activity across the long site. This outline would be significantly enriched, but these program thoughts were the first steps toward the creation of a new place about an old but in many ways young state.

The principal entrance to the Mall would be the arrival area, a formal plaza located immediately north of James Robertson Parkway, bounded by Sixth and Seventh Avenues and the new CSX railroad trestle. Connecting the hill with the expanse of the Mall, the Tennessee Plaza would also provide visitor orientation, a starting point.

Presenting the landscape of Tennessee, the plaza would be symbolic yet representational. A large, flat map of the state, positioned correctly with the long axis of Tennessee in an east-west direction, was proposed. A complete view of the plaza and state map would be purposely best from

elevated positions at the Capitol and from the new Belvedere overlook midway up Capitol Hill. Special lighting would extend this view into evening hours. The plaza would include a vehicular drop-off on the north side of the parkway, and parking would be provided around the periphery, especially for tourists and buses of school children visiting both the Capitol and the new park.

The new railroad trestle viaduct would form a dynamic backdrop to the arrival plaza. Freight trains would be ushered across the new trestle and bridges above Sixth and Seventh Avenues with a new elegance. The area directly beneath the trestle would serve as an orientation center, security station, or perhaps a gift shop, and public rest rooms would also occupy the covered zone.

Immediately north of the open trestle would be an area devoted to Tennessee's rivers and their tremendous roles in the early settlement and continued prosperity of the state. To acknowledge the rivers of Tennessee, we proposed an educational element and a kinetic feature, enticing those standing on the arrival area's big map to venture through the trestle into the rest of the park. We proposed that vertical fountains, one for each major state river, would be positioned directly in front of a polished

Cotton field in West Tennessee   RH

Reelfoot Lake   RH

Farmland in Houston County

Cedar trees in Middle Tennessee

Pasture and crops in Grundy County

Limestone outcroppings

Rural barn in East Tennessee

Lookout Mountain

Smoky Mountains

91

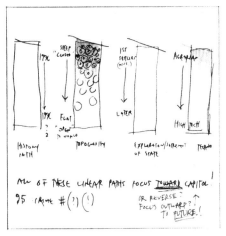

Ideas for a long parcel

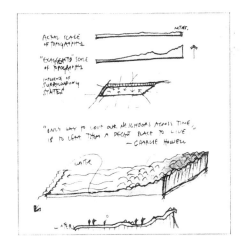

Site as a state profile

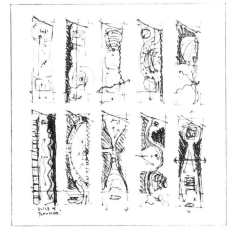

Figure studies

Alternative layouts for the new park

granite wall, a curved surface covered with text about the waterways of Tennessee.

North of Harrison Street, a minor street bisecting the site, would be the location of a flexible outdoor performance space. This area would host performances planned for the Bicentennial Celebrations, ranging from intimate musical or dramatic productions to

larger events. The performance area, an amphitheater, would be slightly recessed into the grade, composed of a series of grass lawn terraces descending down to a stage. When not in use, the performance area would nevertheless be an attractive space. During performances, trains crossing the trestle would obviously need to be diverted

to alternate routes. Specific requirements for this amphitheater would need additional input from performance professionals. The location of the stage would be such that the audience would face Capitol Hill to the south, and from this new amphitheater, the majestic Capitol would appear as the major element on the city skyline above.

A major design debate involved the Lick Branch sewer, its underground path creating an easement that sliced across the Mall between Harrison Street and the proposed performance area. The original Lick Branch had been replaced near the end of the nineteenth century by a gigantic brick sewer, still in place some twenty-five feet below the surface. Structures of any significant size were, for the most part, prohibited on this easement. The brick membrane of this pipe was probably weathered and fragile, creating a subterranean tube of unknown condition and stability. Even now this sewer continues to operate as a combined storm water and sanitary sewer; in layman's terms, everything runs into it. It is the source of an ongoing environmental debate between city and state officials due to its lack of emergency overflow capacity in the event of a major downpour. We struggled with the proper strategy to utilize the land above the

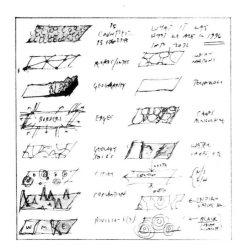
States of the state

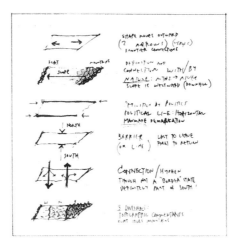
Meaning of the parallelogram

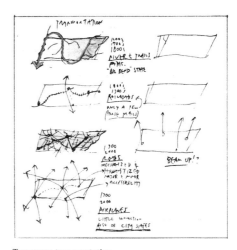
Tennessee transportation

submerged feature, deciding to avoid any substantial construction in this area. The straight line of the fifty-foot-wide easement would therefore exist unnoticed between Harrison Street and the location of the new amphitheater, yet we would recall the original path of the once lovely stream and its tributaries with a pedestrian walkway that would "flow" to the river. We would resurface the creek if only in spirit.

Comprising approximately ten acres, the northern portion of the Mall would become a unique park. Open lawns and shaded groves would accommodate strolling, picnicking, and other passive recreational activities. The park would include focal elements that would reinforce the Bicentennial theme along with the unique history, music, and landscape of Tennessee. Features in this section would be based on the state's heritage, its topography, its vegetation, and its diversity. It would also contain representations of each of Tennessee's ninety-five counties. Portions in this area of the park would be distinctly different in feel and use, pastoral and informal in character to ingratiate visitors with the state's natural beauty and variety. Long forgotten historic features, including McNairy Spring, Sulphur Spring, and

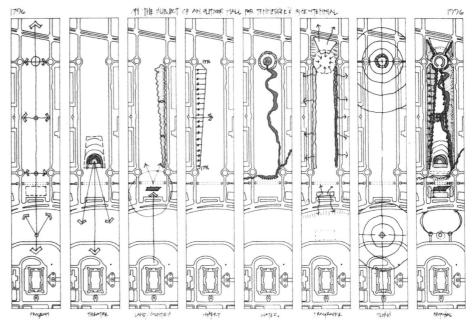
Concept diagrams

others, would also be incorporated into the arrangement.

Development of the large and relatively open northern section offered many creative opportunities. Unlike the essentially featureless National Mall, we would here infuse the park and fill it with many symbolic elements. By virtue of their

extended lengths, the long edges of the park along Sixth and Seventh Avenues provided two unique linear opportunities. Along Sixth Avenue, the eastern edge of the park would become an essay and presentation of the diversity of the state's landscape and vegetation, a Tennessee arboretum. This path would also contain

93

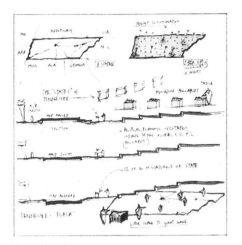
Studies for a big map

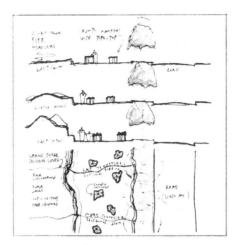
A walk for ninety-five counties

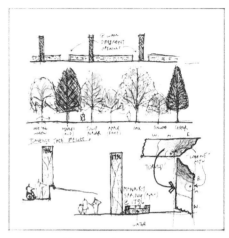
Vegetation and history path

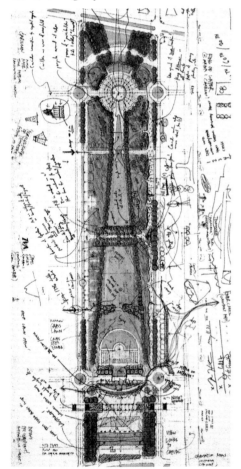
Final schematic layout, May 11, 1993

information about Tennessee's ninety-five counties and symbolic deposits of memorabilia collected from each entity. The trail would work in conjunction with the plantings and symbolic earth forms to create an informal, representative walk across the state—a Walkway of the Counties. A vicinity landmark, an overlook tower, was also initially pondered, and rotaries on the peripheral streets would help calm vehicular traffic.

Along the western edge against Seventh Avenue we proposed the Pathway of History, a granite wall timeline with vertical markers that would present the history of the state. In contrast to the casual, winding character of the county walkway on the opposite side, this timeline would be a rigid and precise composition, an accurate ruler engraved with events from the history of Tennessee. The middle part of the Mall would remain open—a simple, green lawn. A body of still water would occupy part of this central zone, providing the refreshing and reflective qualities expected and needed in a park environment and complementing the kinetic fountains to the south.

Twin diagonal paths, beginning with large flagpoles at the south end of the park, would shift slightly from the strict orthogonal plan geometry to focus on an area at the north end of the park against Jefferson Street. On the two long walkways, we would provide a location where individual Tennesseans could literally put their personal mark on the park, accomplished through the installation of brick-sized, red granite pavers engraved with the names of relatives, friends, or distant ancestors. The paved trails, collectively named the "Path of Volunteers," would focus on a single dynamic event at the north end, a feature that would anchor the overall composition and counterbalance the ingredients of the arrival area and big map at the other end. Composed of a circular plaza and featuring the three stars from the Tennessee state flag, this space, the Court of Three Stars, would contain an acoustical device highlighting the music heritage of Tennessee: a carillon of ninety-five bells.

Given the stature of its purpose and location, the park and all other parts of the Capitol area master plan were designed for visitor safety and an appropriate level of maintenance, with the landscape being regarded as an evolving, sustainable, and cherished resource. Access by visitors who are physically challenged would be an essential requirement. Security lighting of

94

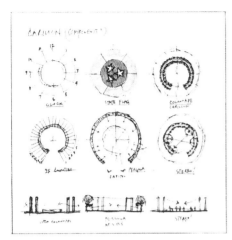

Studies for north-end destination

all areas would be mandatory but done to promote comfort and not merely overkill illumination. Lighting of the Mall and Capitol Hill would also reinforce the dominance of the Greek Revival masterpiece statehouse while accentuating the new outdoor space. An important recommendation was that the park be monitored not by police but rather by Tennessee State Park Rangers, ambassadors of the state known for their friendly demeanor. This would require many discussions between state agencies because the state-park system traditionally maintained only large rural parks, not urban situations such as the Mall.

THE PLAN CONFIRMED

The schematic design phase for the park occurred quickly, adhering to the parameters of the program. Numerous site plan options and adjustments were investigated by the design team, and after several months of intense work, a consensus was reached on May 11, 1993. At about the same time, a dramatic shift occurred in the urban-planning design strategy when state officials announced that they had finalized an arrangement to purchase the American General Tower, obtaining a new inventory of more than 830,000 square feet of office space

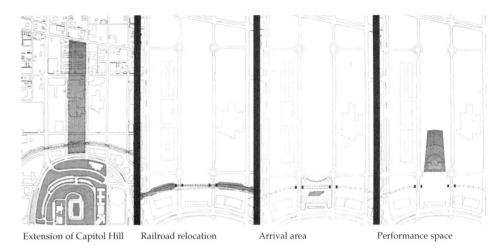

Extension of Capitol Hill Railroad relocation Arrival area Performance space

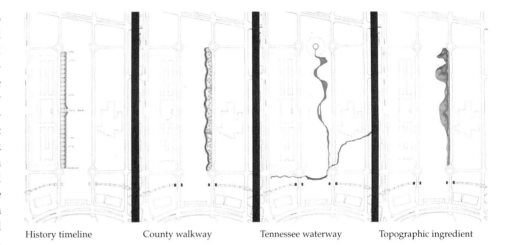

History timeline County walkway Tennessee waterway Topographic ingredient

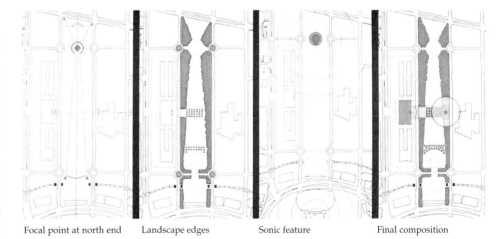

Focal point at north end Landscape edges Sonic feature Final composition

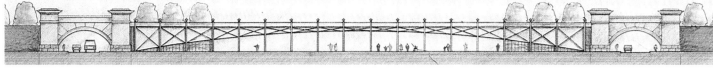

Trestle with bridges at Sixth and Seventh Avenues

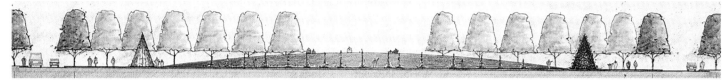

River fountains front arched granite wall

in the signature structure conveniently located close to other existing state buildings. By virtue of its nearby proximity, the tower that had risen too close almost two decades earlier would now become part of the family. Acquisition of this huge building also meant that additional state office facilities would probably not be built near the Mall for many years, if ever. The master plan had sought to populate the vicinity around the new park with several different uses, anticipating that substantial state office space would be a major ingredient. But purchase of the mammoth building, later renamed the "Tennessee Tower," dissolved this potential in the interim and now allowed the preference of placing cultural facilities around the Mall in the future—creating the possibility of an attractive situation not unlike one of the best characteristics of the well-known mall archetype in Washington, D.C. Last minute adjustments were made to the overall plan to capitalize on this significant change and establish a framework for the long-term cultural promise for the periphery of the Mall.

On July 8, 1993, the ambitious master plan and schematic design of the park concept received formal approval by our client, the Tennessee State Building Commission.

Governor McWherter's commitment and steady hand had ensured that the design and execution would rise to the once-in-a-century challenge. Nevertheless, during the commission meeting there was stiff questioning regarding the specific design elements in the plan, the proposed relocation and ownership of Farmers' Market, and of the overall fiscal strategy developed by finance wizard David Manning, commissioner of Finance and Administration. A land swap had been arranged with the city through its development executive Gerald Nicely, ensuring that the state would have ownership of the market property, while day-to-day operations would remain with the city and the market's board of directors. Treasurer Steve Adams insisted that materials in the new park be durable, withstanding use for many generations. Secretary Riley Darnell and Speaker Jimmy Naifeh expressed concern over maintenance and security issues, and Comptroller William Snodgrass quizzed us about accessibility and safety, especially for children and senior citizens. During the presentation, Lieutenant Governor Wilder asked outright, "Young man, does this Mall represent the *sovereignty* of Tennessee?" I paused, not quite sure how to answer. He repeated his question slowly, impatiently,

and then explained that it was very important to him and others involved in governing the state that the Mall express the separate stability and self-sufficiency of Tennessee. Pride and self-reliance were important traits to portray in this endeavor, and his question was legitimate. I answered, "Yes." Would the Mall actually exert a sense of sovereignty, a feeling of distinctive pride? Such was certainly a valid goal. Yet I now know that only with a generation of use and enjoyment of the Mall by state citizens and their visitors would I learn if I had responded in complete honesty.

The plan soon afterward also received important endorsements by the Bicentennial Commission and the Capitol Commission, as well as the spirited support of many legislators, including Senator Douglas Henry and Representative John Bragg. With acceptance of the basic plan by state officials, the major challenge would be the implementation of the final design process necessary to fully realize the intentions of the master plan.

ONWARD INTO FINAL DESIGN

When a major state building project shifts from the category of probability to reality, a curious event also usually occurs, and with the Capitol Area and Bicentennial

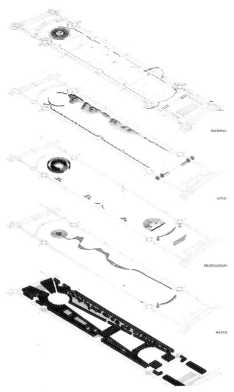

Layers of the park composition

Bicentennial logo   TN200

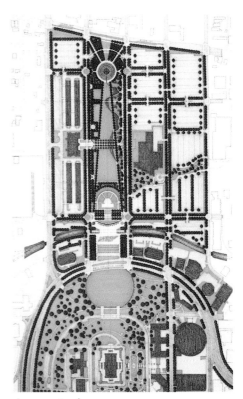

A new master plan

Mall Master Plan the pattern was no different. Instead of a single contract for design and construction work, the project was divided into separate assignments to finalize the already established schematic design ingredients and prepare construction documents. This allowed many more design professionals and general contractors to participate but added complexity in coordination of the endeavor. The master plan was divided into several distinct parts: changes to Capitol Hill, roadway improvements, parking lots, railroad trestle, and the Mall itself. Thanks to the scrutiny of state officials, each section was placed in the hands of committed teams, with members of the original design team distributed to the separate yet interlinked endeavors. Capitol Hill was assigned to Charles Warterfield Jr. Architects; Hodgson & Douglas Landscape

Architects; and Gresham, Smith and Partners as engineers. The dramatic roadway revisions around the Mall were assigned to Barge, Waggoner, Sumner & Cannon Engineers. Extensive new peripheral parking areas and the greenway path were assigned to Gresham, Smith and Partners with Ritchie Smith Associates Landscape Architects. The new trestle and railroad bridges were assigned to Nathan-Evans-Taylor Architects and Stanley D. Lindsey & Associates Structural Engineers. Master plan team member Jon Coddington would remain involved as a consultant throughout the ensuing evolution of the design process. The splitting of responsibilities would result in minor design disagreements and several coordination headaches, yet overall the collection of diverse capabilities worked together quite well. As the official Bicentennial logo was unveiled and Kelly Tolson was appointed head of Tennessee 200, the park design shifted into high gear.

The final design of the Mall was assigned to a new team composed of our firm of Tuck Hinton Architects; original master plan team entity SSOE; and Ross/Fowler Landscape Architects of Knoxville, a talented group previously uninvolved in the Mall project.

This new design team jelled quickly, reconfirming expectations and assigning the separate yet critically interdependent architectural, landscape, and engineering responsibilities. Ross/Fowler Principal Mike Fowler clarified his firm's intention to intensify previous decisions with a level of skill and knowledge demanded by the complexity of both the program and preliminary scheme. The art of our distinct crafts merged but not without several heated discussions. It was perhaps the most productive time in the entire process as the desired images, forms, and features were detailed and finalized for construction. The intensive design phase continued through 1993 into 1994, when construction work began. Other design teams also finalized their respective commissions. The deadline of 1996 now loomed only two years away.

THE MALL ARRIVES

Time does not relinquish its rights, either over human beings or over monuments.

Goethe

Groundbreaking for the Tennessee Bicentennial Capitol Mall occurred on June 27, 1994. Governor McWherter presided over the ceremony, depositing a time capsule full of personal memorabilia under a large granite plaque. Construction first began with the revisions to Capitol Hill by Hardaway Construction Corporation, including the removal of the wide parking terrace and the steep one-way Gay Street extension that had scarred the north slope for three decades. At the same time, Ray Bell Construction Company started construction on the new Farmers' Market on Eighth Avenue. The peripheral roads affected by the master plan were attacked, and the massive construction of the railroad trestle and the new earth-berm adjustments commenced, also by Bell. Other contractors tackled demolition, utility relocation, roadway, and parking-area assignments. Heery International coordinated and supervised the interwoven, complicated construction process. Earlier in March, a new Kroger store had broken ground several blocks north to replace the old one next to the existing Farmers' Market. Construction of this new grocery store was welcomed evidence that city officials with the Metropolitan Development and Housing Authority would pursue their plans to attempt to improve the vicinity north of the Mall through the newly approved Phillips-Jackson Redevelopment Plan.

In the Mall area, the amphitheater was the first element constructed; this work by Bell started in late October 1994. Formal construction of the Mall proper by Hardaway began at the end of 1994. Shortly thereafter on January 21, 1995, the torch of government passed from the McWherter administration to one headed by the new governor, Don Sundquist, and management of the park endeavor landed at the feet of new Commissioner of Finance and Administration Bob Corker, a bright entrepreneur from Chattanooga.

The complexities of construction were formidable. Not only did the numerous contractors have to coordinate their separate assignments, but each had to contend with the unusual nature of the site, a terrain covered with rubble, cinders, and debris from its use as a landfill a century ago. Particularly difficult was the railroad assignment. The project required construction of an entirely separate line, including four bridges, earthwork berms, and a hefty steel trestle, all within yards of the existing railway path and under the

Groundbreaking ceremony

constant scrutiny of CSX railroad officials.

Alignment in construction was crucial. The orthogonal geometry and Cartesian order of the plan mandated constant checking and rechecking to ensure that the new elements—walls, paths, markers, and plantings—would be located as intended. As construction proceeded, the relationships of built and natural components emerged, as did the elements' larger relationships with the Capitol, the new Farmers' Market, and the overall fabric of the city. The dedicated efforts of the numerous contractors were slowly unfolding.

New steps on north slope

View of Mall site from Capitol

Capitol Hill reshaped

Area between parkway and railroad berm

Existing berm and new trestle

Site undergoing transformation

Construction workers enjoying a break

Amphitheater takes shape

Trestle nears completion

100

Farmers' Market site cleared

Park forms emerge

Row of concrete pillars

Area beneath trestle

Construction team and map sample

Completion of map and compass

Snow blankets site in early 1996

Completed decade pylon

Representatives visit on April 27, 1996   BS

Officials at Johnson County disc   BS

Youngsters enjoy capital city marker   GL

Work continued at a brisk pace through 1995. The full establishment of the park was contingent upon completion of the railroad bridges and trestle on the southern end. The new Farmers' Market opened in the summer, allowing demolition of the tired metal sheds of the old market, which had been erected four decades earlier just beneath Jefferson Street. With the bookend obstacles of railroad berm and sheds removed, the final earthwork and shaping of the Mall proceeded. As 1996 finally arrived, the unique transformation of this part of the city was for the first time fully apparent.

A CAPSULE IN TIME

Although the Mall was not yet finished, a major event occurred on April 27, 1996, when the time capsules from all of Tennessee's ninety-five counties were simultaneously lowered into the ground. For each tomb, placed in geographic order along the Mall's east edge Walkway of the Counties, a startling array of material had been assembled by representatives of each county. As citizens from across the state deposited their memorabilia into the dirt and soul of the park, this Tennessee 200 Bicentennial event marked each county's first act of park ownership.

STATEHOOD FESTIVITIES

The Mall was ready just in time for perhaps the most memorable Bicentennial event, the Statehood Festival. After political squabbles about the immediate availability of the park to the public, the Mall was opened on Friday, May 31, 1996, at 8:00 A.M., and visitors slowly filtered into the new park. That afternoon, Nashville resident and Postmaster General Marvin Runyon, joined by Governor Sundquist, former Governor Ned McWherter, Mayor Philip Bredesen, and Bicentennial Commission Chairman Martha Ingram, issued the new Tennessee Bicentennial postage stamp at the first public event held in the new amphitheater. The thirty-two-cent stamp, featuring a twilight photo of the Capitol by Robin Hood, was dedicated and released for public sale, the third time that a William Strickland building had been so honored by the postal service.

Statehood Day, Saturday, June 1, 1996, was spectacular. A large portable stage was erected on the Tennessee Plaza above the granite map of the state. Citizens and their guests arrived to sit on chairs near the map and on the elliptical, sloped north lawn of Capitol Hill. The spacious outdoor yard quickly filled to capacity, and regardless of last minute seating issues, the air was full

of patriotic sentiment. At 6:30 P.M., a special session of the Tennessee State Legislature was convened, a ceremony that included speeches by Lieutenant Governor John Wilder, Speaker of the House of Representatives Jimmy Naifeh, Bicentennial Commission Chairman Martha Ingram, U.S. Vice President Al Gore Jr., and Governor Don Sundquist. A poem in honor of the occasion by poet laureate Margaret Britton Vaughn was delivered in addition to several other moving remarks, songs, and prayers. After the official dedication of the Mall, a thundering cannon salute was issued by the Tennessee National Guard from the Belvedere above the crowd on Capitol Hill and helicopters slowly peeled across the sky. The special legislative session and formal dedication of the Mall was concluded in high style.

The stately dedication ceremony was followed by "Celebration of the Centuries," a musical tribute to the Volunteer State produced by Opryland Productions and directed by Randy Johnson. Performers for this fabulous show included John Ritter, Isaac Hayes, Pat Boone, Amy Grant, Carl Perkins, Sam Moore, Vince Gill, Michael W. Smith, Brenda Lee, Chet Atkins, Ashley Cleveland,

Bicentennial stamp dedication in amphitheater   BS

Hillside fills with spectators   BS

Capitol Hill on June 1, 1996   BS

103

Fireworks from towers light up the sky   BS   BS

Cannon salute by Tennessee National Guard   TSPS

O'Landa Draper, the Harrington Brothers, the Tennessee Children's Dance Ensemble, and the Nashville Symphony. At the conclusion of the musical review, the assembled crowd witnessed one of the most intensive displays of fireworks ever in Tennessee, with colorful blasts and brilliant showers issued not only from the Mall but also from the two bookend office buildings directly east and west of the stage. It was a magnificent closing of the celebration.

After the fireworks, the large audience quietly dissipated, and yet some members took time to step onto the spacious granite map of Tennessee that had been temporarily cordoned off from the public. For most this was their first encounter with an element of the completed park. Citizens shuffled slowly across the engraved surface, looking for their place on the stone quilt. Before the arrival of settlers more than two hundred years ago, wildlife had regularly convened in this area to enjoy the fruits of nature and the resources of a winding stream, and now on this warm evening near the end of the twentieth century, modern inhabitants were now enjoying the fruits of a different era. It was the end of a day this architect shall not soon forget.

BS

BS

"Celebration of the Centuries"

TSPS

105

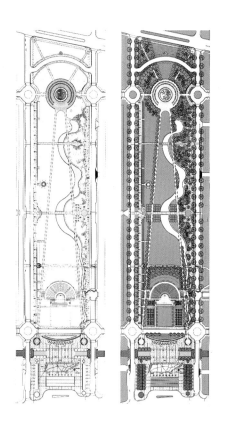

PART FOUR

THE NEW PARK

OVERTURE
CAPITOL HILL AND THE BELVEDERE
TENNESSEE PLAZA
RAILROAD BRIDGES AND TRESTLE
RIVERS OF TENNESSEE
AMPHITHEATER
CENTRAL LAWN
WALKWAY OF THE COUNTIES
PATHWAY OF HISTORY
COURT OF THREE STARS
THE THIRD CENTURY

TENNESSEE PLAZA
Arrival area with gigantic state map

RAILROAD TRESTLE
Steel bridge with Visitors Center beneath

RIVERS OF TENNESSEE
Fountains and curved wall honor state waterways

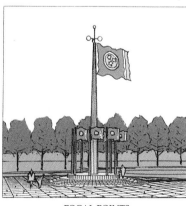

FOCAL POINTS
Dual collection of spires display state flag

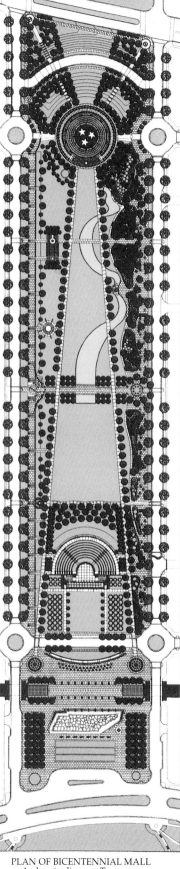

PLAN OF BICENTENNIAL MALL
A place to discover Tennessee

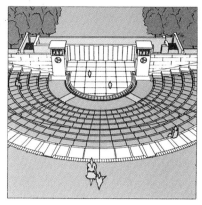

AMPHITHEATER
Greek-inspired performance area facing Capitol

WALKWAY OF THE COUNTIES
Topography and markers present 95 state entities

PATHWAY OF HISTORY
Pylons and 1400-foot wall record state history

COURT OF THREE STARS
Open plaza with 95-bell four-octave carillon

OVERTURE

Acknowledge our obligations to the present and our debts to the past—in order to make a lively and intense whole that is useful in the end and evocative.

Robert Venturi

The Tennessee Bicentennial Capitol Mall was built for state citizens and their guests, forged to honor the Capitol and exalt all that is Tennessee. Similar to Centennial Park, the new park is a permanent gift from government to its constituents. This destination is in Nashville, but its message, meaning, and obligation are purposely influenced by all ninety-five county entities. A large, outdoor vicinity, its security has been bestowed to Tennessee State Park Rangers, who greet visitors and provide a familiar image associated with respect and care for the land. The original intention was to ensure that the park would be in place for use during the Bicentennial year and avoid the year-late situation created a century earlier. With the exception of a few components of the original design, that goal was achieved.

By no means does the Mall showcase all the richness of Tennessee. The built features are exemplars, ingredients that reflect and exhibit with few exceptions the positive aspects of the state. The true diversity of a state shared by more than five million individuals and covering forty-two thousand square miles is beyond comprehension or expression at one location. It was impossible to present all that makes this state special or all the substance that gives it definition. As

Tennessee ambassadors   TDEC

in other areas of the country, Tennessee is also faced with many serious challenges. These include conservation of its precious natural resources and control of rampant highway strip development, with its resulting detestable *sameness* that blurs the valuable distinction between this state and others. The frustrating issues of life at the end of the twentieth century often overwhelm, pushing the individual into a dazed stupor. A park alone cannot eliminate such

pressures, but it can offer a place to relieve, reinvigorate, and renew. Here the refreshments are not only nature but an overview, however brief, of the good things, the meaningful and unique attributes of Tennessee, the colorful, long parallelogram near the middle of the United States. The Mall does not claim perfection in its mission or form. It is in the purest sense simply a distinct destination where one might contemplate the finer aspects of a particular landscape

Before: parking lots and warehouses

Trestle, fountains, flags, and Riverwall   TSPS

Designers Hibdon, Tuck, Kennon, Fowler, Craig, and Hinton   BS

After: changes to the land of the Lick Branch   ML

coupled with interesting aspects of the inhabitants, past and present, of that land.

Now only in its infancy, the full evolution of the Mall will ultimately be influenced by the growth of the abundant vegetation and the use of the many public spaces within. The final impact of the collective built and natural components may not be known for many years, perhaps several decades or generations. As trees mature along the major paths, streets, and open areas, framed visual corridors and composed lawns now only mildly suggested will become fully defined and confirmed. Nature will slowly change and eventually dominate the numerous man-made features of the park. As intended, she will one day

fully recapture this place in Tennessee.

In the following pages, the separate yet interconnected parts of the endeavor are presented, each possessing a distinct origin and meaning, and now a distinct presence and impact. A brief description of the important changes on Capitol Hill initiates this closer examination. Due to the role of the Mall as an extension of the greenery of Capitol Hill, its front is generally considered to be the Tennessee Plaza, the portion at James Robertson Parkway that abuts the base of the adjacent massive earth form. A review of the Mall itself thus begins with this part. Extending north, the Mall's various features together form a journey, a commentary on the

Pathway leads to Tennessee Plaza   BS

characteristics of the state merged with the qualities of the site. A concluding section overviews several preliminary yet fundamental considerations for a third century.

CAPITOL HILL AND THE BELVEDERE

Is this the hill? is this the kirk?
Is this mine own countree?

Samuel Taylor Coleridge

For the occasion of the Bicentennial, Capitol Hill was transformed to return as a welcoming destination for the people of Tennessee. A new hillside was created to reinforce the stately presence of the state-house and expand opportunities for it. The reconfiguration was based on the design of the existing grounds, recommendations of the 1986 *Historic Structure Report,* and review of the dramatic changes that would occur directly north of the Capitol.

The wide, rectangular parking plateau immediately surrounding the Capitol remains relatively unchanged. Removal of selected areas of asphalt was proposed to soften the visual clutter of cars occupying almost every square inch of the plateau. It was also recommended that parked cars be removed from the short drive that winds up to the top of the plateau. This short extension of Seventh Avenue had been renamed Eakin-Weakley in honor of the two women who worked so hard to preserve the ambiance of Capitol Hill, and the upper end of their drive should not be littered with cars.

From the summit of the Capitol, two pedestrian pathways continue to provide access to other government offices and to the city: the south steps that extend to

Charlotte Avenue around the Motlow Tunnel entrance and the steps to the east that extend down to Jackson Plaza and on down to Park Place. The original four corners of Capitol Hill possessed inviting gateways onto the grounds, and the two remaining gates are revived as fitting portals onto the governmental summit. New deciduous trees were planted here and across the entire revised hillside to provide the next generation of vegetation. Evergreen cedar trees were also added in keeping with the spirit and history of the landform originally known as Cedar Knob.

The two stairways leading to the Alvin C. York and Sam Davis statues at the corners are to be reconnected with a walkway system crossing the south grounds. The entrance steps at the Motlow Tunnel located mid-block on axis with the statehouse may be rebuilt, the bunker-like entrance replaced with a more inviting form similar to the one that existed before the revision in the 1950s.

The north and east sides of Capitol Hill are reconnected with a promenade recognizing the state's contribution to national leadership on the highest level. The formal parterre garden surrounding the Andrew Jackson statue directly east of the Capitol is

Master plan of Capitol Hill

improved with pavement repairs, restored fountains, and additional lighting to reinforce the quiet setting. A short path leads directly south to a new statue of President Andrew Johnson by Jim Gray, dedicated on July 20, 1995. It faces east. The walk around Jackson Plaza is extended northward to provide paved access to the tomb

113

Jackson Plaza

Mills's equestrian statue of Andrew Jackson

Polk tomb now accessible

New statue of Andrew Johnson

of President and Mrs. James K. Polk, also designed by William Strickland. Beyond the Polk tomb, a new pedestrian path curves around the north side of Capitol Hill—along the original path of the carriage drive from Park Place—and connects to parking spaces near the State Library and Archives building, providing for the first time handicapped access of Jackson Plaza and the three presidential memorials.

An accessible route on the northeast side of Capitol Hill was proposed in the master plan to meet the American Disabilities Act guidelines and ensure that the entire hill-side would become available to everyone, top to bottom. A series of ramps and steps will zigzag down the hill to reach the inter-mediate terrace near the Cordell Hull Building and eventually extend all the way down the hill to the intersection of Fifth Avenue and James Robertson Parkway. This area is designed for the recognition of Tennessee's governors, with memorial statues or markers to acknowledge each individual. Along this winding path, Cordell Hull and other prominent volun-teers would also be recognized, and the route would honor people who contributed to Tennessee in all walks of life from science

to law and medicine to sports.

To provide an inviting destination for visitors arriving by car, a scenic drive now loops around Capitol Hill from Park Place off Charlotte Avenue, a replacement of the mid-level hillside parking plateau built in the 1950s. The drive connects west to parking areas below the State Library and Archives and Supreme Court buildings. The central area of the drive on the north slope of Capitol Hill is reserved for short-term visitor parking.

With the removal of the wide parking terrace and the elimination of the steep one-way Gay Street, the Belvedere was constructed on the north side of Capitol Hill to create an overlook, similar in spirit to the parterre of Jackson Plaza. The Belvedere allows visitors to look out across the Bicentennial Mall, Germantown, and to the rolling hills beyond. Approximately two hundred feet wide and built of lime-stone to match the Capitol, the Belvedere has edges projecting forward at each end with details sympathetic to the rusticated pattern of the statehouse immediately above. Seen from the Mall, the wide stone overlook purposely appears as a visual extension of the base of the Capitol. A smaller, upper Belvedere is also planned

114

Concept for steps on northeast side

Overlook from Belvedere

Column graveyard at state prison

for the location of the ninety-sixth bell, the final element of the carillon in the Mall beyond.

Below the Belvedere is the great ellipse, a tilted lawn leading to the Mall. Designed to hold a vast crowd, this green bowl utilizes the sloped hill not unlike a scheme suggested by architect Russell Hart in the 1910s. The ellipse form is created by a pair of wide sweeping steps descending from the Belvedere down to the intersections of Sixth and Seventh Avenues on James Robertson Parkway. Only one of the two grand staircases has been installed. The second cannot be completed until the existing high-rise condominium building nearby is demolished. Removal of this structure will also allow establishment of the walkway and ramp system on the northeast side of Capitol Hill, returning the hill and Capitol to everyone.

To act as a base for the north crescent of Capitol Hill, renovations and changes to James Robertson Parkway were essential. It was recommended that the parkway be replanted with a colonnade of large decid-uous shade trees along each side of the street and in the median. The trees would give vertical form to the crescent-shaped parkway, provide shade and seasonal

color, and act as a natural filter to vehicular traffic, creating in total a distinct definition for the Capitol district. There is one distinct open break in the planned street-edge vegetation to emphasize the connection of the Capitol and the new Mall. New side-

walks, lighting, and street furniture were also proposed. Many of the these changes to the roadway currently remain incom-plete. The wide, sweeping boulevard had great promise in the 1950s; that potential still remains unfulfilled.

Ellipse lawn on north slope

115

View from top of cupola, circa 1955 · CW · 1992 · TSPS

Collection of column fragments

Fragments of the original columns that had been removed from the Capitol during the 1950s restoration were incorporated as a special final touch to the changes on Capitol Hill. These large pieces had been stored near the now-abandoned state prison in west Nashville, creating an eerie graveyard suggestive of a Greek ruin. Column fragments selected by architect Charles Warterfield Jr. were retrieved and placed on the hill just west of the Belvedere. Returning from the grounds of a prison, the stones ironically recall the convict labor used to construct the statehouse. The picturesque arrangement of column fragments serves, in the words of Warterfield, "as a memorial to the remarkable men who built the remarkable Capitol building." The column collection, Belvedere, and tilted lawn establish a viable enhancement of the stately Capitol Hill landform and a hyphen joining the statehouse to the new park directly north.

116

1994   TSPS

1996   TSPS

BS

117

TENNESSEE PLAZA

*Now the viewer knows that the frontier is not
"out there," has not been for a long time,
but is here. It is a frontier of mind and
purpose and will.*

Wilma Dykeman

The Tennessee Bicentennial Capitol Mall begins at the base of Capitol Hill on James Robertson Parkway with the Tennessee Plaza, a large outdoor civic room defined on the north by the new steel railroad trestle and focusing south across the street to the magnificent statehouse. The plaza is slightly sloped, and it possesses three grass terraces that gently cascade down from the street to provide a visual buffer for guests arriving at a vehicular pull-off area on the parkway. Though the park is approachable from any direction, this entrance area orients the visitor while making a physical, visual, and thematic connection to William Strickland's signature Capitol building.

The primary feature of this large outdoor area is a giant map of Tennessee. Composed of more than three hundred five-foot-square granite panels, it is one of the largest accurate renditions of a geographic area ever produced. Upon the map's granite surface, every county, city and town, railroad, state and U.S. highway, interstate, and river in the state is engraved. The size was conceived so that children in an elementary class studying Tennessee could fit within the outline of their home county's boundary. Because Tennessee is blessed with beautiful vege-

tation, the map is appropriately green. Pigmentation is used sparingly to highlight county and city names, with gold pinstripes indicating the interstate-highway system. The granite surface is polished to highlight the rivers of the state, and this treatment creates a shimmering, glistening appearance for the numerous waterways, similar to what is seen when traveling across Tennessee in an airplane. Approximately two hundred feet long and fifty feet wide, the map is slightly tilted so that it is more easily seen from both the new Belvedere and the Capitol on the majestic hill immediately south.

Several maps of Tennessee were considered as the guide for the engraved plaza surface. It was necessary to obtain one with sufficient detail and as many small town and community names as possible. The selected plat was a five-foot version previously prepared by the United States Department of the Interior. With a few exceptions and modifications required by both the sheer complexity of the map text and available granite engraving technology, this is the representation of Tennessee that appears on the plaza surface. Although an official version, the government map was not without minor

discrepancies, yet it offered the desired clarity of text, overall accuracy, and readability. The size of text on the map varies mainly to indicate population size, but all the smaller community names are the same letter size even though some of these vary considerably. The patchwork is quite fascinating as the land of Tennessee is sprinkled with many endearing town names: Fruitland and Skullbone in Gibson County, Spot and Only in Hickman County, Carlock and Tranquillity in McMinn County, and Okolona and Camelot in Hawkins County. Reverie is included, the only town in Tennessee located on the western side of the Mississippi River.

Directly east of the map is a large compass raised to seat height above the plaza, clearly indicating the orientation of the map. Engraved upon the surface is information about the reference material used to develop the big rendition of the state and its scale: one foot equals two and one-half miles. And directly south of the map is a new Zero Milestone marker, placed near the boulevard and featuring a playful Department of Transportation "T-Dot."

The large map is impressive yet very difficult to fully comprehend, especially for

ML

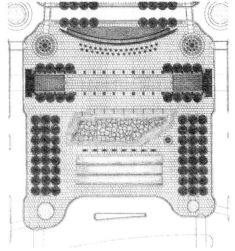
Plan of Tennessee Plaza

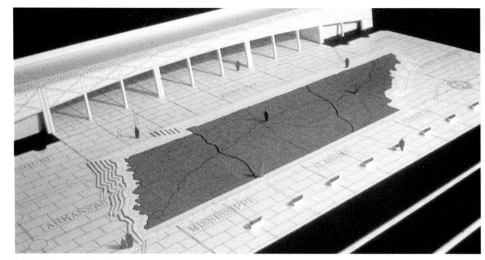
Model of map and trestle

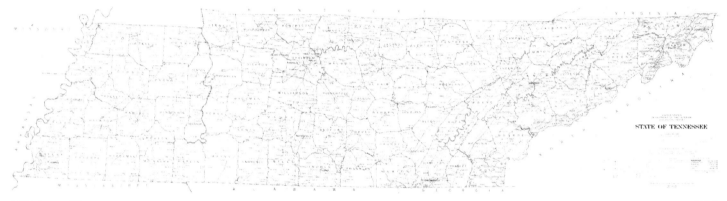
Official map of Tennessee   USDI

individuals walking across the surface for the first time. To assist in a more clear understanding not only of the shape of the state but of the dramatic different qualities of the parallelogram known as Tennessee, eight smaller maps are positioned on the south edge of the map. These solid granite renditions thrust upward at a tilted angle from the surface of the plaza, portraying eight different *states* of Tennessee. With the assistance of several state agencies and regional entities, these markers provide an informative lesson about the different qualities of the

state: geology, early inhabitants, territory, transportation, land cover, recreation, music heritage, and topography. Perhaps the most intriguing rendition is the depiction of the state from a historic map issued when statehood was granted, for this version indicates accurately the layout of the state but with a simple pictorial clarity. The most compelling is a sculptured, exaggerated topographic rendition indicating the variety of different state landforms from the flat areas of the west to the hilly and mountainous areas of the middle and east.

At twilight, the large map reveals a final message. As darkness descends, a small light begins to glow at each county seat of government. The flush-mounted luminaires provide a gentle light source at night while also illuminating visitors walking across the big map. From a distance, the ninety-five pinpoints of light clearly indicate the separate county headquarters evenly spaced across the long state and create a sparkling evening attraction at the new park.

Tennessee markers, map, and trestle   ML

Terraces step down to area of map   ML

View across map to trestle and fountains beyond   ML

Marker celebrates music

Girl studies 1795 map

Exaggerated topography tops eighth marker

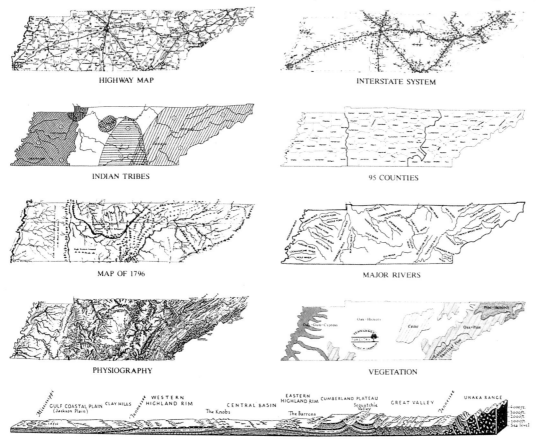

HIGHWAY MAP

INTERSTATE SYSTEM

INDIAN TRIBES

95 COUNTIES

MAP OF 1796

MAJOR RIVERS

PHYSIOGRAPHY

VEGETATION

SELECTIVE STATES OF TENNESSEE

Sources of inspiration for the Tennessee markers

RHP/TDEC

Detail of granite surface

122

Strolling citizens study the state

Visitors ponder information

Zero Milestone with "T-Dot"

Compass

View at dusk

ML

123

RAILROAD BRIDGES AND TRESTLE

We do not ride on the railroad; it rides upon us.

Thoreau

A new railroad trestle replaces the existing earth berm that previously crossed the Mall site and had created a seemingly impenetrable barrier between James Robertson Parkway and available land north. Before the berm, a wood trestle had originally been in place to elevate the railroad tracks above the constant flooding problems around the Lick Branch. The trestle was filled with dirt to become an earth embankment in the early part of the twentieth century. Two busy CSX rail lines continue to traverse this important path.

Two main components constitute the new railroad composition enhanced and finalized in design by Nathan-Evans-Taylor Architects and Stanley D. Lindsey & Associates Engineers: the open steel trestle that runs approximately three hundred feet across the site directly north of the large Tennessee map and pairs of robust limestone bridges at Sixth and Seventh Avenues. The railroad overpass was realigned to cut squarely across the new park and to parallel existing east-west streets. This realignment resulted in a new location shifted north approximately fifty feet from the existing location, and the repositioning also required new overpasses to be built at Fifth and Eighth Avenues. In keeping with the character of the Capitol building, the overpasses at Sixth and Seventh Avenues are sympathetic to the Greek Revival style, massive classical forms clad in limestone.

Spanning the width of the Mall, the steel bridge replaced the existing earth berm. To correspond with the original wood trestle once on the site, each column is flared slightly outward. At twenty-foot intervals, each steel element spans thirty feet. By creating an open trestle, views are possible from the area of the Tennessee Plaza to the Rivers of Tennessee fountains directly north. The top of the railroad bridge structure is articulated with lacy steel railings to partly obscure the lower portion of passing railroad cars. To the east and west ends of the trestle abutments, a simple transition is made from the elevated tracks to the existing berm with a gentle slope enhanced with ground cover.

Repetitive structural elements distribute the massive railroad load in a manner almost identical to the old wood trestle. The underside of the sturdy composition of steel and concrete provides the only generous area of shade in the park, a distinction that will fade as the deciduous trees in the park mature. This area beneath is embellished by repetitive steel arches, decorative forms that connect to the flared primary supports and turn the visual focus to the two glass-enclosed spaces at either end.

The trestle is painted white to give it presence, help reflect light into the area beneath the wide overpass, and complement both the green of the big foreground map and the black of the Rivers of

Bridges and trestle

ML

NETA

Pattern of trestle supports and wide arch

View from Sixth Avenue   CB

Tennessee wall immediately beyond. The visual connection to the wall is also reinforced by a steel arch superimposed across the repetitive vertical supports, a curve that corresponds to the top of the bowed granite wall. Illumination of the steel trestle provides an appropriate nighttime appearance without creating glare or competing with the plaza and Capitol beyond.

Two enclosed spaces are located beneath the trestle against the limestone abutments: public rest rooms at the west end and a gift shop at the east end. Both of these conditioned areas are clad in clear and frosted glass to help minimize the presence while maximizing daylighting within each. Each are structurally independent from the trestle above for separation from railroad vibration and noise.

Rail lines may once again become a substantial part of commuter and passenger movement across the state and nation. If and when this occurs, visitors by rail to the capital city will certainly have a memorable view as they cross this portion of Nashville.

Active lines continue to carry rail traffic

126

Detail of bridge at Seventh Avenue

Visitors center beneath trestle

Detail with flagpole beyond

Twilight trestle

CB

127

RIVERS OF TENNESSEE

Here are your waters and your watering place.
Drink and be whole again beyond confusion.

Robert Frost

Heading north from the Tennessee map, visitors walk underneath the railroad trestle to the Rivers of Tennessee. This wide kinetic water feature was planned to animate the space, draw people from the plaza and the map into the rest of the park, and celebrate the numerous rivers, streams, and waterways of the state.

The Rivers of Tennessee area is comprised of computer-programmed water jets that spray columns of water to ever-changing heights in front of a curved backdrop wall. The background is inscribed with information about the state's rivers and the role they have played in Tennessee history. The curved wall also recalls an earlier nickname for Tennessee as the "Big Bend State," given because of the Tennessee River's course and giant sweep across two sections of the state.

Water issues forth from circular granite disks, each one named in honor of the state's thirty-one dominant waterways, and flows into the trough at the base of the wall appropriately representing the Mississippi. Multiple fountains appear in other parks, and yet here they receive added thematic designations. The top of the backdrop wall slopes down at both sides, opening views and leading visitors to focal areas at the east

ML

Text on curved wall

ML

and west sides of the wall. The information engraved on the polished surface, selected by Lynne Bachleda, includes historic information, quotes, famous sayings, phrases, and poetry relating to the impact of the waterways on state history and develop- ment. Quotes range from a stirring excerpt about the Tennessee River by Donald Davidson to the simple invitation, "I am the river . . . sit and listen to my wisdom," by Ian Menard, a teenager from Williamson County. As one might imagine, a large

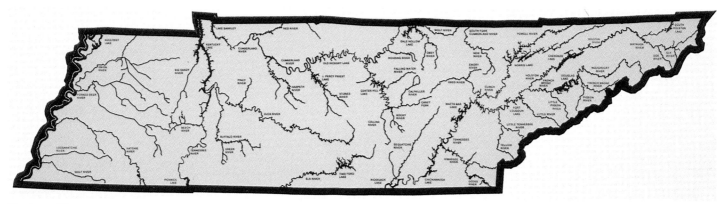

The rivers of Tennessee

Splashing through thirty-one flavors   ML

Flags at focal point spire

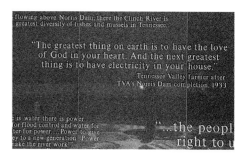

Quotes and facts sprinkled across surface

passage by Mark Twain about the Mississippi is also included, stretched across the base of the wall just above a continuous trough that represents both the river's defining edge and final destination for most of the state's river water. Statements about the impact of the river system on Native American settlements are also presented. The inscriptions, scattered across the wall in varying sizes, juxtapose

the geyser-like fountains that rise and fall from the flat surface of the plaza at varying intervals during the day.

Visitors can also walk up a ramp on the back side of the curved granite wall for views in both directions along the central axis of the Mall. At the apex of the path, the only accessible elevated place in the park, one finds separate engraved statements about the history of both the railroad

system and the Mall property.

Focal points on the east and west sides of the fountains celebrate one of the most recognized symbols of Tennessee, the state flag, featured on tall, dramatic flagpoles. Inspired by Le Nôtre's compositional technique at Versailles and other large gardens, the two gigantic flags and poles frame the view—here with obvious patriotic sentiment—leaving the center open to the landscape beyond. These dual vertical spires also anchor the two south ends of the Path of Volunteers. The American flag does not appear on these flagpoles but instead appropriately caps the summit of the *entire* park composition, the top of the Capitol immediately south.

Pondering the impact of water

131

AMPHITHEATER

The world's a theater, the earth a stage,
Which God and Nature do with actors fill.

Thomas Heywood

To accommodate and accent the importance of the performing arts in Tennessee, a permanent outdoor theater is located north of Harrison Street in the middle section of the Mall. This space, the Tennessee Amphitheater, is centered on axis with the Capitol and provides a flexible location for various types of events. Because the specific long-term use and destiny of this space was not clear when the theater area was originally composed, it was intentionally designed to evolve over time, providing a location not only for celebrations during the Bicentennial but for continued use for concerts, theatrical performances, entertainment shows, graduations, dinner theaters, reunions, political gatherings, and other civic events.

To achieve an appropriate composition for an outdoor theater, the design team looked to the Greeks and Romans. Strickland had embraced the designs of civic and religious buildings and monuments by the Grecian masters as inspiration for his numerous achievements, and the heritage of outdoor theaters of antiquity provided ample models for this part of the project. Several of these marvelous performance areas were studied with the knowledgeable assistance of theater-design

ML

Theater of Epidauros

MM

consultant Duane Wilson of Washington, D.C. Particular attention was paid to the Greek theater at Epidauros, a fourth century B.C. masterpiece, and to the Roman theater of A.D. 50 in Orange, France. A semicircular, concrete adaptation was used, incorporating a modified position of two parascenia, side elements framing the stage proscenium and permanent, low stage wall. The form of the amphitheater honors the architectural precedent of the Capitol while providing flexibility for shows ranging from an audience of a few hundred to a few thousand.

In a departure from the rather steep Greek model, stepped lawns (perrons) were

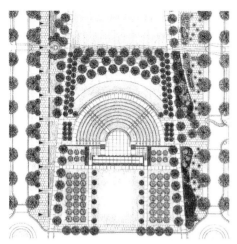

Plan of Amphitheater

Stepped lawns, called perrons

Tower

Model

used, which allow a more gentle and natural seating configuration. The descending series of seven-foot-wide lawn perrons make the space more pleasant and comfortable, and they provide the option for patrons to bring blankets for informal performances or picnics. Each of the concrete-edged perrons is at seat height, making the space immediately available for year-round performance crowds of about one thousand. If filled with movable chairs, the two-hundred-foot-diameter amphitheater will hold up to two thousand spectators.

Another departure from the model of antiquity is the placement of dual towers at the edges of the proscenium that frame the view southward. Lantern-like, these vertical forms are not altogether unlike those that cap the nearby limestone railroad bridges at Sixth and Seventh Avenues. Cookie cutter, stainless steel stars from the state flag (openings for speakers behind) grace the front side below the lightly frosted glass lantern windows and exaggerated cornice. An open lawn north of the terraced seating area extends the capacity, with additional area for larger crowds. Ramps within and behind the stage wall allow the delivery of musical instruments, production crates, speakers,

and other technical equipment and provide handicap access to all parts of the stage and front-row seating.

Most of the Mall is purposely level with the surrounding streets to permit views across the park, not only for observation and safety, but also to permit generous visibility for motorists driving around the periphery. The amphitheater steps down from this principal grade level, submerging into the ground to accomplish several objectives. By being slightly depressed, the space becomes somewhat better acoustically, a difficult challenge for any outdoor venue in the twentieth century reality of urban noise from cars, trucks, airplanes, and, yes, trains. Defined and protected by shade trees at the

edges, the amphitheater becomes a found outdoor room, discovered amongst the other features of the park. And by stepping down out of sight, the amphitheater is not so easily seen—its normally unpopulated appearance not readily apparent to casual visitors of the park.

The amphitheater is not enclosed, although a subtle fence surrounding the periphery might be appropriate to supervise admission and collect for the occasional paid events. This performance space remains open at a dramatic location where one might experience an informal gathering or a grand performance. It was also premature to provide a permanent cover or separate support buildings although such may be required in the future to facilitate ambitious productions. A wood floor for the stage might also be considered in the future. The design does not preclude these or other subtle later additions. A stage backdrop, however, is not needed. The orientation of the theater—audience facing south and performers facing north—places the Capitol in the stage background, providing perhaps the most appropriate of all backdrops as Strickland's masterpiece crowns Capitol Hill on the changing skyline of Nashville.

View of twin amphitheater towers, Harrison Street, and Riverwall

CENTRAL LAWN

I believe a leaf of grass is no less than the journey-work of the stars.

Walt Whitman

Of the numerous reasons for the construction of the Bicentennial Mall, none was more important in the initial stages of conception than to provide an unobstructed view of the State Capitol through the creation of a long, green lawn extending north. The Mall evolved into a much more intriguing educational destination, but the center of the new park retains the essential open character of its historic mentor, the National Mall in Washington, D.C., by providing an unobstructed, unprogrammed spacious field available for use for a variety of activities.

The layout of the meadow narrows from the south end to the northern terminus at the Court of Three Stars, creating a forced visual perspective. The converging formal composition is edged and framed by the contrasting shady spaces on both sides and by the two sidewalks that collectively form the Path of Volunteers. This linear path was designed to contain brick-sized, red granite pavers engraved with the names of Tennessee ancestors, citizens, and even descendants through a fund-raising program organized by Tennessee 200. The ends of the dual fourteen-hundred-foot sidewalks will feature granite plaques for Governors

BS

Aerial view of park

TSPS

137

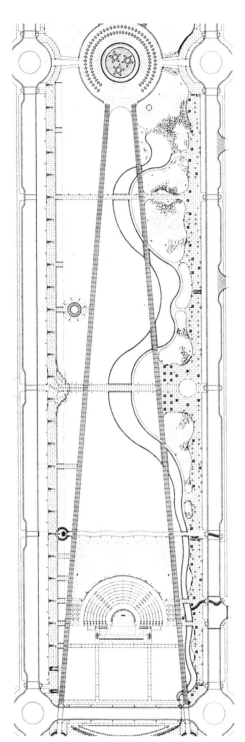

Plan of Path of Volunteers

Path to be completed

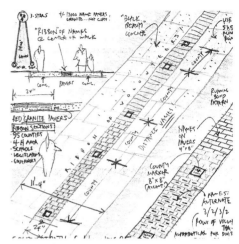

Concepts for granite name pavers

McWherter and Sundquist and for the Ninety-eighth and Ninety-ninth General Assemblies. The seventeen-thousand-name pavers will be installed in 1997, placed to form a ribbon at the center of the long diagonal walkways and arranged by county. Tennessee's public schools and 4-H clubs will also be featured on the path.

To the west is the rigid, linear Pathway of History; to the east is the less formal Walkway of the Counties. In the open lawn itself, recreational activities such as picnicking, kite flying, frisbee throwing, and informal games can be enjoyed. The long, truncated yard is interrupted at midpoint by a cross-axial path through an orchard of flowering trees. Aligned with the former path of Jackson Street, a second cross axis traverses the lawn, connecting visitor parking areas east of the park with the long-overdue Tennessee World War II Memorial and with Farmers' Market directly across Seventh Avenue. These tree-lined paths and the amphitheater directly south are positioned so that none compromise the grand, open vista of the Capitol. Glimpses under the tree canopy of the Central Lawn are visible to visiting motorists traveling on Sixth and Seventh Avenues. Dramatic views of the Capitol on

Tennessee 200 brochure

TN200

138

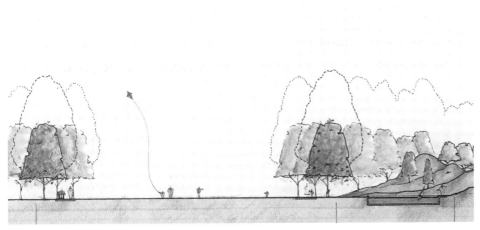

Illustration of lawn at north end

Walkway edged with oak trees

the skyline will be afforded from the gracious open meadow. Here, future generations will have the opportunity to play in the backyard of the Capitol.

To challenge the symmetry of the lawn and introduce a much-needed open body of water to the park, an additional feature was originally proposed that has yet to be constructed. This ingredient, the Tennessee Waterway, will be an uninterrupted sinuous pool—a quiet, slow-moving stream that would begin in the higher forms of the East Tennessee topography and travel in and out across the Central Lawn to terminate at a symbolic dam at the main cross-axial path. By virtue of its curving and wandering profile, it will complement the formality of the main lawn and also confirm and exalt Tennessee's earlier "Big Bend State" sobriquet. Almost every major park in the world, including the National Mall, features a major open body of water of some configuration, and it should be included as intended at the Mall, not only for the reflective and calming effects, but also to acknowledge Tennessee's water-use heritage. Tennesseans consider themselves to be proud yet friendly people; the mixture of formal and informal geometries will also help signify this duality.

Reflecting pool in Washington, D.C.   GTB

Similar to features found elsewhere throughout the park, this water path would espouse an educational component, with markers or features explaining the roles of the Tennessee Valley Authority, the U.S. Army Corps of Engineers, and other institutions in changing the course of water utilization in the state. Funding of the waterway, although now detained, is imperative for a cohesive completion of the Central Lawn in particular and the overall Mall experience in general.

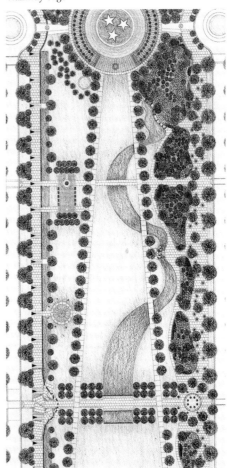

Plan of future Tennessee Waterway

WALKWAY OF THE COUNTIES

The fertile soil of Tennessee
Grew more than corn, tobacco, and cotton,
It grew a crop of people who are
Trailblazers, child raisers, flag wavers, soul savers.

Margaret Britton Vaughn

To celebrate the rich cultural heritage and diversity of landscape found across Tennessee, the eastern edge of the Mall is devoted to these special characteristics with the Walkway of the Counties. This area stretches north from Harrison Street to the Court of Three Stars. It is a commentary on the beautiful and varied landscape of Tennessee and a tribute to the ninety-five smaller governmental entities that comprise the state.

Tennessee is a rich, diverse state, quite unlike any in the nation. To the west, the state is bordered by the largest river in North America. To the east, it is bordered by the second tallest mountains on the continent, with open plains, basins, hills, and plateaus spanning between the two opposite ends. Not only does the land change, but so does the vegetation, and Tennessee is home to an amazing variety of plants, trees, and flowers. The north and the south edges of the state are defined primarily by man, as if this great parallelogram was carved out as a fabulous sample, a slice of America, possessing within it the diversity of nature in the eastern-middle part of the United States. This characteristic was important to present at the Mall in an abstract yet genuine manner. The tribute to the landscape and vegetation was combined with another primary goal of the park: to populate the Mall with a symbolic and authentic presence of all the counties in the state of Tennessee.

The walkway begins on the southeast side near Harrison Street corresponding to the western end of the state. The ground plane is essentially level at this end and becomes progressively more rolling and hilly, rising to the highest mounds as the adjacent path reaches the north end of the park. This changing topography reflects the varied landforms found as one travels across the state. A medley of native

The ninety-five counties of Tennessee

TDEC

ML

141

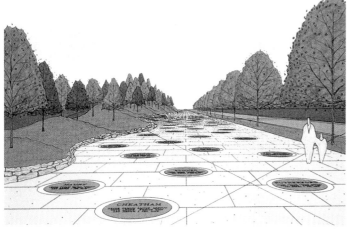

Perspective illustration of the walkway

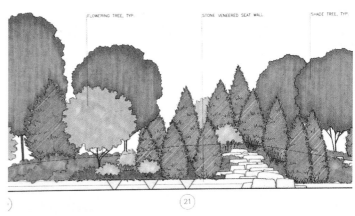

Elevation illustrating diversity of plant materials   R/F

Overview of topographic features along Sixth Avenue   ML

vegetation has been selected to correspond to the landforms, establishing here a Tennessee arboretum. The walkway is also divided into the major geophysical regions within Tennessee. The width of the walkway varies from twelve to twenty feet and is defined by a sinuous seat-height wall at the western side of the meandering path. The experience is informal and comfortable with trees planted not only in the peripheral areas and symbolic mounded earth forms, but also within the path. Visitors can here wander not only against the landforms but also under and through the trees of the state.

Landscape architect design team member Mike Fowler best explains the details:

From the flat lands and bald cypress trees of the west near Harrison Street, past the rolling hills and cedars of Middle Tennessee and on to the hemlock clad slopes symbolizing the mountains of the East Tennessee near the Court of Three Stars, this great cross section celebrates the differences in topography and plants that characterize the three grand divisions. While the transition from flat lands to mountains will seem familiar to most Tennesseans, many of the native plants will be unusual, such as the

Horsetail from West Tennessee

Column fragments

Dividing line at grand division

distinctive scouring rush (a.k.a. horsetail), the colorful Tennessee coneflower, the fragrant cumberland rosemary, and the bigleaf magnolia. Whether unusual or common, the plants selected are native to the area of the state that they represent and are able to adapt to the local project environment.

In addition to the plants and topography, the rock work and stone walls also contribute to the story of the natural environment of Tennessee. The low stone walls are of Tennessee Quartzite, which was quarried near Crossville. Although Tennessee Quartzite ranges from buff brown to grey, only grey stones were used in the walls. The rocks in the planters are symbolic of typical rock outcroppings found in Middle and East Tennessee. The rock outcrops in Middle Tennessee are typically slab like and horizontally layered, while many distinctive rock outcroppings in East Tennessee are made up of a tumble of boulders left from the mountain building process eons ago.

Original column fragments from the Capitol are located at the midpoint of the walkway. Similar to a collection on Capitol Hill, they recall the tremendous endeavor 150 years ago to erect the statehouse. Fragments here also honor historic preser-vation architect Charles Warterfield Jr. and many others who have fought throughout their careers to preserve and honor William Strickland's masterpiece building.

Evenly distributed along the fourteen-hundred-foot length are ninety-five walkway surface granite plaques, each representing a county. The four-foot granite disk presents a brief history and a map indicating the county location in the state. Beneath is buried the large time capsule with memorabilia and objects collected for the occasion of the Bicentennial by Tennessee 200.

The material in the now-submerged time capsules is fascinating. One has no problem finding variety in Tennessee as these capsules contain an astonishing array of objects, from letters to flags, buttons to photographs, maps to belt buckles, moon-shine to Holy Bibles. The markers and time capsules beneath populate the walkway and provide both a symbolic and valid presence and ownership of the landmark park by each county.

When the stainless steel time capsules were buried on April 27, 1996, representa-tives from all counties helped lower their respective treasures into the ninety-five underground tombs for posterity in a

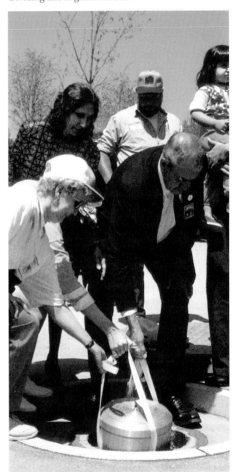
Cannon County capsule lowered into tomb

143

Shelby County representatives

Williamson County representatives

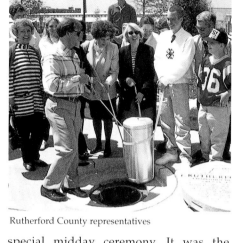

Rutherford County representatives

special midday ceremony. It was the largest and most diverse burial of memorabilia collected from such a vast area. The capsules will be unearthed and opened at the occasion of Tennessee's Tricentennial on June 1, 2096.

Again, Fowler provides a clear summation of the intentions for this component of the Mall:

Through topography, planting, rock outcrops, county markers, and interpretative signage, this area of the Mall is intended to add to the sense of place and awareness of the natural environment of Tennessee. Unlike the History Wall to the west, time here is only marked by the slow change of the seasons: the first blooms of dogwood and redbud, the blossoms of summer, the blaze of maples and sumacs in the fall, and the holly berries of winter. Hopefully time will be kind to the Walkway of the Counties and that as the trees mature and plantings change, the sense of a cross section of Tennessee will only deepen and become more meaningful to those who visit.

Variety of time capsule contents

TN200

Walkway of the Counties looking south

Pathway of History

Histories make men wise; poets, witty;
the mathematics, subtile; natural philosophy, deep;
moral, grave; logic and rhetoric, able to contend.

Francis Bacon

All history is modern history.

Wallace Stevens

The west side of the park contains a feature that records the history of Tennessee from early to modern times, the Pathway of History. This linear sidewalk, extending over fourteen hundred feet along the west side of the Mall against Seventh Avenue, is a timeline, a chart showcasing a history of more than two centuries. It is composed of two primary ingredients: a continuous, low granite wall and a row of vertical granite pylons. The history of the state is recorded on the polished granite wall forty-eight inches tall. Text on the surface is high enough to be easily read, yet the wall is low enough to allow pedestrians and motorists on Seventh Avenue to look over the top into the interior of the park. The wall is a continuous element, a script of facts and emotions to be engraved for future generations. Accomplishments, triumphs, problems, tragedies, historic events, war, peace . . . all will be engraved upon the polished surface. This wall contains openings primarily to acknowledge special events that have occurred in the history of the state, also allowing movement to and from the interior of the park. The pylons create an edge, a fence on the western side, and modulate the path into uniform fifty-foot segments. All the pylons were erected, but only small

ML

sections of the wall itself were finished in 1996; completion of the entire timeline is now scheduled to occur sometime in 1997.

The black granite pylons are purposely thin—the triangular shape and sharp white edge defying thickness when seen from the walkway. These twenty-nine elements are purposely set apart from the wall to allow the text of history to flow uninterrupted across the reflective granite surface. Inspiration for the form of the vertical markers had several sources, from the ominous black monolith in Stanley Kubrick and Arthur C. Clarke's prophetic film *2001: A Space Odyssey* to the unbuilt pylons of Freedom Plaza in Washington. Except for a single date at the top, no other information is included on the polished black surface. Although an easier date division was considered (1810, 1820, etc., instead of 1816, 1826, etc.), the *six* increment seemed challengingly appropriate, with references to the founding of the nation in 1776, Tennessee statehood in 1796, the Centennial in 1896, and, of course, the Bicentennial year. The repetitive pattern of stark black pylons creates a definitive edge, almost an opaque fence against Seventh Avenue.

The first four pylons divide ancient history in Tennessee into large segments as

Perspective illustration

Model

recommended by history consultant, Lynne Bachleda. With the 1766 pylon, the decade timeline pattern begins and continues to the end of the path. Every fifty-foot section of the wall is devoted to a ten-year period in state history, uninterrupted for the predominance of the long, straight path.

147

March of time

Statehood area at 1796

McNairy Spring fountain

STATEHOOD FOUNTAIN

At the timeline location of 1796, the first in a series of special-event markers is located. The timeline pattern was such that the important event of Tennessee statehood in 1796 occurred at the same place as the historic location of McNairy Spring, one of the tributaries of the Lick Branch. Although the site of McNairy Spring was not excavated to find its precise location, there is evidence that it is directly below and still flows, its waters now diverted into the subterranean 1892 brick sewer beneath the site. The space of the Statehood Fountain is inwardly focused, a circular outdoor room with a symbolic circular fountain gushing water to recall the original spring. This enclosed space is suggestive of a time when pioneers and settlers attempted to look inward, examining and defining themselves to discover and claim an identity, a new state. Sixteen stars surrounding the fountain and a lone drinking fountain unite the availability of refreshing fresh water with a toast to the establishment of the sixteenth state two hundred years ago. A wiggling path suggests the historic route of the small stream as it flowed eastward across the site into the larger Lick Branch and beyond into the Cumberland River.

Pylons along Seventh Avenue

148

Model of path between markers 1846 and 1876

CIVIL WAR AREA

At the midpoint of the walkway, in alignment with the main cross-axis path west to the new Farmers' Market, the course of events is shattered by the tumultuous events of the Civil War. Here the wall cracks and shifts at events where secession and war are foreshadowed, and the wall is symbolically blown into vertical fragments as the War Between the States begins and the state is torn apart. Recorded on the fragments are battles, events, and emotions of the war, selected by Bachleda and officials of the Tennessee State Museum. These fragments memorialize the inconceivable disruption and divisiveness that occurred during the conflict. A single marker located in the center of the cross axis recalls the trauma of the times. On the marker above a stirring quote by Robert Penn Warren, the prominent engraving of "North" and "South" (and, more precisely, "Union" and "Confederacy") challenges the visitor to struggle with the same issue faced by Tennesseans nearly 150 years ago: One must choose a side. As history proceeds through to the end of the war, the wall segments are reunited, Tennessee reenters the Union, and the wall is healed as Reconstruction occurs and adjustments

Wall cracks to foreshadow war

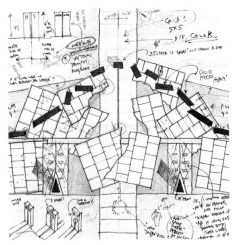
Concept of the disruption

North/South marker

Events of the War Between the States

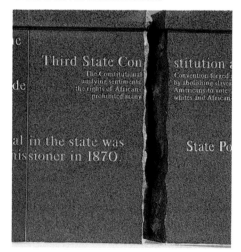

Healing after the war

are made in the political structure and society of the state.

CENTENNIAL MARKER

When Tennessee celebrated its one-hundredth anniversary, a racetrack in Nashville was transformed into a wonderful showcase of culture and achievement, the Tennessee Centennial Exposition. This exposition was an astonishing accomplishment, especially when considering the devastation of the Civil War that disrupted so much of the state only a generation earlier. The fabulous collection of numerous temporary buildings has long since vanished into

memory, except for the rebuilt Parthenon, the picturesque Lake Watauga, and the surrounding grounds of Centennial Park. It was important to remind Tennesseans and their visitors of this wonderful, often forgotten achievement when the state not only presented itself to the world but also looked outward to the promise of the upcoming twentieth century. The Centennial Marker is, therefore, a round form, a series of stepped platforms over thirty feet in diameter at the base. The height of each step matches those of the replica Parthenon. Around the circular walkway is an evocative quote from Governor Robert Taylor

150

Centennial Exposition   TSLA

Markers celebrate exposition

Governor Taylor's quote   VP

recalling the recovery and achievements of a state that only a generation earlier had suffered tremendous social and economic devastation. Radiating out of this walkway are eight compass markers featuring engraved photographic scenes from the Centennial Exposition. Among the engravings are panoramic views of the sprawling affair, scenes documenting the gaiety and success of a celebration that attracted almost two million visitors and close-ups of several key structures including the Negro Building and the Machinery Building. In this place, one celebrates Tennessee accomplishments a century ago. In contrast to the inward Statehood Fountain of 1796, here the focus is outward, to the nation, to the world.

WORLD WAR II MEMORIAL

Moving northward along the Pathway of History, visitors can anticipate arriving at the Tennessee World War II Memorial. The Mall was selected from many available sites for this long-overdue memorial to the courage and sacrifice of soldiers from Tennessee. Although the 1952 State Library and Archives building was erected in honor of veterans of the war, it has never been perceived as such. This future memorial will be located just east of the history wall,

Centennial marker

appropriately between the 1936 and the 1946 granite date pylons. Illustrating the impact and extent of the worldwide conflict, an enormous, rotating granite world globe will be the primary feature of this memorial. Ten massive granite monoliths nearby will depict major battles and events, and the pavement will be sprinkled with gold stars in remembrance of the 5,731 Tennesseans lost in the war, a reminder of the touching but almost forgotten Gold Star Mothers program. Groundbreaking for the memorial, attended by Governor Sundquist, former governor Ned McWherter, other key state

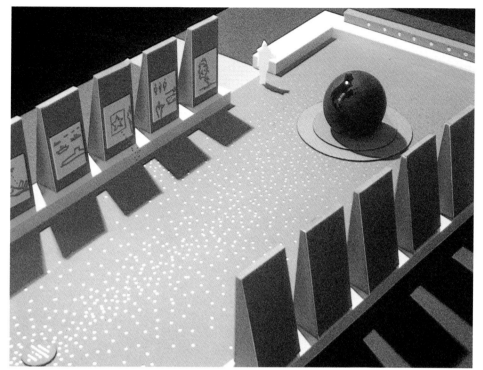

Model of World War II Memorial

Governors McWherter and Sundquist   GCA

officials, and members of the World War II Memorial Trust organization, occurred on a hot July 1, 1996. The memorial will be finished in the fall of 1997.

When the Pathway of History is completed, it will create a dynamic educational and aesthetic element in the park. The ambitious timeline ends at 1996 with two pylon markers that frame the west entry to the Court of Three Stars. These dual elements straddle the entrance to the court, and text related to the Bicentennial Celebration will be presented on seat-height walls. Of course, the history of Tennessee does not end with the Bicentennial, and the inscriptions will terminate at the northern edge of the path with a small marker that challenges future generations to conceive a tricentennial inheritor to the Mall.

World War II Memorial Trust and officials   GCA

ML

153

COURT OF THREE STARS

*For there is a music wherever there is a harmony,
order, or proportion.*

Sir Thomas Browne

An impressive variety of distinct musical forms and traditions have emanated from Tennessee, and this is a well-known, distinguishing characteristic of the state. The Court of Three Stars near Jefferson Street honors this identity as a tribute to the music heritage of Tennessee. A circular area, it is the important northern anchor of the park and balances the significance and attraction of the big map and fountains at the south end. It is also the northern terminus of both the Central Lawn and the two diagonal walks that together constitute the Path of Volunteers. Here the timeline of the Pathway of History and meandering Walkway of the Counties also both conclude or begin depending on one's point of origin. This gathering space commemorates the richness of music found in Tennessee while harmonizing with other thematic components of the Mall.

The plaza receives its visual spirit from the Tennessee state flag. Tennessee is two centuries old, yet it was not until 1905 that the General Assembly selected a design by Captain LeRoy Reeves as the official state flag. His design was a red flag containing in its center three white stars in a circular blue field. Reeves's intentions were clear in his original description for the design:

ML

"The three stars are of pure white, representing the three grand divisions of the state. They are bound together by the endless circle of the blue field, the symbol of being three bound together in one—an indissoluble trinity." Here Reeves's layout becomes enlarged more than ever before as the three stars from his flag become the main feature at the center of the circular paved court. Rendered in subtle shades of granite, this flat plaza was the only part of the intended composition finished in 1996.

In the near future, the Court of Three Stars will change considerably. The plaza will be surrounded by two concentric rings of limestone columns. Each column will be four feet in diameter and approximately twenty-five feet tall. The collection of columns will be slightly raised on a circular plinth above the three-star plaza, this elevation creating a continuous seat edge inside the C-shaped enclosure. The assemblage of vertical elements will be similar in spirit to that found at the National Arboretum in Washington, D.C., where original stone columns from the U.S. Capitol building form a memorable outdoor composition. Ninety-five chimes or bells—one for each county in the state—will be mounted within the tops of the columns, and as a group, the bells of

State flag as patriotic carpet

different pitches will form a musical instrument called a carillon. Unlike a typical carillon where the bells are mounted together high in a tower, the chimes here will be placed in a horizontal composition, allowing visitors to walk outdoors through the sound in a unique acoustic chamber.

The bells will play automatically during the day, operated by a computer

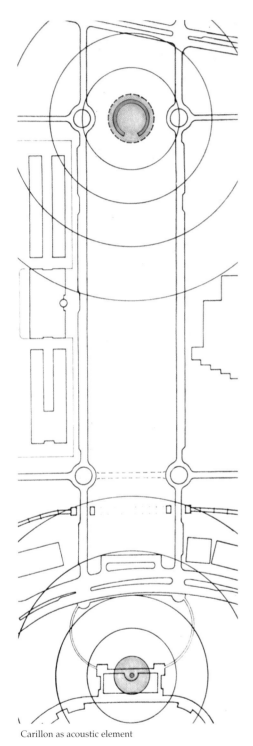

Carillon as acoustic element

Columns at National Arboretum   JL

Disc at entrance to court

located in a small round structure nearby. This building will also contain a carillon console of manual batons, allowing a guest musician, a carillonneur, to play special selections. The instrument will not be designed to be very loud, only very good, to insure that it does not overly disturb the nearby residential neighborhoods of Germantown and Buena Vista. A short enunciation, perhaps every hour, will serve as a scheduled acoustic event similar to the timed kinetic fountains of the Rivers of Tennessee.

On the plinth surrounding the stars, the granite seat-height wall is proposed to be engraved with names of musicians who have had a dramatic impact on the music history of the state. All types of music developed and composed in Tennessee will be included from gospel to country, classical to bluegrass, jazz to blues. The central axis of the Mall and the carillon will remain open to Jefferson Street, not only for a generous view into the park and the Capitol to the south, but also to enhance the expected potential relationship to a significant future civic building that may be built at some point in the future directly across the street. The height of the columns will be high enough to provide an important sense of enclosure for people in the court, but low enough that motorists and pedestrians on Jefferson Street will still have an unobstructed view of the Capitol. In addition, a single ninety-sixth bell is proposed for the north face of Capitol Hill. This largest bell will answer the collective ringing of the ninety-five-bell carillon much as state government in the Capitol is to answer to the collective voices of the people. The resulting acoustical connection across the vast distance will add a new dimension to the visual experience already established. The carillon is scheduled to be finished in the near future, although the exact completion date is unknown at this time.

Tall granite monoliths at the intersections of Sixth and Seventh Avenues and Jefferson Street establish the north edge of the park and announce the presence of the Mall. These corner markers invite pedestrians to cross the busy street at the intersections where the street is purposely textured with concrete pavers to alert motorists. Standing as sentinels and located on a roadway that continues to evolve, these elements recall the long-forgotten historic entries onto the grounds of the distant Capitol, a final gesture to the creators of the magnificent statehouse and its grounds.

Site of future carillon

Model

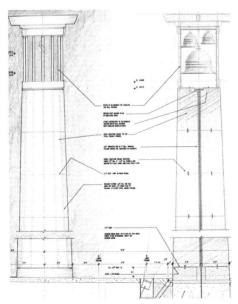

Column details

Perspective illustration

Jefferson Street monolith

157

THE THIRD CENTURY

Who can tell what another century will unfold?
I think I see a vision of the future opening before me.
I see triumphs in arts, and achievements in science,
undreamed of by artisans and philosophers of the past.

Governor Robert Taylor, 1897

What is the destiny of the Mall and its surrounding properties? Similar to the planning dilemma before the arrival of the new park, much is left to be done. The original master plan prepared by our team in 1993 considered this issue and made several broad recommendations, but implementation will require a constant review of the actual impact of the park. Only with a comprehensive overview and a logical redevelopment plan will the district around the Mall grow in proper fashion to insure that this vicinity north of the Capitol continues to evolve into a useful and exciting destination.

In July 1996, John Ferguson succeeded Bob Corker as commissioner of Finance and Administration, and Larry Kirk was appointed assistant commissioner overseeing Capital Projects Management, the state agency responsible for planning, construction, and future development around the Mall. This department delivered the park on schedule; their task now would be to complete the remaining unbuilt park components and capitalize on the centurial occasion at hand.

At this point, the Mall is a gift, an urban planning shot of adrenaline. Alone it will not transform, but taken as the front engine of a comprehensive scheme, it should help

ML

establish the promise for a third century. Located immediately north of the existing downtown central business district, where previous development had been limited to industrial and commercial operations, warehouses, and parking lots, the Mall creates a unique opportunity and responsibility to carefully plan for development during the next century of Tennessee statehood.

Future buildings and activities in the vicinity of the park should focus toward it, providing views from new structures while creating active, beneficial edges. Buildings should also reinforce the primary original goal of the Mall: to preserve and emphasize views of the Capitol. Development must instill a pattern of consistency that will, in turn, form a distinct Mall district and an identifiable sense of place.

Buildings immediately adjacent should respond directly to the character and mission of the park. The new Farmers' Market was erected west of the Mall on Seventh Avenue, composed of a central building and open-air sheds extending north and south to the nearby side streets of Jackson and Harrison. This facility, designed under the direction of Seab Tuck, has already become what was intended: a shopping destination unique to Nashville,

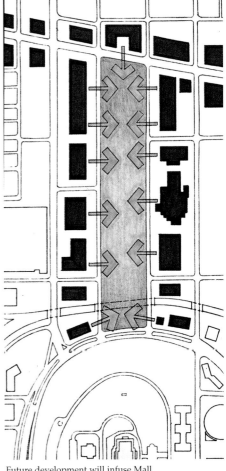

Future development will infuse Mall

Farmers' Market   ML

Interior hall   VP

one which helps to add vitality and stability to the neighborhood while attracting visitors to the vicinity of the park.

The State Data Center presently occupies about one-fourth of the property on the east side of the Mall. This is somewhat unfortunate due to the building's low scale and its purposely restricted use. The single entry faces south, yet future additions or alterations should redirect attention and entry toward the Mall to create activity and a distinctive edge against Sixth Avenue. Ideally, the processing activities here will soon yield to more inviting future uses.

The three prominent parcels around the north end of the park along Jefferson Street will require very careful programming and design. All are of paramount importance due to their potential to reinforce the Court of Three Stars, create an enclosure and terminus for the north end of the Mall, focus and intensify views back to the Capitol, and create strong corner statements on the busy

street. These sites should be reserved for buildings possessing important civic, cultural, or governmental activities, with attention given to functions that would continually bring use and life to the Mall. Such residents of these properties might include a new Tennessee state museum, a new state library and archives, a Tennessee futurespace educational center, an agricultural research center, a state technology and science museum, a transportation demonstration facility, an environmental center, an energy and conservation research center, a Tennessee music center, a government learning center, a Tennessee sports history center, a federal facility (museum, research center, or archives), or a local facility (museum, science center, branch library, or school).

In a brief design exercise in 1995, our firm explored the possibility of locating a new Tennessee State Museum at the northern end of the Mall across Jefferson

Street. This site, currently occupied by the Onyx Building and the recently renovated Elliott School, represents a monumental position for the location of a structure that would anchor the new park in a manner similar to that by which the Lincoln Memorial anchors the west end of the National Mall in Washington. The sheer prominence of this site mandates that a building of only the *highest* civic purpose be allowed to occupy the property. By virtue of this position, any new structure here would become equated with the majesty and presence of the Capitol at the other end of the Mall. A new state museum would certainly fulfill such a prerequisite.

Yet corresponding with the desire for a terminus to the linear park is an equal intention to leave the end of the great axis open, thereby maintaining an unobstructed spatial and symbolic gesture to the landscape beyond. Thomas Jefferson, for whom the adjacent street was named, would probably have endorsed this attitude. Development of an appropriate composition that accomplishes both goals will therefore be quite challenging. Our sketchy, hypothetical design proposed a form transparent at the center, essentially an open hall defined by a bowed-glass loggia. Dual opaque

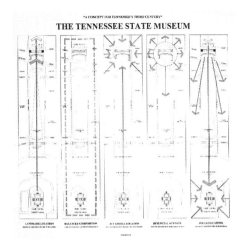

Concept diagrams

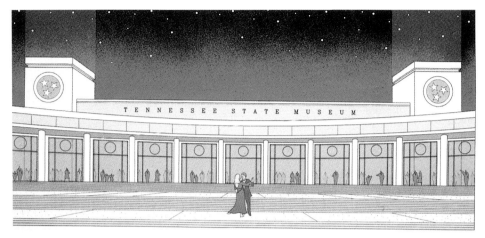

Conceptual perspective of south facade

towers would bracket the building composition and thereby work with other twin elements in the new park—railroad bridges, flagpoles, amphitheater towers, and carillon columns—to frame a vista to the hills beyond and, by reference, toward the frontier. Although the historic structures on the site represent an immediate hindrance, one or both could conceivably be incorporated into the final composition. An equally intriguing direction might be to simply establish here a park as an extension of the Mall, an edifice of nature. This commanding Jefferson Street site offers a very rare civic design opportunity, one that must not be missed.

Remaining sites adjacent to the Mall should be developed with mixed-use buildings, including commercial, institutional, educational, and cultural activities. Retail occupancies would be acceptable, but only if of a special nature such as the new market. Predictable retail products found with ease in shopping malls and strip centers elsewhere should have no business here. Warehousing, service, or industrial activities should not be allowed unless there is a special component that would provide a unique activity or an educational destination, such as the display of a revolu-

tionary manufacturing or technological process. Regardless of the specifics of form and placement, all future peripheral structures must infuse the Mall with vitality and, in so doing, enrich the park with year-round activity and use.

Though the localized impact of the Mall on James Robertson Parkway is limited to the section between Sixth and Seventh Avenues, state buildings populate much of this corridor, creating an opportunity to extend the animation of the park to the street. With increased growth, the parkway at the base of Capitol Hill should receive the attention it deserves, and a concerted effort should be exerted to enhance the road through the addition of more street trees, coordinated lighting, and street furniture. This obligation is especially evident and crucial at the contorted west end of the corridor. The boulevard still has the potential to be much more than a busy vehicular thoroughfare.

Similar care and planning should also be extended to Eighth Avenue, the predominant historic entry into the downtown from the northern part of the city, and to Jefferson Street, the busy thoroughfare extending west to the campuses of Tennessee State and Fisk Universities. Both roadways should be

altered from their current freeway-like profiles to become stately boulevards possessing generous trees, landscaped medians, and safe pedestrian crosswalks.

Another phase of development should occur along Fifth Avenue, a street now bordered in this area mainly by parking lots. This is the most logical, direct pedestrian route to and from downtown, and it also serves as a primary vehicular path to Jefferson Street. Successful activities along this street could be a mix of residential, retail, institutional, educational, cultural, and office use. As the area matures, new construction along Third and Fourth Avenues could evolve in a similar fashion. Development on Jackson Street, east of the Mall, also has similar potential. This cross street offers particular promise, its east end conceivably terminating at the same location where the Lick Branch once opened into the Cumberland River. Throughout the revived area, new emphasis should be given toward the river, connecting the emerging neighborhood to this natural amenity. Great care will be necessary to establish use and building guidelines encouraging proper design responses and clearly prohibiting inappropriate activ- ities or heroic, unrelated forms. High-rise buildings that would block views

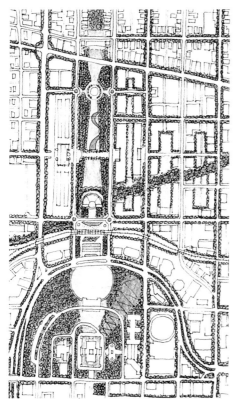
Diagonal greenway recalls stream

Path near Fourth Avenue

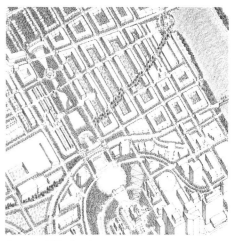
A new neighborhood

History on Jefferson Street

of the Capitol should not be allowed. The area will undoubtedly continue to evolve, and simple, straightforward mid-rise structures—buildings with consistent street edges and that could be easily altered within and adapted over time—should form the basic fabric of this new neighborhood.

One of the most promising aspects for future urban growth in this vicinity is the acknowledgment of the historic Lick Branch as the basis of a new greenway. Although the original stream was buried over a century ago, the sewer pipe remains beneath the soil, creating a straight utility easement on the surface. It is along this restricted path that the new greenway is planned, a winding pedestrian trail and linear park that mimics the historic creek. Only a short, two-block section of the trail

was finished by 1996, including a small fountain placed at the original location of Sulphur Spring near Fourth Avenue. In the future this corridor, which honors both the original inhabitants and early settlers from Europe, should extend east to the river and also west to forge a thin yet inviting green ribbon across a reemerging part of Nashville.

The Mall presents both the state and the city with the kind of opportunity that comes along only once every few generations to redevelop a large, centrally located piece of urban real estate. However, this

occasion can only be fully realized with close cooperation of government agencies and involvement of the private sector. The long-term development of the vicinity around the Mall will necessarily involve financing from state government, intergovernmental grants, city funds, private contributions, and project revenues. Since federal funds continue to be limited, new innovative strategies have been devised in several other cities to complete large-scale development through privatization of the process. A number of cities have used this approach, and a similar technique was utilized to some degree when Capitol Hill was revised in the 1950s. Yet perhaps the closest recent model is the successful Pennsylvania Avenue Development Corporation in Washington, D.C. As our nation's capital city provided an important precedent for the basic form of the park, so too might its evolution prove valuable for the continued growth of our state equivalent. With thoughtful planning and design, strong political leadership, and innovative financing, the third century of the area surrounding the Bicentennial Mall might match in its future what the park achieves now in spirit and in form: a long-lasting gift for all Tennesseans.

State Capitol and Tennessee Bicentennial Capitol Mall

TSPS

Epilogue

Jon Coddington

To write an epilogue one must consider beginnings. What was the initial germ or seed of an idea that can bring understanding to the completed project? It is the seed that provides the initial nourishment that allows growth to occur, and within the genes of the seed are the instructions for the eventual form and identity that the matter will eventually assume. There were two important distinguishing characteristics that constituted the seed for the Bicentennial Mall: the commitment that it was to be a collaborative effort and the establishment of a sensibility rather than a prescription that would guide the project's evolution.

The idea of a collaborative effort is all too novel in today's built environment, but it is essential in the making of sustaining civic places. The Mall's collaborations that resulted were multifaceted and individual contributions are indistinguishable. However, there is no doubt that the Mall was a creative and dynamic collaboration between the people and its government, private enterprise, the academy, and most importantly, the creative talents of the state. But given the nature of the project, there were other collaborations as well, particularly the collaboration of the past,

present, and future. Those of us involved with the project knew it was beyond the imaginative capabilities of any one person or group of people. The Mall represents a collective vision, and through the collaborative efforts of all, a truly civic space has emerged that tells a story in physical form of a place and its people. But all creative collaborations need to be informed by a spirit or sensibility that is not limiting, but liberating, while still giving direction and focus.

What was needed was not prescriptive theory nor the specificity of a particular design that might have later restricted the full exploration of the possibilities of the project. Instead the team concluded that an attitude and sensibility toward the project that could simultaneously reside in the past, present, and future was required. It was within this spirit that the Bicentennial Mall as we know it today was conceived, and it was within this spirit that the team wrote the following to serve as a guide for those who would work on the program, master plan, and final design:

The project is to be a celebration of both past achievements and those yet to come. Thus, the project will have not only technical dimensions

to it, but ethical dimensions as well, for inherent in the project is the commitment to leave a place better than the way it was found. As the State approaches its Bicentennial, there is an opportunity to bequeath to future generations a project which we will wish to be remembered by. It is an opportunity similar to that which confronted the State when the Capitol Building was initially conceived. Then, both the leaders and the people of the State committed themselves to a lasting standard of excellence, and the landmark Capitol is the tangible result of that commitment. In the spirit of the upcoming Bicentennial, we are obligated to do the same. In the end the project is intended to do with material what Wordsworth did in words: "Others will love what we have loved, And we will teach them how."

With these words an attitude was established and a sensibility struck that continues to inform the project.

It is not surprising that the Mall has gained additional significance because it was conceived and executed with a sense of confidence, grace, and style that we have not seen in recent years in government-initiated projects. The Mall is an affirmation of the collective will; though recognizing the importance and integrity of the individual, it nevertheless declares that we as Tennesseans are inextricably linked to a larger collective, ongoing culture and civilization.

It is significant that the centerpiece of the Bicentennial was not a static building or an ephemeral event but rather a park that will grow, change, and evolve over time. As with any significant landscape design, the project is an act of faith, for many of us who were directly responsible for the project will not be here when it reaches full maturity.

The Bicentennial Mall was designed for Tennesseans and for those visiting the state. The park is a place for participation and observation, both of which are art forms in themselves. By cultivating these arts, the park allows us to learn how to transform information into knowledge and combine facts with beliefs to create value linked to the specificity of place. The three themes that bind the park—Tennessee's people, music, and landscape—simultaneously distinguish Tennessee from and connect Tennessee to the world. For Tennessee's culture to remain vibrant, it must be receptive to a wide range of external sources and ways of interpreting the world while still retaining a core that distinguishes it from all other cultures. It must remain modern while still returning to its roots. These roots can never be precisely defined, only explored. Similar to culture and the world of ideas, a park must have a vibrant ecology: a rich and varied web of things and relationships from many places that can survive, flourish, and be transformed by their new surroundings. However, in its most intimate center, a park, like its culture, must retain that which is of its place. Both a park's and a culture's virtue resides in its stubborn uniqueness, in its resistance to generalization, and in its resistance to our

final knowledge of it. Each deals in a gentle declarative of the affirmation of life and its tapestry of dependent relationships.

The park gains distinction and significance because of its placement at the foot of the Capitol and within the larger city fabric. The symmetry and classical language of the Capitol finds its complimentary opposite in its informal grounds, which were originally conceived by William Strickland to be a "stroll park for the people of Tennessee." The design of the Bicentennial Mall also incorporates these formal and informal design strategies. Both the Capitol and its grounds need each other to be complete. In this regard, the whole is greater than the sum of its parts. So it is with a park and the city. A park is nature's critique of the city just as the city is a critique of the wilderness. A city, with its accompanying culture, honors humankind. A park honors the world. A park is where architecture and nature meet. It is this edge condition—a state of in-between—that is essential to understanding the park and its relation to the city. The park positions itself between the garden and the wilderness, between the beautiful and the sublime, between the finite and the infinite, between restraint and freedom. In this state of in-between, a park provides its inhabitants with both prospect and refuge, mystery and legibility. It provides the freedom to be an observer and a participant, and with these qualities and responsibilities, more subject matter for culture and its arts is created. However, a park in the city is in complementary opposition to the arts—a park is matter that generates spirit, whereas the arts are spirit that generates matter. In either case, both show value, and value takes thought and care to create and maintain. To survive, they are dependent on the genius of the one and the many. In the end, they are as the land and sky, for nature and culture must

connect and touch everything we do.

In this regard an epilogue cannot yet be written about the Mall, for the city is not yet complete as it meets the park. Historically, the city has been where the heart of civilization resides, and the success of the mall will be measured by how, as a catalyst, it helps shape and form the city around it. The purpose of a park is not just to provide greenspace in the city but, more importantly, how it can help create and shape community and its consequent culture. The newly opened mall has been acclaimed as a delightful place. But in the end we must think of it as Robert Frost would have us think about the purpose of a poem—that it begin with delight and end in wisdom. Thus it is our hope that the Mall is not an end in itself but a beginning of something larger and that these words do not constitute an epilogue but an introduction.

166

APPENDICES

TENNESSEE BICENTENNIAL CAPITOL MALL
A. GENERAL DESCRIPTION
B. CHRONOLOGY
C. TENNESSEE COUNTY TIME CAPSULES

General Description

The Tennessee Bicentennial Capitol Mall is located north of the State Capitol in Nashville between Sixth and Seventh Avenues, stretching north over 2,200 feet from James Robertson Parkway to Jefferson Street. The Mall, more accurately an urban park, received its fundamental inspiration from the world-renowned National Mall in Washington, D.C., and yet it also contains unique and dramatic features based on the special qualities of the Volunteer State: its people, its history, its landscape, and its music. These elements range from literal to symbolic representations, providing an unusual and exciting learning experience for children, state citizens, and visitors alike. The Mall is the centerpiece of the ambitious $55-million Capitol Area Master Plan, an extensive project that included the redevelopment of the north slope of Capitol Hill and the enhancement of the flat land on the east and west sides of the new park. This latter area once contained the historic but now vanished French Lick mineral deposit and the Lick Branch, a meandering stream instrumental in the early settlement of Nashville. Implementation of the comprehensive master plan and construction of the Mall forever preserve an unobstructed,

dramatic view of the State Capitol while establishing a meaningful, educational place in honor of two hundred years of Tennessee history.

The long, nineteen-acre Mall begins at the base of Capitol Hill at James Robertson Parkway with the Tennessee Plaza, an arrival area between the sweeping, radial boulevard and elevated CSX railroad tracks. This area features an accurate granite map of Tennessee. One of the largest delineations ever made, the engraved hardscape depicts federal highways, state roads, rivers, the ninety-five counties, and virtually every city and town in the state. Tiny uplights at county seats create a fascinating illuminated pattern at dusk. Immediately in front of the flat map, eight sculptural granite renditions of Tennessee protrude from the plaza surface, each portraying a different characteristic or informative *state* of the state.

A new railroad trestle creates an impressive backdrop to the Tennessee map. The open steel bridge, a replacement of previous earth-berm railroad tracks, serves as a gateway into the expanse of the Mall. Public rest rooms and a gift shop occupy small structures tucked beneath the trestle's skeletal profile, while lime-

stone clad abutments replace the dilapidated bridges that once spanned Sixth and Seventh Avenues.

Just beyond the new trestle is an area dedicated to the rivers of Tennessee and their impact on the early settlement and continued development of the state. This space contains thirty-one vertical water fountains, one for each of the predominant rivers in the state. The Riverwall, a sweeping granite surface with inscriptions and quotes about Tennessee's waterways, serves as an educational and poetic backdrop to the numerous fountains. The curved wall recalls the earlier nickname, "Big Bend State," a term based on the graceful flow of the Tennessee River across the profile of the state. At both ends of the wall are identical focal points containing multiple flagpoles, taller elements that guide visitors onward into the central areas of the Mall.

North of the Tennessee Plaza and just beyond Harrison Street, an outdoor performance area is positioned at the center of the Mall. This area is composed of terraced lawns, called "perrons," descending to a large stage in a classic theater shape derived from Greek and Roman models. Dual limestone towers edge the stage and frame dramatic views directly south of the Greek Revival style Capitol building. The outdoor theater has the capacity for approximately two thousand spectators with overflow areas available for additional seating on the adjacent sloped lawn.

As visitors move north beyond the performance area, they encounter two distinctly different areas along the perimeter edges of the Mall, the Walkway of the Counties along Sixth Avenue and the Pathway of History along Seventh Avenue. Complementing these tree-lined peripheral concourses is a large, open lawn at the center of the park. This spacious area is edged by the Path of Volunteers, a sidewalk featuring 17,000 granite name pavers.

Engraved discs recognize the special contributions of Tennessee's ninety-five counties and populate the walkway surface of the Mall's eastern edge to form the Walkway of the Counties. Each granite disc displays a map and historic information about the county entity, and beneath, a time capsule containing items collected for the Bicentennial is entombed in one of the most ambitious and unique burials of memorabilia ever. The arrangement of these ninety-five county markers from south to north along Sixth Avenue corresponds to the approximate location of each county, with demarcations at the three grand divisions of the state. Directly adjacent to this informal walkway, topographic features of the state are portrayed in symbolic fashion. The southern end contains relatively flat areas typical of the western part of the state, while the northern end contains representations of the mountainous eastern region of the state; a representation of the gentle hills of the middle of the state connects the other two sections. Native trees, shrubs, ferns, grasses, and wildflowers along this

walkway present the great diversity of vegetation found across the state. The walkway and its adjacent plantings therefore represent a slice of the state, showcasing the variety of land and people found across Tennessee.

In contrast to the informal, meandering quality of the east side, the west side of the Mall possesses a very rhythmic, precise representation of historic state events at the Pathway of History. A fourteen-hundred-foot-long, chest-high granite wall is engraved with historic events that have occurred during the past two centuries. Included will be an area devoted to events before the arrival of settlers from Europe, such as information on Native American settlements and their impact on the rich cultural heritage that comprise a complete history of the state. Each ten-year period on the linear path is marked with a tall granite pylon emphasizing the march of time at a larger scale, and nodes along the length of the wall highlight particularly important events such as Tennessee statehood in 1796 and the Centennial in 1896. The wall is symbolically broken at the timeline location of the tragic conflict of the Civil War, aligning this traumatic event with the axial path that both bisects the Mall and connects it to the new Farmers' Market directly west across Seventh Avenue. An evocative "North/South" marker at the midpoint of the path requires visitors to choose a side, much as Tennesseans had to during the divisive, terrible war. Although several key features of the Pathway of History are now finished, the majority of the engraved horizontal linkage of historical events is yet to be completed. The long-overdue Tennessee World War II Memorial, a stirring composition located at the appropriate timeline location along the

path, will be finished in late 1997.

The concluding feature of the Mall is the Court of Three Stars, a focal gathering area positioned at the northern end of the Mall near Jefferson Street. It will serve as a tribute to the musical heritage of Tennessee. In the near future, columns will be located in a circular configuration around a flat granite plaza containing three large stars, a familiar image from the state flag. The numerous cylinders will be arranged to create a sense of enclosure, with a large opening facing the distant statehouse. Chimes will be located at the top of the columns, and the resulting collection of bells will create a unique carillon, equipped to be played by a carillonneur or to play programmed music. The carillon will also signal the passing of each hour of the day, a further connection to the time theme found throughout the park. A single, large ninety-sixth bell is also proposed to be located in the distance on the north side of Capitol Hill to answer the ringing of the collective chimes in the Mall, creating a symbolic and acoustic connection to reinforce the dramatic visual relationship between the new urban park and the historic statehouse.

The Mall's comprehensive master plan was adopted in 1993, and construction of adjustments to Capitol Hill and areas around the Mall were completed in 1995. The new Farmers' Market, a relocated replacement of the outdated facility that had previously blocked the grand vista of the Capitol, was also finished the same year. Dedicated during the Tennessee Bicentennial Statehood Day festivities on June 1, 1996, the Mall is open for all visitors as a state park. The History Wall and Path of Volunteers are both scheduled for construction in 1997, a century after the one-year-detained 1897 Tennessee Centennial Exposition.

APPENDIX B
TENNESSEE BICENTENNIAL CAPITOL MALL

Chronology

The following is a list of dates significant to the history, design, and development of the Tennessee Bicentennial Capitol Mall and surrounding area.

500 million B.C.—The area of Middle Tennessee is occupied by a shallow sea.

435 million B.C.—The area of Middle Tennessee is pushed upward. The shallow sea recedes into major rivers across the exposed surface.

66 million B.C.—The Central Basin of Middle Tennessee is formed.

1.6 million B.C.—Glaciers north of Tennessee create alternating climatic conditions across the state.

10,000 B.C.—Paleo Indians hunt and camp in areas of Tennessee.

8000 B.C.—Indians of the Archaic period occupy areas of Tennessee; some groups successfully incorporate agricultural techniques.

1000 B.C.—Indians of the Woodland period establish permanent settlements in Tennessee.

447 B.C.—Pericles begins work on the Parthenon at the Acropolis in Athens, Greece. This most cherished of all Greek buildings is designed by Ictinus and Callicrates and features within a colossal statue of Athena by Phidias. In 1897, a stucco and wood copy of the Parthenon is erected in Nashville as the centerpiece of the Tennessee Centennial Exposition.

350 B.C.—A theater designed by Polycleitos is built in Epidauros, Greece. Together with a later Roman theater of A.D. 50 at Orange in present-day France, these spaces become examples for an amphitheater built in the Bicentennial Mall.

334 B.C.—The Choragic Monument of Lysicrates is built in Athens. It later becomes the model for towers atop several buildings designed by architect William Strickland in the nineteenth century, including the Tennessee State Capitol.

A.D. 900—Indian tribes of the Mississippian period flourish across Tennessee.

1200—The area near the Lick Branch, directly north of what will later become downtown Nashville, is densely settled by Indians until 1400.

1635—A ball-and-mallet game is played on Pall Mall, a street in London. By ellipsis, the term *Pall Mall* is later shortened to *mall*, a term defining a promenade or linear walkway.

1692—Martin Chartier, one of Robert Cavelier LaSalle's men, travels through parts of Middle Tennessee and later to Virginia.

1714—Frenchman Charles Charleville opens a trading post north of the Lick Branch near present day Jefferson Street to conduct business with Indians.

1715—Shawnee Indians are driven from Middle Tennessee by Chickasaw and Cherokee tribes. Abundant hunting ground around area of the Lick Branch is held by no single Indian nation.

1720—English traders from Carolinas venture into Middle Tennessee.

1762—James Stuart and Nicholas Revett publish *Antiquities of Athens* in England. A documentation of structures from ancient Greece, this book becomes an important guide for many Greek Revival architects, including William Strickland.

1763—A long hunter named Henry Scaggs visits the future area of Nashville. Other long hunters travel through the area, and word of the abundant resources of the area is communicated to the Carolinas.

1768—A survey by Thomas Hutchins of land near the Lick Branch indicates an old Shawnee fort built in 1672 on the banks of the Cumberland River near what will later become Jefferson Street.

1769—Jacques Timothé Boucher de Montbrun settles in the area near Charleville's original outpost. He establishes a successful trading operation and later becomes known as Timothy Demonbreun.

1770—White visitors find Timothy Demonbreun's outpost and refer to the large nearby salt spring and creek flowing into the Cumberland River as the "Great French Salt Lick" or simply "French Lick."

North Carolina judge and land speculator Richard Henderson engages explorers David Boone and Kasper Mansker to visit the future area of Nashville.

1779—Judge Henderson engages several additional explorers, including James Robertson and George Freeland, to visit land near the French Lick in the spring. They return to the Watauga settlement in East Tennessee to tell of their favorable impressions.

James Robertson leaves the settlement on the Watauga River in October to lead pioneers across land to the site of the French Lick. They arrive on December 25. The winter is so cold that the river is frozen, and the settlers cross the river's surface to the bluffs on west side and build a fort.

George Freeland and others erect a cabin and station close to a spring near what will later be Eighth Avenue in the future Germantown section of Nashville.

1780—John Donelson's flotilla of settlers, which had departed East Tennessee in late-December 1779, arrives on April 24 to join James Robertson's group. It is the founding of the settlement Nashborough, named in honor of General Francis Nash and later becomes the city of Nashville.

The Cumberland Compact is signed on May 13. This document establishes the first civil government in Middle Tennessee.

1781—Felix Robertson, son of Charlotte and James, is born on January 11. His birth is the first documented of a white child born in Nashborough, and he later becomes a doctor.

Cherokees attack Freeland Station on January 15.

Settlers successfully defend Fort Nashborough during the Battle of the Bluff on April 2. Only seventy original settlers survive the severe fighting.

1784—In honor of Brigadier General William Lee Davidson, Davidson County is created by North Carolina legislature, and the name of the largest settlement in Middle Tennessee is changed from Nashborough to Nashville.

A survey of land by Thomas Molloy depicts the division of land in and around the area of the Lick Branch and Nashville.

1786—A survey by David McGavock of "Plantations on Cumberland River" shows 640 acres around French Lick as "public land," complying with a North Carolina law that at least 640 acres around a salt spring or salt lick must be public property.

1788—William Strickland is born in New Jersey.

1789—The first bridge built in Nashville, composed of logs and split timbers, is erected across the Lick Branch near the stream's outlet into the Cumberland River.

1790—Anthony Hart constructs a salt works to package salt found at Sulphur Spring, the main spring on the Lick Branch.

1791—Judge John McNairy receives a land grant of two hundred acres in north Nashville, including a spring on the site of the future Bicentennial Mall.

Pierre Charles L'Enfant proposes a design for the new capital city of the United States. His scheme for Washington, D.C., includes a linear park that will evolve into the National Mall. This park becomes one of the planning models for the Bicentennial Mall.

1796—Tennessee is admitted to the United States as the sixteenth state on June 1. The General Assembly of Tennessee meets in Knoxville, and John Sevier is elected as the first governor.

1797—David Morrison is born in Pennsylvania. He works as a builder and travels to Nashville in the 1820s. He brings his knowledge of Greek Revival style architecture to Middle Tennessee.

1801—The seal of Tennessee is adopted by the General Assembly.

1803—At age fourteen, William Strickland is an apprentice to Benjamin H. Latrobe, architect of the original U.S. Capitol.

1804—The land around the French Lick and Sulphur Spring is no longer public property. The first city cemetery is located overlooking the Lick Branch.

1808—Strickland makes his first important architectural drawings for a Masonic hall in Philadelphia.

1812—The General Assembly meets in Nashville for the first time.

1813—In May, Strickland's hypothetical design for a monument in Baltimore honoring George Washington is exhibited in Philadelphia.

1814—James Robertson dies near Memphis on September 1 and is buried at the Chickasaw Agency there. In 1825, his remains are reinterred at the Nashville City Cemetery.

1818—Strickland wins a design competition for the Second Bank of the United States in Philadelphia. The exterior of this Greek Revival structure is based on the Parthenon. The building is completed six years later.

1825—Strickland meets with General Lafayette in Philadelphia. He travels to England in the same year.

Philip Lindsley becomes president of the University of Nashville. He is credited with describing Nashville as the "Athens of the West." Later the phrase becomes "Athens of the South."

General Lafayette visits Nashville.

1826—Strickland designs a Washington Monument for Philadelphia. It is never built.

1828—Strickland supervises the restoration of the steepled tower above Independence Hall in Philadelphia.

Andrew Jackson is elected president of the United States.

1830—Nashville annexes land between what is now Jo Johnston Avenue and Hamilton Street.

1831—President Jackson hires David Morrison to redesign his home, The Hermitage. Morrison's changes incorporate Greek Revival elements, the first time such treatments occur in a Nashville building.

1832—Strickland designs perhaps his most original building, the Merchants' Exchange in Philadelphia. The building is finished two years later.

Andrew Jackson is reelected president.

1833—A map of Nashville by Ayers illustrates the path of the Lick Branch and the names of many streets. Several east-west streets north of Cedar Knob are named after U.S. presidents.

1834—After a fire, The Hermitage is rebuilt for a fourth time, based on design by William Hume and Joseph Reiff. Colossal order columns create a much more impressive Greek Revival facade than the Morrison renovation of 1831.

1835—The State of Tennessee Union Bank is built in Nashville. The Greek Revival design by David Morrison is patterned after Strickland's 1824 Second Bank of the United States in Philadelphia.

1836—National competition for the Washington Monument in Washington, D.C., is won by Strickland's friend and fellow Greek Revival advocate Robert Mills.

1837—Financial panic hits the northeast area of the United States, causing many civic and commercial projects to be canceled.

Strickland is selected to design a new sarcophagus for the tomb of President George Washington at Mount Vernon which had been built in 1831, over three decades after the president's death in 1799.

1838—With his family, Strickland tours Europe, including a visit to Rome.

Nashville annexes land from Hamilton Street north to Jefferson Street.

1840—Severe flood in Cairo, Illinois, causes cancellation of a major civil engineering project designed by Strickland.

1841—Strickland helps edit a book published in London, *Public Works in the United States.*

Major flooding of Cumberland River occurs. Lick Branch floods entire vicinity between Crawford and Jefferson Streets. During the next century, frequent flooding of this creek and surrounding lowlands limits significant development in this section of Nashville.

1842—Strickland is elected to the Royal Institute of Civil Engineers in England.

1843—By act of the General Assembly, Nashville becomes the permanent state capital on October 7. On December 11, four acres on Campbell's Hill, previously known as Cedar Knob, become state property as the location for a capitol building.

1844—The Tennessee Capitol Commission is formed by the state legislature on January 30 to oversee the design and construction of a permanent statehouse.

Strickland presents plans on April 21 for the substantial enlargement of the United States Capitol in Washington, D.C. His plans are not accepted.

Dissatisfied with Robert Mills's 1836 competition-winning scheme for the Washington Monument, Congressman Zadock Pratt of New York submits an alternative design by Strickland to Congress on May 25. Strickland's substitute proposal is not accepted, and later construction eventually begins on Mills's original design on July 4, 1848. The 555-foot obelisk is not completed until December 6, 1884.

On June 16, the Capitol Commission authorizes an invitation letter to be sent to Strickland requesting his interest in designing a statehouse in Nashville.

Several architects, including Gideon Shryock, Adolphus Heiman, and James Dakin, present plans for a new statehouse to Capitol Commission members. Strickland does not visit Nashville but submits a sketch.

James K. Polk is elected president of the United States.

1845—On April 2, Strickland receives a second formal invitation from the Capitol Commission urging him to visit Nashville and present plans for a statehouse. Strickland accepts the invitation.

Strickland arrives in Nashville on April 29.

Strickland presents plans, specifications, and an estimate for the new Tennessee statehouse to the Capitol Commission on May 20. His scheme is accepted.

Andrew Jackson dies at The Hermitage on June 8.

A contract between the state and Strickland is signed on June 18 authorizing him to complete the design and construction of the new statehouse.

The cornerstone for the Tennessee State Capitol Building is laid during an elaborate Masonic ritual on July 4.

1846—Gideon Shryock files a formal protest to the Capitol Commission on May 12 requesting payment for his unsuccessful design for the Tennessee statehouse.

1847—St. Mary's Cathedral on Fifth Avenue is dedicated on October 31. The architect is Adolphus Heiman. The cathedral's tower is somewhat similar to the cupola atop the Capitol; this and other factors create the false impression in the early part of the twentieth century that William Strickland was the original architect.

1848—Wilson County Courthouse is built in Lebanon, Tennessee. The Greek Revival style courthouse designed by William Strickland features a Choragic Monument tower similar to the one at the Tennessee State Capitol.

1849—On April 28, the cornerstone is laid for First Presbyterian Church on Church Street in Nashville. The Egyptian Revival style building is designed by William Strickland.

James K. Polk dies of cholera in Nashville on June 15. Later, Strickland designs a tomb for President and Mrs. Polk.

1851—The Great Exposition, an international exhibition of emerging advances in technology and industry, is held in London. It begins a pattern of expositions throughout the western world that lasts for many decades.

In February, Nashville Gas Company is established with gas works in buildings located at the north end of Market Street (later known as Second Avenue) near where the road crosses the Lick Branch.

First Presbyterian Church is completed and dedicated on Easter Sunday, April 20.

1853—The Tennessee Legislature meets for the first time in the new but yet-to-be-completed Capitol on October 3.

Capitol Planing Mill, a woodworking shop, is established by J. W. McCullough at the corner of what is now Jo Johnston and Seventh Avenues.

1854—William Strickland dies unexpectedly on April 6 in the City Hotel. After an elaborate funeral on April 8, he is buried in the northeast corner of the Capitol, above the now hidden cornerstone. Strickland's son Francis is appointed to succeed his father as architect of the Capitol on June 3.

The Nashville and Chattanooga railroad is opened.

1855—The Capitol is finished with the exception of interior work and the exterior terraces.

Francis Strickland designs the Davidson County Courthouse, a rectangular structure

somewhat similar to his father's design for the Capitol, minus the tower.

1857—Holy Rosary Cathedral site at the northeast corner of the Capitol grounds is purchased by the state.

After two years of disagreements with the Capitol Commission, Francis Strickland is dismissed as architect of the Capitol on May 1.

1858—On December 4, H. M. Akeroyd is appointed to oversee final work on the Capitol.

1859—On March 19, the final stone is laid on the lower terrace. The Tennessee State Capitol building is finished fourteen years after it was started.

The Church of the Assumption in Germantown is dedicated on August 14. Brick from the demolished Holy Rosary Cathedral on Capitol Hill is used in the construction. A steeple is added thirteen years later.

The Louisville and Nashville railroad is completed and connects the two cities. This line includes a wood trestle north of Capitol Hill across the future site of the Bicentennial Mall.

1860—Civil engineer J. P. Hayden is hired to survey Capitol Hill and recommend stabilization measures. Landscape gardener William Pritchard develops a design for the enhancement of the entire site, and his controversial design is accepted in October.

1861—The Civil War starts on April 12.

Governor Isham Harris proclaims Tennessee's secession from the Union on June 24.

1862—With the anticipated arrival of Union forces, much of Nashville's population flees in panic on February 16.

Union forces occupy Nashville on February 24. "Old Glory," owned by Captain William Driver and one of the most famous of all

U.S. flags, is hoisted above the east portico of the statehouse.

On March 3, Andrew Johnson of Greeneville is appointed military governor of Tennessee.

The Capitol becomes a Union headquarters and is called "Fort Andrew Johnson" in recognition of the military governor from East Tennessee.

Union soldiers stationed in Nashville bring baseball to Tennessee, playing the game in an open field near Sulphur Spring.

A building for Saint Cecilia Academy, a grammar and high school for girls, is completed north of Germantown. Other sections are added to the school building in 1880 and 1913.

1863—The Capitol is used as a hospital following the Battle of Stones River near Murfreesboro.

1864—The Battle of Nashville occurs in the southwest section of the city. Union officers reportedly watch the fighting from the tower of the Capitol.

Abraham Lincoln is reelected president on November 4. Former Tennessee senator and acting Union military governor Andrew Johnson is elected vice president.

1865—The War Between the States ends on April 9.

Andrew Johnson becomes president on April 15, one day after the assassination of Abraham Lincoln.

Federal occupation of Nashville ends on July 1.

W. G. Bush and T. L. Herbert Companies are founded on Van Buren Street in Germantown. During the next century, these companies occupy many properties in Germantown and near the Lick Branch.

1866—The first baseball game in Nashville between organized teams is played in September on the open field near Sulphur Spring.

Fisk School, later to become Fisk University, is founded for the education of emancipated slaves.

A horse-drawn streetcar route opens connecting downtown Nashville and Germantown.

1867—Belleview Public School opens near Jefferson Street and Summer Street (later known as Fifth Avenue) for the education of children of emancipated slaves.

1868—The railroad to St. Louis is completed. The railroad company becomes Nashville, Chattanooga, and St. Louis Railway (N. C. & St. L.).

1870—The state legislature passes an act to improve the Capitol grounds, and John Bogart of New York is hired to develop a workable scheme.

Work begins on a factory for Tennessee Manufacturing Company on Spruce Street (later known as Eighth Avenue) under supervision of the company's president, Samuel D. Morgan. Other sections are added in the following decade.

1871—Fisk Jubilee Singers begin national tour to raise money for their school, which will become an important institution on Jefferson Street.

Landscape architect John Bogart begins reconfiguration of Capitol Hill.

1873—Cholera epidemic strikes Nashville. Similar epidemics have occurred five times in the forty years before. This epidemic kills over one thousand residents.

Vanderbilt University is established. Together with other institutions of higher learning, it helps confirm Nashville's growing reputation as the "Athens of the South."

1875—Jubilee Hall is completed at Fisk School on Jefferson Street. It is the first permanent building in the United States for the higher education of African Americans.

1876—United States Centennial Exposition is held in Philadelphia. This event begins the

era of expositions in America, one of which will be the Tennessee Centennial Exposition in 1897.

1877—Bogart's scheme for the reconfiguration of Capitol Hill is finished.

1879—Nashville Sulphur Spring Company is incorporated. This company bottles the pungent water from Sulphur Spring and also offers baths in the supposed healing waters.

1880—Nashville Centennial Exposition is held from April 23 to May 30 in a large temporary building at the corner of Broad and Spruce Streets. The highlight of the celebration is the May 20 dedication of an equestrian statue of Andrew Jackson by Clark Mills on the east side of Capitol Hill.

Long-time Capitol Commission Chairman Samuel D. Morgan dies on June 10.

A triangular marker is placed on Capitol Hill to honor the three governors surnamed Brown from Giles County.

1881—An exposition is held in Atlanta. Due to its success and the growing popularity of expositions in general, two others are held in this city, one in 1887 and one in 1895.

Wilson County Courthouse in Lebanon, designed by William Strickland, is destroyed in December by fire.

On Christmas Eve, Samuel D. Morgan's body is moved from the original cemetery plot to a burial tomb in the southeast corner of the Capitol.

1882—*Manufacturing and Mercantile Resources of Nashville* compares Sulphur Spring's healing waters to the famous ones at Hot Springs, Arkansas.

1883—A successful exposition is held in Louisville.

1884—Early in the year, the Cumberland River floods, inundating area of the Lick Branch and other parts of Nashville.

1885—The first professional baseball game in Nashville is played on the open field near Sulphur Spring.

A successful exposition is held in New Orleans.

1886—John Geist opens a blacksmith shop on Jefferson Street. This street continues to develop as Germantown flourishes as a residential community north of Sulphur Spring.

1887—McEwen's Steam Laundry, located at the corner of Crawford Street and Summer Street (later known as Fifth Avenue), is one of the city's largest. A historian notes that "twelve hundred dozen collars and cuffs are cleaned daily . . . [for] thousands of people."

1888—Bird's-eye view drawing of Nashville published by H. Wellge & Company of Milwaukee shows continued lack of development of the area of the Lick Branch.

1889—The Lick Branch is channelized so that water and sewage flow more freely into the Cumberland River. The area around the creek is now known as Sulphur Bottoms.

Universal Exposition is held in Paris, France. This successful fair devoted to the achievements of industry leaves two important permanent gifts: the Eiffel Tower and a linear urban park, the Champ de Mars.

1890—An individual dies after falling from one of the upper esplanades of the Capitol.

Bruton & Condon Snuff Company erects a building on Harrison Street west of Spruce Street. This structure is the first of many added during the next century. The company later becomes American Tobacco in 1900 and then United States Tobacco in 1922.

1891—The tomb of President and Mrs. James K. Polk, designed by William Strickland, is moved from the original location at Polk Place to the northeast corner of Capitol Hill.

Report in March by Harry McDonald of Louisville identifies severe deterioration on exterior and interior of the Capitol. McDonald supervises the installation of protective railings on the esplanades of the Capitol between the columns of the porticos.

1892—The Lick Branch is excavated and enclosed in a large, brick sewer. The historic creek vanishes from sight.

1893—World Columbian Exposition in Chicago opens on May 1. This exposition and its "White City" of temporary neoclassical structures becomes the model for many subsequent expositions and also for the City Beautiful Movement in urban planning. More than 25 million people visit the fair. The Tennessee Centennial Exposition of 1897, patterned after this northern example, would later be referred to by some as the "Fair White City of the South."

1894—Structure for Odd Fellows Lodge is built at northeast corner of the intersection of Jefferson Street and Vine Street (later known as Seventh Avenue).

1896—Tennessee Centennial. For many reasons, economic and political, the official anniversary celebration is delayed.

1897—Tennessee Centennial Exposition is held in the west part of Nashville. The exposition includes the erection of many temporary buildings, including an accurate replica of the Parthenon. President William McKinley officially opens the celebration from Washington on May 1 by sending a signal to Nashville over telegraph wires.

Tennessee Day is held on June 1, 101 years after statehood in 1796.

The Negro Building is officially opened on Negro Day, June 5.

On June 11, President McKinley visits the exposition.

Almost 55,000 attend the fair during Confederate Veterans Days, June 23 and 24.

Tightrope walker "Arion" entertains crowds throughout the exposition. He falls to his death one year later.

Nashville Day is celebrated on September 11, and attendance swells to 41,558.

The largest one-day attendance is a surprising 98,579 on "Thomas Day," October 28, in honor of John W. Thomas, president of N. C. & St. L. Railroad and president of the Exposition Company.

The fair officially closes on October 30. Total attendance is a staggering 1,786,711.

Service industries in the area around Sulphur Bottoms continue to flourish.

1901—Athletic Park Stadium, built beside Sulphur Spring between Fourth and Fifth Avenues, becomes the home of Nashville Volunteers professional baseball team.

McMillan Commission adopts a plan for the reconfiguration of Washington, D.C., based on L'Enfant's concept of 1791. Soon afterward, the grand expanse of the National Mall is completed.

1902—New steps from Charlotte Avenue to the Capitol are built on the south side of Capitol Hill.

An extensive cleaning and repair program is authorized in April to resolve the exterior condition of the Capitol.

1903—Third Baptist Church is built on Monroe Street, one block west of Spruce Street (later known as Eighth Avenue) and Germantown.

1904—On July 26, the announcement is made that the twelve-story First National Bank building will be erected on the southeast corner of Church and Cherry Streets. It will be the city's first skyscraper.

Carnegie Library is completed and opened to the public on September 19 at corner of Union Street and Polk Place on the site of James K. Polk's residence. Later, it is demolished for construction of the Ben West Public Library.

A city ordinance is enacted on December 22 to change names of streets running north and southwest of the Cumberland River.

1905—A design by Captain LeRoy Reeves is adopted as the official flag of Tennessee.

1906—Monroe Street Methodist Episcopal Church is erected in Germantown, and St. Paul's Lutheran Church is built three blocks north on Eighth Avenue.

The Stahlman Building, designed by Carpenter & Blair with Otto Eggers of New York, is erected on Union Street as the city's second skyscraper.

1907—A "Governor's Mansion" is authorized by the legislature, and the Williams Residence, directly south of the Capitol on Seventh Avenue, is purchased on July 10. It remains the official residence of the state's chief executive until 1923 when it is demolished to make room the War Memorial Building.

Henry and Lawrence Neuhoff erect a large meat-packing plant on the Cumberland River. Over the next fifty years, several additions are made to this facility.

In October, a tree and marker are placed on Capitol Hill by Watauga Chapter of Daughters of American Revolution in memory of early pioneers.

1908—Athletic Park Baseball Stadium near Sulphur Spring is renamed "Sulphur Dell" by sportswriter Grantland Rice.

International Harvester Company, which had occupied a site at Harrison Street and Seventh Avenue for several years, moves to Second Avenue.

1909—Statue of Sam Davis, "Boy Hero of the Confederacy" by George J. Zolnay, is dedicated on the southwest corner of Capitol Hill.

The city establishes Morgan Park in Germantown in honor of Samuel D. Morgan.

1910—Nashville Spring and Mattress Company is located between Harrison and Hamilton Streets and remains there for twenty years.

Hermitage Hotel, designed by J. Edwin Carpenter, is completed at corner of Sixth Avenue and Union Street.

1912—YMCA Building is erected on Union Street across from the War Memorial Building.

1914—Noel and Company Ice Manufacturers, which will supply ice to Nashville for many decades, is built on Tenth Avenue.

1915—Mrs. John (Elizabeth) Eakin and Mrs. Robert (Margaret) Weakley present their idea to the Centennial Club for preserving and beautifying the grounds surrounding the Capitol.

Another Carnegie Library is built on Monroe Street, one block west of Eighth Avenue near Germantown.

1916—YMCA announces plans to build a Negro YMCA at the corner of Park Place and Charlotte Avenue.

Nashville architect Russell Hart develops plans of the Capitol area for Centennial Club, including the suggestion of an amphitheater on the north slope.

Named in honor of teacher and Methodist minister Reverend Collins Elliott, a new Elliott School is built on the corner of Jefferson Street and Sixth Avenue. This structure by Marr & Holman replaces an earlier building of 1873.

The only no-hitter baseball game ever played at Sulphur Dell Stadium occurs on July 11. Nashville Vols beat rival Chattanooga 2–0.

The Tennessee Capitol Association is chartered by Elizabeth Eakin and Margaret Weakley on December 21, one week after Mrs. Eakin's purchase from YMCA of property at the corner of Park Place and Charlotte Avenue. This organization is formed to advocate protection and enhancement of property around the Capitol.

1917—The *Nashville Banner* publishes a drawing on January 13 by architect Harry Frahn of a hypothetical vertical enlargement of the Capitol.

Elizabeth Eakin purchases property at corner of Seventh and Charlotte Avenues to prevent an out-of-town publishing company from erecting a building on the site. Through the next five years, she will continue to purchase other lots on Capitol Hill.

1918—World War I ends on November 11. More than 116,000 Tennesseans serve during the war, and 2,965 are killed.

1919—Tennessee General Assembly Public Act of 1919 authorizes the creation of a park south of the Capitol as a memorial to the veterans of the Great War. The property is later given to the city for use as a public park to be known as Victory Square (better known as War Memorial Park). State authorities do not relinquish the property to the city until 1953.

James E. Caldwell establishes the Nashville Union Stock Yards on Second Avenue near path of Lick Branch sewer.

1920—The temporary stucco and wood Parthenon in Centennial Park is demolished and work begins on a permanent concrete replacement. The architect for the reconstruction is Russell Hart.

1921—Legislature approves funds to reimburse Elizabeth Eakin for her purchases of land around Capitol Hill.

1924—Fehr Public School is built at north end of Germantown.

"Zero Milestone" marker is dedicated on May 12 near the Capitol by the Nashville Automobile Club. Distances on state highways are hereafter measured from this point. In the late-1950s it is removed for construction of the Cotton States Annex Building. The marker is later misplaced and lost in the 1980s.

1925—Statue of Edward Ward Carmack by Nancy Cox McCormack is erected on the south side of Capitol Hill in the middle of the 1902 steps connecting to Charlotte Avenue.

The War Memorial Building is built in honor of Tennesseans who fought and died in

World War I. Edward Dougherty is the architect. The statue of Nike in the building's central courtyard is by Belle Kinney.

Andrew Jackson Hotel and Cotton States office building are built on Sixth Avenue directly across from War Memorial Building.

1926—On October 10, a large three-figure sculpture by Belle Kinney is unveiled at the south end of the War Memorial Building to honor, as stated on the statue, "the heroic devotion and self-sacrifice of the women of Tennessee during the War Between the States."

In December the worst flooding in Nashville's recorded history occurs. At some points, the Cumberland River expands to three miles in width. This flooding continues into January 1927.

1927—Sulphur Dell Stadium is revised and turned around such that home plate faces northeast. A new covered grandstand, designed by Marr & Holman, is built.

On July 27, "7–27–27," a triangular time capsule is buried on Capitol Hill by Nashville Council No. 1 of Royal and Select Masons.

1928—The Tennessee Manufacturing Company on Eighth Avenue becomes the Werthan Bag Corporation.

1930—In honor of the Sesquicentennial of Nashville, a downsized replica of Fort Nashborough is erected on the bluff above the Cumberland River.

1931—The concrete Parthenon in Centennial Park is completed.

1933—The mockingbird is selected as the state bird, and the iris is selected as the state flower. The passion flower had already been designated the state flower in 1919, and the apparent confusion is settled in 1973 by naming the passion flower as the state *wildflower*.

1934—A concrete "Coast and Geodetic Survey Marker" is placed on Capitol Hill.

1935—A large brick building is added to the U.S. Tobacco Company complex on Harrison Street. Later, a large sign advertising "Bruton Snuff" is placed on the roof.

1936—Elizabeth Eakin dies penniless, and the state does not completely resolve reimbursements to her estate until 1945.

Several offices inside the Capitol are renovated, including the governor's suite. This work is supervised by Emmons Woolwine and John Howard Clark.

1937—The Tennessee Supreme Court Building is completed at the corner of Seventh and Charlotte Avenues. The architects are Marr & Holman, and the contractor is Rock City Construction Company.

The Cumberland River overflows, flooding parts of downtown Nashville.

Davidson County Public Building & Court House is erected. Its north facade fronts what is now James Robertson Parkway. The architect is Emmons Woolwine with participation of New York architect Frederic Hirons, and the contractor is J. A. Jones Construction Company.

Cheatham Place public housing development is completed on Eighth Avenue across from Werthan Bag factory. It is the city's first public-housing project.

1939—On October 3, a marker is placed on Capitol Hill by American Legion Post 5 to honor "American War Mothers of the Great War."

1940—The Tennessee State Office Building is finished at corner of Park Place and Charlotte Avenue. It is later renamed the John Sevier State Office Building in honor of Tennessee's first governor. The architect is Emmons Woolwine, and the contractor is Niles Yearwood.

The Nashville Housing Authority classifies 92 percent of the houses between Capitol Hill and the railroad to be in "unfit and substandard" condition. This action helps validate the massive urban-renewal project that will commence ten years later.

1945—World War II ends on August 14. More than 369,000 Tennesseans serve during the war, and 5,731 are killed.

Chapter 114 of *Tennessee Public Acts, 1945* includes "Slum Clearance and Urban Renewal Act of 1945," a provision that authorizes the removal of dilapidated structures around the Capitol.

Tennessean Cordell Hull, who served as U.S. secretary of state longer than any other person in American history, receives the Nobel Peace Prize.

R. L. Wiles opens a new feed mill store in the Sulphur Dell area at the corner of Third and Whiteside Avenues, moving from its previous 1913 location on Second Avenue South.

1946—For the Tennessee Sesquicentennial, the U.S. Postal Service issues a commemorative three-cent stamp featuring Andrew Jackson, John Sevier, and the Capitol.

1947—The General Assembly appropriates funds on March 12 to build a new Library and Archives building in honor of Tennesseans who fought and died in World War II. Additional funds are required and appropriated on April 11, 1949, and March 13, 1951.

1949—Preliminary studies are made by the City Planning Commission for the long-awaited removal of slums around the Capitol.

The U.S. Congress approves the "Housing Act of 1949." One week later, officials from Nashville receive approval for the massive urban renewal of ninety-six acres surrounding the Capitol.

1950—Selected structures are demolished between the Capitol and the railroad, and the reshaping of Capitol Hill begins.

On November 11, Armistice Day, a plaque is unveiled at War Memorial Park by *Nashville Banner* in memory of Tennessee Air National Guardsmen killed in a plane crash on July 23, 1950. The bronze plaque is later relocated to Legislative Plaza.

1951—On March 9, the Tennessee Supreme Court upholds the "Slum Clearance and Urban Renewal Act of 1945" in the case of *Nashville Housing Authority* v. *The City*.

1952—The cornerstone is laid for Cordell Hull State Office Building on Park Place. This large building is finished in 1954. The architects are Hart and McBryde, and the contractor is Creighton-MacDonald.

City of Nashville Capitol Redevelopment Plan, developed by Clarke, Rapuano and Holleran of New York, is adopted.

Tennessee State Library and Archives on Seventh Avenue directly west of the Capitol is finished and dedicated. The architect is H. Clinton Parrent Jr., and the contractor is Rock City Construction Company.

Old Hickory Dam is built on the Cumberland River by the U.S. Army Corps of Engineers, helping to stabilize the flow of the river and significantly reducing the potential for devastating floods in many areas of Middle Tennessee, including the area north of the Capitol.

1953—The General Assembly appropriates funds for the repair of deteriorating limestone on the exterior of the Capitol.

Although demolition and site work are already well underway, the official Capitol Hill Redevelopment Dedication ceremony is held on November 6.

1954—Farmers' Market relocates in October from area near the Davidson County Courthouse to its new location north of downtown and bordered by Jackson and Jefferson Streets and Sixth and Eighth Avenues. A large grocery store is later built at the corner of Eighth and Jefferson next to the open sheds of the market.

1955—Major flood in March inundates lower parts of the newly cleared Capitol Hill redevelopment area.

The General Assembly creates the State Building Commission to replace the earlier

Capitol Hill Area Commission and to oversee all future state building projects.

First Presbyterian Church on Church Street becomes The Downtown Presbyterian Church.

1956—Work begins on major repair and restoration of the Capitol, including the replacement of most of the exterior Bigby limestone with Oolitic limestone from Indiana. This work is finished four years later. The architects are Victor G. Stromquist with Woolwine, Harwood and Clark.

Metro Manor apartment building is built on James Robertson Parkway at Fifth Avenue.

Davidson County Agricultural Extension Service building is erected on Jefferson Street beside Farmers' Market. Three years later the building is named in honor of Oscar Farris.

1957—Interior renovations of the Capitol take place. The crypt level is excavated and transformed into offices.

The Life & Casualty Tower, the tallest building in the Southeast, is opened on April 30. It is the first structure in Nashville to fully challenge the visual prominence of the Capitol. The skyscraper is designed by Edwin Keeble and built by J. A. Jones Construction Company.

A large water and sewage treatment plant is built northeast of Germantown. Over the next four decades, it is expanded several times. The often malodorous facility and others, including several meat-packing plants, help to permanently alter the character of the vicinity.

1958—The Motlow Tunnel is built beneath south side of the Capitol, creating an enclosed, conditioned entry from Charlotte Avenue to the statehouse.

The Federal Reserve Branch Bank is completed in November on Eighth Avenue above the western end of James Robertson Parkway. The architect is Henry J. Toombs of Atlanta.

1959—Nashville Gas Company builds a new service center at the site of its previous gas works on Second Avenue.

1960—The area immediately around the Capitol is altered by the installation of a new road connected to Seventh Avenue and the construction of a parking plateau surrounding the statehouse.

A Holiday Inn motel is built on James Robertson Parkway at the corner of Eighth Avenue. Other motels, including Travel Lodge and Ramada Inn, are soon built nearby.

1961—Capitol Towers is built on James Robertson Parkway at the southwest corner of Fifth Avenue. John Doggett of Memphis is the architect. It blocks views of the Capitol from motorist on the boulevard.

Municipal Auditorium is completed on James Robertson Parkway. The architects are Marr & Holman.

In September, students from Tennessee State and Fisk Universities march from campuses on Jefferson Street to the Capitol and Metro Courthouse to protest the dismissal of fellow classmates who had been expelled from school for "freedom riding."

In the fall, more than six hundred new trees are planted on the massive landform of Capitol Hill.

1962—The Tennessee Education Association building, designed by Taylor & Crabtree, is completed at the northeast corner of James Robertson Parkway and Sixth Avenue.

1963—Central Services Building designed by Marr & Holman is completed, an unusual below-grade, hyphen-like structure located between Sevier and Cordell Hull buildings. Its plaza top, with substantial earth topping to help shield a subterranean atomic bomb shelter, does not block view of Capitol from the east.

The last baseball game is played at Sulphur Dell Stadium on September 8, Nashville

Vols winning over Lynchburg in both games of a doubleheader.

Percy Priest Dam is built on Stones River. Similar to the Old Hickory Dam, it further helps stabilize the Cumberland River.

1964—Sulphur Dell Stadium becomes Sulphur Dell Speedway, an auto-racing track.

1965—Significant portions of the interstate highway system are built in Davidson County; this work continues for many years.

Ben West Public Library is completed at corner of Union Street and Polk Place, designed by Taylor & Crabtree and built by W. F. Holt & Sons.

1966—The last section of property of the massive Capitol Hill Redevelopment Plan is sold to private interests after sixteen years and the administrations of three mayors and three governors. The $9.6-million project has resulted in twenty-five new structures and dramatic changes to the area north of the Capitol.

On November 18, a plaque is placed on the Supreme Court building in honor of Elizabeth Eakin and Margaret Weakley. In later years, the section of Seventh Avenue on Capitol Hill is renamed Eakin-Weakley Drive.

After being used unsuccessfully for car races, miscellaneous outdoor events, and automobile storage, the Sulphur Dell Stadium is demolished and the site is cleared to become a gravel parking lot.

1968—A proposal is developed for the city by Clarke, Rapuano and Holleran for the area between James Robertson Parkway and Jefferson Street. It includes office developments and a municipal stadium.

Television station Channel Five-WLAC building, designed by Earl Swensson Associates, is completed on James Robertson Parkway.

A statue of World War I hero Alvin York by Felix de Weldon is unveiled on December 13 at the southeast corner of Capitol Hill.

1969—The title for War Memorial Park is returned from the city to state government. This property is to be used for construction of Legislative Plaza.

Andrew Jackson State Office Building, designed by Taylor & Crabtree and built by Melton Construction Company, is completed on Demonbreun Street at the corner of Fifth Avenue.

Architect Robert Church of Knoxville submits a design for a large parking garage on Capitol Hill. His scheme includes the idea of a linear park to the north, perhaps the first concept for what will later become the Bicentennial Mall.

On September 10, a plaque is placed on Capitol Hill in honor of the seventy-fifth anniversary of the founding in Nashville of the United Daughters of the Confederacy in 1894.

1970—Elliott School on Jefferson Street is closed.

The National Life Tower is finished directly west of the War Memorial Building. It is designed by Skidmore, Owings and Merrill of Chicago and built by H. C. Beck Company.

1971—Major sections of Interstate 40 and 265 are finished, slicing through prominently black neighborhoods west and north of Germantown.

First Baptist Church Capitol Hill is built on James Robertson Parkway. The architect is Quincy Jackson.

Andrew Jackson Hotel is demolished on June 13. Explosive charges placed within level the twelve-story building in seconds.

University of Tennessee at Nashville opens a large building on Charlotte Avenue near the western end of James Robertson Parkway. The facility, designed by Earl Swensson Associates, later becomes the downtown campus of Tennessee State University.

The Capitol receives National Historic Landmark status on November 11 from the United States Department of the Interior, the highest recognition given to a historic structure in the country.

1973—Metrocenter office and industrial park, a development by Victor Johnson and R. C. Mathews, opens north of Germantown near Interstate 265. The master plan is by Robert Lamb Hart of New York.

1974—Activities at the Nashville Union Stock Yards cease. The main brick building reopens as the Stock-Yard Restaurant in 1980.

Legislative Plaza is finished, a subterranean state office building beneath a large urban plaza located directly south of the Capitol. It is designed by Steinbaugh, Harwood and Rogers and built by Sharondale Construction Company.

1975—The Cumberland River floods.

Hyatt Regency Hotel is built on Union Street directly across from the War Memorial Building. John Mastin & Associates of Atlanta is the architect. It later becomes the Crowne Plaza hotel.

A tree and concrete marker are placed on Capitol Hill by the National Society of Colonial Dames in Tennessee in honor of two hundredth anniversary of George Washington's acceptance of command of American colonial army.

1976—During national Bicentennial celebrations, a reenactment is held of the journey of settlers who left East Tennessee and traveled to Nashville in 1780.

The Tennessee flag is accidentally published upside down by the U.S. Postal Service in "Flags of America" stamp series.

A replica of Liberty Bell is placed on the east side of Capitol Hill in recognition of the nation's Bicentennial.

"Still on Patrol" plaque is placed on Legislative Plaza by U.S. Navy Submarine veterans to honor 374 officers, 3,131 men, and 52 subs lost during World War II.

1978—A time capsule is buried on Capitol Hill by Governor Ray Blanton.

1979—U.S. Postal Service issues the first four-stamp block of a series honoring American architecture. Included is the Merchants' Exchange Building in Philadelphia by William Strickland.

1980—Nashville Bicentennial is celebrated.

Nashville! magazine features a hypothetical proposal by Earl Swensson Associates for Sulphur Dell, including a massive arena and a linear brick plaza above underground garages for state employees.

1981—U.S. Tobacco Company headquarters at corner of Eighth Avenue and Harrison Street is finished in August. It is designed by Burkhalter-Hickerson Architects.

The James K. Polk Building is finished. This giant structure on Deaderick Street contains an office tower for state government, the Tennessee State Museum, and the Tennessee Performing Arts Center. It is designed by Taylor & Crabtree and built by Mercury-Bell.

1982—Alan LeQuire begins work on the enormous statue of Athena that will fill the principal chamber of the Parthenon in Nashville's Centennial Park. It is finished seven years later.

National Life Tower is purchased by American General Insurance Company and renamed American General Center.

A 1931 Nashville Gas Company steel-cage storage tank, located on Third Avenue across from Wiles Feed Mills, is demolished.

1983—Riverfront Park is dedicated on July 10. It is one of several ambitious projects advocated by the Century III Commission, established in 1978 for Nashville's Bicentennial in 1980.

A plaque is placed on Legislative Plaza in honor of the USS *Nashville* by surviving members of its crew.

A plaque is placed on Legislative Plaza by Camps of Greater Nashville, Woodmen of the World, to commemorate the location of Andrew Johnson's residence while he was military governor of Tennessee.

1984—James Hoobler, director of Tennessee Historical Society, makes a report in March to state officials calling for the restoration of the Capitol.

Leaking roof of Capitol is repaired, and failing stonework on exterior is addressed by the Ehrenkrantz Group, led by Michael Emrick.

A tree marker is placed on Capitol Hill in memory of Martin Luther King Jr.

Roy Harrower of Memphis and Bruce McCarty of Knoxville submit separate conceptual plans for the development of state-owned land north of the Capitol.

1985—Landscape architect Joe Hodgson develops the idea for a narrow rectangular park in midst of state-owned property directly north of the Capitol.

By executive order from Governor Lamar Alexander on May 14, the Capitol Commission is established to oversee the Capitol building and surrounding properties.

The Metropolitan Development and Housing Authority commissions a study for the mixed-use development of 171 acres of land in the Sulphur Dell area.

Rachel Jackson Building is finished on corner of Deaderick Street and Sixth Avenue.

Vietnam Veterans Park is dedicated on November 10 at the south end of the War Memorial Building to honor the 49,000 participants and 1,291 killed from Tennessee. Landscape architect is Joe Hodgson, and contractor is American Constructors Inc.

1986—Numerous events are held across the state during "Homecoming '86," a year-long celebration of Tennessee heritage.

Historic Structures Report is issued in January as a thorough documentation of the history of the Capitol and includes recommendations for future restoration projects. The report is by Mendel, Mesick, Cohen, Waite and Hall Architects.

On May 5, six cedar trees are planted in a row on the southeast corner of Capitol Hill in remembrance of the Holocaust.

On May 26, a three-figure statue by Alan LeQuire is added to Vietnam Veterans Park.

Riverfront Apartments are built on First Avenue beneath the existing Kerrigan Ironworks shed. Developers are Nelson Andrews and Miles Warfield, architects are Tuck Hinton Everton Architects, and contractor is Orion Building Corporation. This residential complex straddles the historic outlet where the Lick Branch once flowed into the river.

The restoration of the former state library in the Capitol is finished.

In December, work begins on an extensive remodeling of the Parthenon in Centennial Park. Architects are Gresham, Smith and Partners, and contractor is Alexander & Shankle Construction Company. This work is finished in September 1988.

1987—On January 17, Ned McWherter is inaugurated governor. Under his administration the seeds for the Tennessee Bicentennial of 1996 are planted.

State Data Center, designed by Gresham, Smith and Partners and built by Lacona Construction Company, is completed on Fifth Avenue, north of Harrison Street.

Volunteer Plaza State Office Building, designed by Yearwood, Johnson, Stanton & Crabtree and built by Turner Construction Company, is completed on James Robertson Parkway at the corner of Fifth Avenue. It is later renamed Davy (David) Crockett Tower.

Stockyards Business Center is built on Second Avenue. The two-building facility developed by R. C. Mathews straddles the subterranean Lick Branch sewer.

Odd Fellows Lodge at corner of Jefferson Street and Seventh Avenue is restored to become an art gallery. It is renamed the "Onyx Building" by owner Carlton Wilkinson.

1988—John Bridges of Aladdin Industries shares idea of a linear park north of Capitol with several local officials.

R. D. Herbert & Sons moves from its location on Harrison Street between Sixth and Seventh Avenues to a new facility on Third Avenue near Morgan Park.

City Center office tower is finished on Sixth Avenue diagonally across from Legislative Plaza. It is designed by Stubbins Associates of Boston and Gresham, Smith and Partners, and is built by Holt Southeast Corporation.

Restoration of selected interior areas in the Capitol, including the original Supreme Court Room, is completed. The architects are Warterfield-Goodwin Associates and the Ehrenkrantz Group. Although recommended, the House and Senate chambers are not restored.

Nashville Gas Company sells its facility on Second Avenue and consolidates its operations at a new headquarters in Metrocenter.

1989—Governor McWherter assigns early planning of statewide Bicentennial events to Executive Assistant Jim Hall.

Aladdin Industries Executive Victor Johnson shows John Bridges's concept for a linear park to Governor McWherter and his staff.

Local television stations broadcast an announcement that land north of the State Capitol might become a park to commemorate the 1996 Bicentennial Celebration.

1990—Several schemes are developed by Robert Lamb Hart of New York and by in-house state planners for office buildings on the north slope of Capitol Hill and for a linear park.

1991—During Subarea 9 planning session of the Citizens' Advisory Committee on April 5, preliminary plans are discussed regarding the possibility of new state office buildings located on the north slope of Capitol Hill and spanning over James Robertson Parkway. The idea is not warmly received.

"Tennessee Bicentennial Celebration: Laying Foundations" booklet by executive planning director Jim Hall is issued in May.

A design team is assembled in Nashville on September 18 and 19 by Jerry Preston to review the previous plans and possibilities of land north of the Capitol, including area of proposed Mall. The team is composed of Charles Warterfield Jr., Jon Coddington, David Johnson, Bob McKinney, and Kem Hinton.

The Subarea 9 "City Center" Plan for downtown Nashville is adopted by city officials on November 7. It includes a sketch of the open lawn idea for the Bicentennial Mall.

The Holiday Inn structure on James Robertson Parkway is demolished. Other nearby motels are soon afterward also demolished.

A new Tennessee Education Association building is completed on Third Avenue at the east end of Harrison Street. The state purchases the 1962 TEA building on James Robertson Parkway next to the future Bicentennial Mall, and the building becomes the home of state-park officials in 1996.

1992—By executive order on June 1, Governor McWherter establishes the Tennessee Bicentennial Commission. Shortly thereafter he announces the members of the commission, a bipartisan group that will oversee the specifics of the statewide Bicentennial Celebration in 1996.

Korean War Memorial on Legislative Plaza is dedicated on July 4 to honor the 93,000 participants and 843 killed from Tennessee. The sculptor is Russ Faxon, and contractor is Dixie Stone Company.

The first meeting of the Bicentennial Commission is held in Nashville at the Capitol on August 12. Martha Ingram is chairman. The rough concept is presented for the Bicentennial Mall as an open lawn extending north from the Capitol.

The master plan team composed of Tuck Hinton Architects and Jon Coddington, Charles Warterfield Jr., David Johnson, Bob McKinney, and Ritchie Smith is hired on August 27 to develop the program and design for Capitol Hill and North Capitol Complex (area of Bicentennial Mall).

Members of the Mall design team and governor's staff travel to Memphis on December 14 to meet with West Tennessee representatives of the Bicentennial Commission regarding the design of the Bicentennial Mall. Similar sessions occur in Chattanooga on December 18 and in Knoxville on December 21.

Jefferson Street Bridge is blown up on Mother's Day, Sunday, May 10. A new concrete ramp bridge is to replace the lacy but decaying steel structure.

1993—An all-day session is held on January 13 between state and city officials to plan the new Farmers' Market structure with market consultant John Williams.

On January 20, Tennessean Al Gore Jr. is inaugurated as the forty-fifth vice president of the United States.

The Bicentennial Commission meets on January 25 at The Hermitage in Nashville. The commission focuses on developing statewide activities to celebrate the Bicentennial.

Gateway Plaza state office building is completed on James Robertson Parkway at corner of Eighth Avenue. A virtual copy of the Volunteer Plaza building two blocks east, this building is later renamed the Andrew Johnson Tower.

A special community presentation regarding the potential impact of the Bicentennial Mall is given on March 8 at Monroe Street United Methodist Church in Germantown. Governor McWherter attends.

The Downtown Presbyterian Church, designed by William Strickland, receives National Historic Landmark status on April 19 from the United States Department of the Interior. Only five other structures in Davidson County, including the Capitol, have received this highest recognition.

On May 3, state officials and members of the Mall design team meet with CSX railroad officials in Jacksonville, Florida, to discuss revisions of the existing railroad.

After exploring several alternatives, the design team reaches a consensus on May 11 for the final schematic layout of the Bicentennial Mall.

On May 12, the state announces a purchase agreement to acquire the American General Center.

The master plan for the Bicentennial Mall is presented to state officials, including Governor McWherter, on May 26.

The Bicentennial Commission meets on June 2 at Fisk University. The master plan for the Bicentennial Mall and Capitol Hill is unveiled.

The master plan for the Bicentennial Mall and Capitol Hill is approved by the State Building Commission on July 8.

A final review of the Mall and Capitol Hill master plan with the Capitol Commission occurs on July 23.

Tennessee Treasures, a traveling exhibit of artifacts from the Tennessee State Museum, begins its ninety-five-county journey in Jonesboro on September 8.

On September 27, Kelly Tolson becomes executive director of Tennessee 200, the nonprofit entity that implements the activities of the Bicentennial Commission. Cindy Bean becomes director of public relations and marketing, and later Carolyn Brackett becomes director of statewide projects.

Davidson County Agricultural Extension structure is demolished, one of the first to be removed to create a grand vista of the Capitol from Jefferson Street.

From Third to Eighth Avenues, Jefferson Street is widened, and a new bridge is built across the Cumberland River.

1994—Contracts are signed in January between the state and several design firms for work on Capitol Hill, the railroad, streets, parking areas, and the Bicentennial Mall.

Located on the south side of Werthan Bag Corporation, the only remaining public spring supplying natural sulphur water is closed on March 18.

Groundbreaking begins on March 28 for the new Kroger grocery store on Eighth Avenue to replace the existing dilapidated store next to Farmers' Market.

A Bicentennial Mall model-building contest, sponsored by Heery International, is held at McGavock High School on April 30. Models of the new park by elementary and high school students are later displayed at Bellevue Center shopping mall.

A contract is signed between the state and Ray Bell Construction Company on June 23 for construction of four new rail bridges and a railroad trestle across site of the Bicentennial Mall.

Groundbreaking ceremony for the Bicentennial Mall is held on June 27. Governor McWherter deposits a time capsule of personal memorabilia.

The area of the future Bicentennial Mall is excavated by archaeologists from the Division of Archaeology, Tennessee Department of Environment and Conservation.

A contract is signed between the state and Hardaway Construction Corporation of Tennessee on October 7 for substantial work on the north slope of Capitol Hill.

A contract is signed between the state and Ray Bell Construction Company on October 21 for construction of the amphitheater within the area of the Bicentennial Mall.

On November 8, Don Sundquist of Memphis is elected governor.

A contract is signed between the state and Hardaway Construction Corporation of Tennessee on December 16 for construction of the Bicentennial Mall.

1995—Don Sundquist is inaugurated as governor on January 21. Chattanooga entrepreneur Bob Corker succeeds David Manning as commissioner of Finance and Administration, and Bill McDonald succeeds Jerry Preston as assistant commissioner overseeing Capital Projects Management, the state agency responsible for design and construction. Jim Dixey succeeds Ed Belbusti as the state's project manager of the Mall.

"Tennessee Waltz" fund-raiser for State Museum is held at the Capitol on March 25. Conceptual plans for a new state museum at the north end of the Mall across Jefferson Street are displayed for the first time.

Tenants begin moving to new Farmers' Market on Eighth Avenue on June 19.

Dancy Jones becomes vice chairman of Tennessee 200 board of directors on July 18.

On July 20, a statue of President Andrew Johnson by Jim Gray is unveiled on the southeast side of Capitol Hill. It faces east.

Bison Meadows Park is constructed in August on Hillsboro Road. This unusual park reminds passersby of historic animal trails that led to the Lick Branch. The landscape architect is Tara Armistead, and the sculptor of the wireframe bison is Alan LeQuire.

Bicentennial county flags are unveiled during a ceremony on August 18 at Bellevue Center shopping mall. A tour of the Bicentennial Mall construction site later in the day coincides with a reenactment at the Capitol of the 1920 adoption of the Nineteenth Amendment.

Renovation of Elliott School is completed in October to become one of several Dede Wallace Center facilities in the city. This

structure is renamed in honor of Ella Bullard Hayes. Michael Emrick is the renovation architect.

The new Farmers' Market—located on Eighth Avenue between Harrison and Jackson Streets, designed by Tuck Hinton Architects and built by Ray Bell Construction Company—is formally dedicated on October 21.

In November, the top surface of Legislative Plaza is officially renamed "War Memorial Plaza."

1996—On January 11, the U.S. Postmaster General Marvin Runyon unveils the design for Tennessee Bicentennial stamp at a ceremony on the east steps of the Capitol. The thirty-two-cent stamp features a photograph by Robin Hood of the statehouse and Andrew Jackson statue.

Work begins to repair and restore the roof and decorative concrete sculpture on the Parthenon. Architects are Gresham, Smith and Partners with Quinn Evans Architects, and the contractor is Orion Building Corporation. The ambitious restoration project will take several years to complete.

Tennessee First Lady Martha Sundquist plants a tulip poplar tree in the Bicentennial Mall at the south end of the Walkway of the Counties on Arbor Day, March 1. Each county also receives a tulip poplar and a Bicentennial plaque to honor the occasion.

A statewide program is launched on March 8 in Knoxville to encourage individuals to help document Tennessee's history. The project includes a survey of World War II veterans.

On April 1, Justin P. Wilson succeeds Don Dills as commissioner of the Department of Environment and Conservation. Maintenance and security of the Bicentennial Mall is later inherited by this department after the new park opens.

Civil War Heritage Trail begins on April 20 in Nashville to recall the events and sites of the divisive conflict and its impact on Tennessee.

"Bicentennial Sampler" opens at Tennessee State Museum. This exhibit from April 26 to July 28 presents artifacts related to Tennessee's first two hundred years.

Time capsules from all ninety-five counties are buried at the Bicentennial Mall on April 27. It is the largest number of time capsules ever buried at a single location.

Tennessee Bicentennial Arts and Entertainment Festival is held in Nashville from May 2 through May 25. This elaborate series of performances includes events at the Tennessee Performing Arts Center, Fisk University, the Hermitage Hotel, and Ryman Auditorium.

Bicentennial Greenways program begins on May 3 in Nashville. The statewide project plans to create two hundred new miles of greenways in Tennessee.

After a week of strained relations between the Bicentennial Commission and Governor Sundquist, the Mall is opened to the public at 8:00 A.M. on Friday, May 31.

After similar ceremonies in Knoxville and Memphis, the Tennessee Bicentennial postage stamp is dedicated and issued in the Tennessee Amphitheater on May 31.

This is the first public use of the outdoor amphitheater at the Mall.

On June 1, Tennessee celebrates its official Bicentennial with Statehood Day festivities at the Mall, including a special convening of the General Assembly followed by an all-star music review. Fireworks cap the spectacular day.

At midday on June 1, Confederate Memorial Day is observed at Sam Davis statue by the Sons of Confederate Veterans.

Groundbreaking ceremonies for the Tennessee World War II Memorial are held at the Mall on July 1.

John Ferguson succeeds Bob Corker as commissioner of Finance and Administration on July 1. Larry Kirk succeeds Bill McDonald as assistant commissioner overseeing the Capital Projects Management organization.

On July 4, the *Spirit of Tennessee* Bicentennial Train begins to trek across the state from Union City. The exhibit touts the state's accomplishments in trade development and travels to thirty-seven locations before completing its journey on November 15 in Nashville.

On September 15, a new "Zero Milestone" marker is placed at the south end of the Mall at the vehicular pull off from James Robertson Parkway.

"Celebration of French Lick on the Cumberland" is held on October 5 in Nashville. A statue of early settler Timothy Demonbreun by Alan LeQuire is unveiled.

A master plan for Hope Gardens, a residential district directly south of Jefferson Street and west of Eighth Avenue, is completed in October by Everton Oglesby Askew Architects with Duany & Plater-Zyberk of Miami.

Nashville Arena, for most purposes a replacement of the Municipal Auditorium on James Robertson Parkway, opens with a special Amy Grant/Nashville Symphony Christmas concert on December 18.

On December 31, Wiles Feed Mills on Third Avenue closes when its owners retire; transition in the area of the Lick Branch continues.

From its opening on May 31 to the end of 1996, the Bicentennial Mall attracts more than a quarter of a million visitors.

TENNESSEE COUNTY TIME CAPSULES
BURIED APRIL 27, 1996
From *A Capsule in Time*
Published by Tennessee 200
Compiled and edited by Cindy Bean

ANDERSON

1. Student essays
2. Anderson County budget
3. County school systems technology plan—Anderson County, Oak Ridge, Clinton
4. Holy Bible, listing all Anderson County churches
5. Anderson County Bicentennial calendar
6. Anderson County historical sketches—by Kathleen Baker Hoskins
7. *Anderson County—Its Cities, Towns, and Points of Interest as of 1940, Updated 1986*, published by Bonnie M. Page
8. Anderson County Bicentennial Committee —newspaper article
9. List of Anderson County Bicentennial events
10. Clinton Chamber of Commerce brochure
11. Oak Ridge Chamber of Commerce brochure
12. News clipping—picture of the Anderson County Bicentennial flag
13. Anderson County birthday coin
14. Article on the founding of Norris
15. Pellissippi Genealogical & Historical Society Journal
16. Football programs from area high schools
17. Lockheed Martin, Sapphire Project and Sea Wolf
18. Bicentennial hand fan

BEDFORD

1. Picture of famous athletes from Bedford County
2. Historic newspaper from Bedford County
3. Bell Buckle magnet
4. Rabbit cup
5. Tennessee Walking Horse Disk
6. *A Pictorial History of Bedford County*
7. Winning children's essays about the future
8. Shelbyville Chamber of Commerce information
9. Bedford County map
10. Web school magazine
11. Bell Buckle Christmas flyer
12. Bell Buckle Craft flyer
13. Historic Bell Buckle flyer
14. Postcard of Bell Buckle
15. Shelbyville brochure
16. Pencils and explanation sheet
17. Tennessee Walking Horse article
18. Letter from county executive
19. Letter from the mayor
20. Picture of the courthouse
21. County budget
22. *Door to the Past*
23. Bedford County phone book
24. Bicentennial poem
25. *The Light in the Kitchen Window*
26. Examples of historic society quarterly

BENTON

1. Program from the Glover's Trace Chapter Daughters of the American Revolution's American History Month Banquet, February 23, 1996
2. "Video History of Benton County," 1992
3. *200 Years of Tennessee Cooking*, cookbook by Benton County Genealogical Society in Camden, 1996
4. Tennessee County History Series, Benton County, Jonathan K.T. Smith, Esq., 1979
5. Benton County Sesquicentennial envelopes with cancellation stamps and postage stamps from Tennessee's Homecoming '86, and the Ameripex stamp collecting show in Chicago
6. County seal
7. Letter from Jimmy Thornton, county executive
8. Letter from the city of Big Sandy
9. Letter from the town of Camden

BLEDSOE

1. Lincoln school letter and photograph
2. Scenic 127 map
3. Harvest festival brochure
4. Discover Pikeville brochure
5. Bledsoe County brochure
6. Bethal Church bulletin
7. 1996 Old Farmers Almanac
8. Bledsoe phone book
9. Slides of Bledsoe County Courthouse
10. Fall Harvest Festival pictures
11. Video tape of Bledsoe County
12. Bledsoe County program for *Tennessee Treasures*
13. Fast draw brochure
14. *Top Gun* magazine
15. Vision 2000 plan for the county
16. 1995 Christmas parade pictures
17. Candidate benefit night flyer
18. Resolution to restore theater
19. Picture of county flag

20. Chamber of Commerce banquet program
21. Fall Harvest meeting card
22. Tourism brochure
23. Vaugn House brochure
24. Bledsoe County map
25. *Bledsoe County Tennessee* by Elizabeth Parham Robrett
26. Article on extension agents
27. Article on parade
28. The *Bledsonian News*, January 4, 1996
29. Fall Creek Falls brochure
30. Rodney Atkins brochure
31. *Shopper*, December 19, 1995
32. Pictures of pumpkins
33. Pictures of *Tennessee Treasures* exhibit
34. Pictures of Fall Creek Falls
35. Postcards

BLOUNT

1. Tennessee marble—three tiles, one brick—history of Blount County marble
2. Items from Nippondenso Tennessee, Inc.—starter for Dodge Ram Truck, alternator for Chrysler/Dodge minivan, instrument cluster for Chrysler/Dodge minivan, engine electronic control unit for Ford Probe, company profile and brochure
3. Commemorative coin
4. Tennessee, with Blount County seal and city of Maryville seal
5. Aluminum sample—from Aluminum Company of America
6. Booklet—ALCOA Tennessee Operations: Exploring New Worlds of Technology
7. History of City of Alcoa—*The Story of Alcoa, 75 Years, 1919–1994*
8. Brochure about the Polly Toole Statue
9. Scrapbook of *Daily Times* newspaper articles 1992–1995
10. Scrapbook of pictures from Blount County Bicentennial events
11. Picture of Blount County Bicentennial flag with history
12. Official programs from Tennessee 200 celebrations
13. Brochure—Walking Tour of Louisville Historic District
14. Postcards
15. *Interactive: Blount County Chamber of Commerce Membership & Buyers Guide* magazine—1995
16. Tennessee Valley Authority Annual Report, 1934

17. Tennessee Valley Authority Annual Report, 1994
18. Report to the Congress on the Unified Development of the Tennessee River System, March 1936
19. *Loyal Mountain Troopers: The Second & Third Tennessee Volunteer Calvary in the Civil War* by Charles S. McCammon
20. *Blount County Remembered: The 1890s Photography of W. O. Garner*
21. *History of Blount County, Tennessee, from War Trail to Landing Strip, 1795–1955* (Revised), by Inez Burns
22. *A Chronicle of Our Heritage*, three volumes
23. *Blount County Tennessee* magazine, 1991–1992, 1994
24. Automobile license plate
25. Blount County budget, fiscal year 1995–1996
26. Blount County street map
27. Blount County Investment Opportunities brochure
28. School brochures
29. Blount County Area Manufacturers and Non-manufacturing Industries Directory
30. Brochure—The Spokesman, Blount County Chamber of Commerce
31. *Homes* magazine, November–December 1995
32. Brochure—Foothills Land Conservancy
33. Program from the dedication of the Maryville Bicentennial Memorial, December 10, 1995
34. Color copy of Blount County Bicentennial logo
35. Color copy of Blount County Bicentennial flag

BRADLEY

1. Letter from county executive
2. School board list
3. Elected officials list
4. Tennessee 200 committee list
5. Bicentennial flag
6. Letter from the Main Street organization
7. Project Pride: 1996 Olympic Committee listing
8. Project Pride T-shirt
9. *Bradley County Weekly* newspaper
10. *Cleveland Daily Banner* newspaper
11. Wood carving of a Cherokee Chieftain
12. Cleveland T-shirt
13. United Way Annual Report

14. Cleveland-Bradley Regional Museum Packet
15. Cleveland-Bradley Goals 2000
16. Brochures on local sites and industries
17. Cleveland city schools and Bradley County schools—report cards
18. Bradley County Chamber of Commerce brochures
19. Cleveland city government documents
20. Cleveland telephone book
21. TECD material
22. Bradley Memorial Hospital booklet
23. Cleveland State Community College literature
24. Lee College literature

CAMPBELL

1. Seeds
2. Emergency directory
3. Total Quality Partnership—Hopes for the Future
4. Campbell County map
5. Cableview information
6. Campbell County economic statistics
7. Interstate exit directory
8. Campbell County Chamber of Commerce Guidebook
9. Campbell County phone directory, March 1995–1996
10. South Campbell County Rotary Club information
11. Hack Ayers Auction and Real Estate calendar
12. *La Follette Press*, December 28, 1995
13. La Follette United Methodist Church bulletin, December 31, 1995
14. Photographs of life in Campbell County
15. City of Jellico information
16. Fishing lure—used for trout and bass fishing
17. Bic disposable razor
18. University of Tennessee key ring
19. Staple remover
20. Campbell County board of commissioners resolution appointing Time Capsule Committee
21. Article—interview with Leslie Tamer and photograph
22. Campbell County Bicentennial Woman of the Year photograph
23. Coal
24. City of La Follette Centennial poster 1897–1997
25. Cigar

26. City of Jacksboro calendar
27. Campbell County flag
28. City of Jellico information
29. Video—"1995 Travel Tour of Campbell County"

CANNON

1. *Cannon Courier* newspaper
2. Cannon County Sesquicentennial Homecoming '86 booklet
3. *History of Cannon County* by Robert L. Mason
4. Directory for Woodbury Lions Club 1995–1996
5. 1996 season program for the Arts Center of Cannon County
6. Program for Cannon County's opening ceremony for *Tennessee Treasures*
7. Bank of Commerce 50th Anniversary newspaper
8. Cannon County *The Good Ole Days* newspaper, May 4–7, 1994
9. 1996 budget for Cannon County
10. 1994 subdivision regulations for Cannon County
11. Map of Cannon County
12. 1994 Annual Financial Report for Cannon County
13. *Cannon County History, 1836–1995*
14. Cannon County schedule of events, from the county executive's office
15. Photograph of the Cannon County High School class of 1995

CARROLL

1. Ralph J. McDonald print "The Bethel College Wildcat"
2. *History of Huntington,* July 1986
3. *History of Carroll County,* 1972
4. *History of Carroll County,* 1986
5. Resolution 2–02–96 and 2–01–96

CARTER

1. Photographs of county schools
2. Photographs of local government buildings
3. Photographs of churches
4. Key to the city of Elizabethton
5. Elizabethton telephone directory
6. Essays from class of 1996 from city/county schools
7. Photographs from students from Eastside School

8. Daughters of the American Revolution yearbook
9. *From a Window on Hattie Avenue*
10. *Later History of Carter County, 1865–1980*
11. Hymnal
12. Bicentennial brick badge
13. Tennis ball
14. Postcards
15. "I love Elizabethton and Carter County" badge
16. "The Bridge at Betsy" poem
17. 1996 calendar of East Tennessee
18. Carter County coloring book
19. Brochures
20. Area maps
21. Range yearbook
22. Caldwell Springs Baptist Church information
23. Winter Fest 1995 information
24. *Elizabethton Star*
25. Christmas cards
26. Business cards
27. Map of Tennessee
28. T.A. Dugger Junior High School yearbook
29. Folder from East Side School
30. Plans for 1996 school year from West Side
31. Plans for 1996 school year from Harold McConnick
32. Folder of minutes and agenda of county court and county commission meeting
33. Police and Fire Department shoulder patch
34. 1996 almanac
35. Sheriff's Department shoulder patch
36. Sheriff's Department calendar, key ring, pen
37. Central School yearbook
38. Materials from First Freewill Baptist Church
39. Central student's work

CHEATHAM

1. Cheatham County flag
2. Lockert Law Firm calendar
3. *Ashland City Times,* January 31, 1996
4. Cheatham County Homecoming '86 calendar
5. Attabry Automation hat
6. Linda Fizer hat
7. Ashland City Summerfest '95 T-shirt
8. Letter from Mayor Mary Jenkins
9. 3-Star folders
10. 3-Star brochure
11. 3-Star logos

12. 3-Star news release
13. "1994 in Review," 3-Star
14. County executive letter, photographs, state of county newspaper article
15. 1989–1995 fact books
16. Bicentennial county map
17. Main street drawing
18. Chamber of Commerce directory
19. Chamber of Commerce coffee mug
20. Chamber of Commerce newsletter
21. Chamber of Commerce invitation
22. Cheatham County special events calendar
23. Cheatham County seal
24. One pen
25. Three pencils
26. Virginia Van Hook package
27. Photograph of Genealogical Society president
28. Genealogical materials
29. County poem
30. Litter bag
31. Historic poster
32. List of elected officials
33. VFW roster
34. Photograph of bridge
35. Tomato seeds
36. 4-H materials
37. R.E. West cap
38. Belt buckle
39. Letter
40. Brochure
41. Elsa Lockert Mainstreet card
42. Business cards
43. *Ashland City Times,* January 24 and 31, 1996
44. The *Advocate,* February 10, 1996
45. WQSV Radio Valley Views broadcast
46. Ministerial Association information
47. State Industries: truck, brochure, and photographs
48. Tennessee Association of Churches newsletter
49. Phone Pals brochure
50. United Way brochure
51. County commission and state senator and representatives listings
52. Cheatham County school system lists
53. Letter from State Representative Mike Williamson
54. *Tell Us A Story, Daddy* by the Rev. Dr. David R. Davis
55. Poster of the Cumberland River Bridge
56. Poster of Sidney's Bluff with a 1995 calendar
57. Letter and photographs from County Clerk W. J. Hall

CHESTER

1. *Chester County Tennessee*, 1882–1995
2. Letter from County Executive Anthony Bolton
3. List of county officials
4. Various documents describing areas of Chester County

CLAIBORNE

1. Special editions of newspapers
2. 1890 newspaper—first edition
3. Speedwell Academy letters
4. School essay
5. School enrollment list
6. Lincoln Memorial University information
7. County photographs
8. Bicentennial button
9. Educational Excellence Award
10. Telephone book
11. County seal
12. Commercial Bank calendar
13. Volunteer 200 Day bandanna
14. Newcomer's guide
15. Church list
16. Ladies Birthday Almanac
17. County Bicentennial Committee listing
18. Claiborne County Bicentennial events listing

CLAY

1. *The Story of OshKosh B'Gosh*
2. Holly Creek Resorts brochure
3. Dale Hollow Marina brochure
4. Horse Creek Dock and Resort brochure
5. Dale Hollow Marina rates
6. Dale Hollow National Fish Hatchery brochure
7. Dale Hollow Dam brochure
8. Cumberland River brochure
9. Cedar Hill Resort brochure
10. The American Bald Eagle brochure
11. Celina brochure
12. Pallet Pro, Inc., brochure
13. Two articles on Clay County history
14. Celina data sheet
15. Dale Hollow Lake map
16. Honest Abe Log Homes brochure
17. Honest Abe Log Homes floor plan
18. Braky Beaver brochure
19. OshKosh B'Gosh boy's and girl's outfit
20. Drawing of *Celina Steamboat*
21. Celina Ferry sketch and article
22. Photograph of friends at a football game
23. Writings about Bob Riley—Legend of the Upper Cumberland
24. *Artists of Tennessee, Volume II*
25. *History of Clay County, Tennessee, 1870–1986*
26. *Clay County, Tennessee—1880 U.S. Census*
27. Celina photographs
28. Drawing of Clay County Courthouse
29. Drawing of the Swinging Bridge
30. Drawing of the Henry Horton Bridge

COCKE

1. Wood turning spindle
2. List of employees, labels, and coupons from Hunt Foods Company
3. Brochure and catalog from Lisega, Inc.
4. Brochure and spiral-wound paper tube from Sonoco Products Company
5. Lawn mower tire and coupling spider from ACE Products
6. Newcomer guidebook for Newport/Cocke County
7. Kiwanis Club pin
8. DPRC pin
9. Letter from Cocke County executive, Harold Cates
10. Letter from mayor of Newport, Jim Robinson
11. Letter from mayor of Parrottsville, Mike Gilbert
12. Holy Bible
13. Christy Mission puzzle
14. Letter from the Cocke County School Superintendent
15. Brief history of the Economic Development Commission
16. Chemical sample from the Flura Corporation
17. Moonshine still whittled by Bruce Williamson
18. Letter and coin set from R. J. Tucker, president of the Cocke County Bar Association

COFFEE

1. County executive's gavel
2. Photographs
3. Folders
4. Don Northcutt's Marble Artwork—Spear's Homeplace
5. Agricultural history record
6. 4-H history record
7. 4-H emblem
8. Proclamation of dedication of Highway 41 to James R. Brantley
9. Brantley pewter horse
10. George Dickel bottle
11. Directory of manufacturers
12. County budget
13. County map
14. General information on the city of Tullahoma
15. Coffee County phone book
16. School system pin
17. *Trees of Christmas*
18. Coffee County wood block map stamp
19. *Newsleader*
20. *Manchester Times*
21. *Tullahoma News*
22. Coffee County cemetery records and maps
23. School yearbooks:
    New Union Elementary School 1994–1995
    Hickerson Elementary School 1995
    Jones Elementary School 1994–1995
    East Coffee Elementary School 1995
    North Coffee School 1994–1995
    Hillsboro Elementary School 1994–1995
    Coffee County Middle School 1995
    College Street Elementary School 1994–1995
    Westwood Junior High School 1995
    Coffee County High School 1995

CROCKETT

1. *All About Crockett*, Fall 1995
2. *West Tennessee Cotton Festival*, 1993
3. *Crockett County Courthouse Centennial, 1874–1974*
4. *West Tennessee Industrial Association View*
5. Spec building photograph
6. Crockett County telephone book, 1995–1996
7. Chamber Bucks
8. $2 bill
9. Uncirculated proof set
10. Bicentennial silver dollar
11. Six historical photographs
12. *Paper Trails*, 1995—A Genealogical Publication
13. 1995 Crockett County High School graduation composite
14. County map
15. Brochures
16. Cotton bale
17. *Cookin' in Crockett*
18. Cotton bowl
19. Chamber of Commerce sticker

20. Two boxes of slides and reference sheets
21. Letter from Chamber of Commerce and employees
22. 1994 Christmas edition of the *Crockett Times*
23. Letter from Jim Jerman, county executive

CUMBERLAND

1. Samples of Crab Orchard stone found in Cumberland County
2. Hammer handle from Turner, Day, Woolworth Handle Mill
3. Telephone directory
4. *Cumberland County's First 100 Years—History of Cumberland County* by Helen Bullard and Joseph Marshall Krechniak
5. Centennial Issue of *Crossville Chronicle*, July 12, 1956
6. *A History of Pleasant Hill Academy/Cumberland County Pioneer School* by Emma F. Dodge
7. 1995 *Lifestyle* Magazine, Vol. 6
8. *Doctor Woman of the Cumberlands* by May Cravath Wharton, M.D.
9. Brochures of various scenic historical and industrial sites in Cumberland County
10. Cumberland County map
11. *USA Weekend*, December 1–3, 1995
12. Automobile mileage charts
13. 1996 Buick catalog
14. 1996 Pontiac Firebird catalog
15. 1996 GMC Truck catalog
16. 1996 Jeep catalog
17. Cumberland County Bicentennial calendar, 1996
18. Holy Bible
19. American flag
20. Tennessee 200 Cumberland County pin

DAVIDSON

1. The *Tennessean*, January 1, 1996
2. The *Nashville Banner*, January 1, 1996
3. *Nashville Scene*, Annual Manual for 1996
4. *Where to Be Scene*, Winter 1996
5. Music City's Best, 1995–1996 Nashville Area Chamber of Commerce Business Directory
6. *Grand Ole Opry*, picture history book
7. Political buttons collection
8. Photographs of Chief Emmett Turner
9. Letter about Chief Emmett Turner prepared by Kenneth W. Sanders

10. Letter from Ed Benson, executive director of the Country Music Association
11. "New Stars, Superstars, and Legends" souvenir program from the Grand Old Opry
12. "Independence Day" song recorded by Martina McBride
13. Domestic Violence mission statement
14. Nashville's Agenda—"21 goals for the 21st century," with photograph and video
15. Tatting samples, photographs and articles about Willie Smith Scott
16. Letter and photographs from Wynona D. Lurie
17. Partnership 2000 Annual Report
18. Letter from John Egerton, metro historian
19. *Nashville Life* magazine, with feature article about John Egerton
20. Letter and photograph from John L. Connelley
21. Letters and photographs from students of Davidson County schools—Buena Vista/Jones Paideia Magnet School, Tusculum Elementary School, Sylvan Park Elementary, Apollo Middle School, Maplewood High School
22. Letter, essay, photograph, and symphony performance program from Houston Turntine
23. Letter and photograph from Vice Mayor Jay West
24. Letter and photograph from Donna Mancini
25. Letter and photograph from Representative Bob Clement, district congressman
26. Letter and photograph from Dennis C. Bottorff, Chamber of Commerce chairman
27. *Nashville Quarterly*
28. Nashville population data
29. Music City USA information
30. Health Care industry information
31. Red Grooms-carousel
32. Menus from famous Nashville restaurants—Rotiers, Pancake Pantry, Varallo's Restaurant, Sweet's, and the Loveless Motel and Restaurant
33. Summer Lights T-shirt
34. Garth Brooks compact disc
35. Pathways to the Future-overview of all area educational institutions
36. Letter from Dr. Henry Ponder, president, Fisk University
37. Letter and photograph from Joe B. Wyatt, chancellor, Vanderbilt University

38. Original score composed by Michael Kurek, and photograph and biography
39. Greenways photograph and brochure
40. Nashville Arena—photograph of dedication and model, arena project overview, "Arena News," mouse pad for a computer
41. Tennessee Stadium—proposed stadium rendition, sticker, PSL application
42. "Nashville Live," print by Phil Ponder
43. Words and Music program and tape
44. "King of the Road" tie
45. Nashville pendant
46. Photographs and slides taken by Metro Photographer Gary Layda
47. Poster of BR5-49, the house band at Robert's Western World, 416 Broadway
48. Poster of Martha White Bluegrass Night at the Ryman Auditorium
49. "Play Like Marty" poster, autographed by Marty Stuart
50. Coins from Mayor Bredesen
51. Wood art—Nashville Arts Music Dance Theater
52. Nashville wood bass guitar
53. Nashville mini-bell
54. Nashville pin
55. "Pick Nashville" pick
56. Ryman Auditorium hat pin
57. Hard Rock Cafe pin
58. Wild Horse Saloon hat pin
59. Nashville bumper sticker
60. Three Nashville postcards
61. Tennessee Repertory Theatre program
62. Nashville Vacation Guide
63. Nashville map
64. Various brochures for Nashville sites
65. Teddy bear
66. Davidson County time capsule dedication photograph
67. Listing of 1996 Bicentennial projects in Davidson County
68. Photograph of Davidson County Bicentennial Committee
69. Photograph of Davidson County Time Capsule Committee
70. Channel 5 business card
71. Hardaway Construction business cards
72. Two Susan B. Anthony coins used in vending machines at Hardaway Construction
73. Hardaway Construction T-shirt
74. Granite chip from the Bicentennial Capitol Mall site
75. The *Tennessean*, April 11, 1996, article about sealing of time capsules

DECATUR

1. Coins and currency, 1995
2. Deck of playing cards, limited edition from Coca-Cola company
3. Merry Christmas Tennessee ornament
4. Cassette tape by Jay Larrin
5. Matchbook from Decatur County Bank
6. Farmer Bank statement
7. Letter from mayor of Decaturville
8. Elks newsletter
9. Flag designing information
10. City of Parsons brochures
11. Church bulletins
12. Parsons Junior High, Parsons High School annuals
13. Decatur county information
14. Decatur County Chamber of Commerce brochure
15. State of Tennessee wages and benefits information
16. Scotts Hill statement, Mayor Alderman
17. Business cards
18. Townsend cookbook
19. Extension cookbook
20. VFW roster
21. Northside FCE Homemakers roster
22. Elks cookbook
23. *Reflections and Images*
24. Letter from county executive
25. Historical newsletter
26. Transparencies of Decaturville and Parsons businesses
27. *Decatur County Bicentennial Cookbook*
28. Parsons telephone directory
29. *Decatur County Fair* 1995
30. *History of Parsons and surrounding areas* by Lillye Younger
31. Captain N.A. Wesson Chapter 2396 of the United Daughters of the Confederacy roster
32. Delta Kappa Gamma of Decatur County roster
33. Decatur County Retired Teachers Association roster
34. 1996 yearbook—Family and Community Education, Agriculture Extension Service
35. Parson Chapter-Order of Eastern Star roster
36. Decatur County-Riverside High School Handbook
37. Map of Decaturville
38. Parsons Lions Club roster
39. 1994–1995 statistics of Decaturville
40. Tennessee Community Data—Chamber of Commerce
41. Decatur County library information
42. Decatur County historical society information
43. Information from the sheriff's office and E–911
44. Decatur County Bank—officers, employees, and statement of condition.
45. Brochures of various areas in Decatur County
46. Job Training Partnership Program
47. Fred's Pharmacy with Decatur, Perry, and Henderson County physicians information
48. Menu from Old Post House Restaurant
49. Poem written by Decatur County resident, J. D. Dodd
50. Photographs of present-day people and places
51. The *News Leader*—Parsons
52. Barbie doll replica of the original of 1960
53. Souvenir handkerchief from Volunteer 200 Day

DEKALB

1. DeKalb County telephone book
2. Webb's History of DeKalb County
3. Pictorial History of DeKalb County
4. Pictures of landmarks, town squares, schools
5. 1995 Fiddlers Jamboree souvenir program
6. 1996 Fiddlers Jamboree brochure
7. DeKalb County medal of honor recipient, Charles P. Cantrell
8. Chamber of Commerce data sheet
9. Industrial, tourists, and business brochures
10. 1995 DeKalb County High School annual
11. Map of DeKalb County
12. Map of Center Hill Lake
13. Fishing lure
14. Small pottery vase by Susan Demay
15. Slides by local potter Susan Demay
16. Biography of Congressman Joe L. Evins
17. Glass paperweight
18. Commemorative Sam Houston Tree Ceremony information
19. Children's book
20. Cookbook
21. Small children's toys
22. *Smithville Review*
23. DeKalb County Fair booklet
24. Official White House photograph of Community Chorus and Vice President Albert Gore Jr.
25. 1996 calendar from DeKalb County sheriff's department
26. Photographs of resident country music stars
27. Souvenir scarf
28. Commemorative stamps
29. Poster
30. Library card
31. Currency
32. ATM card
33. Voter registration card
34. Gideon Bible

DICKSON

1. Article of the I-840 North Connection in Dickson County, *Dickson Herald*
2. Article on the school building plan, *Dickson Herald*
3. 1995 Christmas Program from Edgewood United Methodist Church
4. Letters from mayors throughout the county
5. Letter from county executive, Bill Field
6. Letter from Tom Waychoff, president and CEO, Dickson County Chamber of Commerce
7. Letters from the Dickson County Bicentennial Committee
8. Photograph of the Dickson County Bicentennial Committee
9. Song and letter from Alda Marie Harrell
10. Slides: Presbyterian Church in Montgomery Bell, Montgomery Bell Homestead, Charlotte Courthouse
11. Two pieces of slag with history from Jackson Furnace
12. Selected articles from the 1995 Fact Book, *Dickson Herald*
13. Essays from three students at Charlotte Junior High
14. *A History of Dickson County* by Robert E. Corlew
15. *Bicentennial Cookbook*, Dickson County Family and Community Education Clubs
16. *Cumberland Furnace*, George E. Jackson
17. *Dickson County Historical Overview*, Sherry Kilgore
18. "Reflections of Our Past," *Dickson Herald*
19. American Eagle Coin Set, First Federal Bank
20. Tennessee 200 commemorative coin, Peoples Bank
21. 1996 Olympic Coin, Peoples Bank
22. $2 bill, Union Planters Bank

23. $2 bill, Farmers & Merchants Bank
24. State of Tennessee paperweight, First Union Bank
25. $1 U.S. currency collection, Bank of Dickson
26. Bank of Dickson hat
27. Real Estate monthly
28. *Property on Parade*
29. Map of Dickson and Charlotte
30. Chamber of Commerce brochures
31. Chamber of Commerce newsletter
32. Unmistakably Dickson County—Chamber of Commerce Directory
33. Charlotte brochure
34. Ministerial Fellowship brochure
35. 1995 Old Timers Day brochure
36. Afghan
37. Cumberland Furnace cap
38. Letter from Michael Davenport
39. Songs "Come Home to an Old Friend" and "Happy Birthday, My Old Friend, Tennessee" by Alda Marie Harrell

DYER

1. Dyersburg Jaycees hat
2. Register of deeds election campaign hat for Kim Walker
3. Dyersburg Corporation hat
4. Photograph of Chelsea Paige Wilson
5. Small cotton bale
6. Brick from Dyer County Courthouse
7. Three Kim Walker Jaycee pins
8. Bicentennial key chain
9. CMT pin
10. American Business Women's Association membership pin
11. Dyer County telephone book, February 1996
12. Area phone book, 1995
13. First Citizens National Bank 1994 Annual Report
14. Dyersburg State Community College—1996 spring class schedule, sports programs 1995–1996
15. Photograph of Old Dyersburg High School
16. Two Dyer County Christmas ornaments
17. Various business cards
18. Methodist Youth 1930s Debate program
19. Article—"Dogwood Festival Honoring Bicentennial"
20. Article—"Mrs. Willie Hatch making potpourri from local flowers," May 24, 1989
21. Dyersburg Jaycees Chimes for Charity Foundation financial statement, through September 1995

22. Dyer County budget, June 30 1995–1996
23. Postcard of First Methodist Church
24. Cookbook published by Janice Stafford
25. 1994 Dyersburg City Directory
26. Print depicting Dyer County buildings
27. *U.S. News & World Report* magazines—December 1995–January 1996 and February 12, 1996
28. Class photograph, drawings from Mrs. Teresa Cook's third grade class, Dyersburg Primary School
29. Class photograph of Mrs. Sarah Goldsby's third grade class, Dyersburg Primary School
30. Photographs and stories from Mrs. Pressler's third grade class, Dyersburg Primary School
31. Dyer County map
32. 1995 Dyer County tax rate
33. Chamber of Commerce services guide
34. *Dyersburg Tennessee: The Heart of the Land of Plenty*, published 1924
35. Church bulletin, Methodist Episcopal Church, South
36. Jaycees application
37. *Dyersburg News* newspaper
38. *State Gazette* newspaper
39. Photograph of watermelon cutting at Old Dyersberg High School
40. Photograph of monument in front of courthouse
41. Photograph of downtown Dyersburg
42. Photograph of First Methodist Episcopal Church, South
43. Photograph of Alvin C. York
44. Photograph of Minglewood/Minglewood Box Factory
45. Photograph of Illinois Central Railroad Train in 1930s
46. Photograph of Dyersburg Hospital and Dr. Watson's home
47. Photograph of a tombstone
48. Various old newspaper articles

FAYETTE

1. "Fayette County on the Grow" notebook with county statistics and history
2. Fayette County 1996 photographic calendar
3. Various letterhead stationery
4. Various business cards
5. Tennessee House of Representatives coloring book
6. State of the State address by Governor Don Sundquist

7. Tennessee House of Representatives information book
8. Brochures of Fayette County historic homes
9. Fayette County Chamber of Commerce membership directory
10. Photograph of Braden mayor and others

FENTRESS

1. Carved mule and letter of explanation
2. Bicentennial Committee listing
3. Fentress County Hospital letter
4. City of Jamestown information and letter
5. History of education submitted by county school superintendent
6. Clarkrange High School data
7. Jamestown Rotary Club roster and pin
8. Photographs of local sites
9. York Institute data
10. Letter from county executive
11. Brochures from points of interest in Fentress County
12. *History of Buffalo Cove* by Will Peavyhouse
13. *Knobs of Tennessee* by A.R. Hogue
14. *Jamestown—Then and Now* by Hazel Wheeler
15. *Hill Country History*, by Wilma Pinckley
16. Bible and tin carried by Ray Chism through World War I
17. Piece of coal and local story on Wright's Store
18. Churches in Fentress County listing
19. Paper on Crinoids by Phillip Brannon
20. History of the Chestnut Tree by Henry Hoover
21. Canceled check by Alvin C. York, donated by Edward York
22. *History of newspapers in Fentress County* by Bill Bowden
23. York Institute annual
24. History of York Institute
25. *Leader Times*, 1975
26. Indian fossil

FRANKLIN

1. Picture of Jo Ann Brinkley and Margaret Lynch, Franklin County Bicentennial Committee chairpersons
2. Chamber of Commerce brochures
3. Picture, biographical information, and letter from county executive, Clinton L. Williams
4. List of members of the Franklin County Bicentennial Committee

5. *Herald Chronicle* newspaper, includes picture of Editor Charles Sons and brief history of Franklin County and its future
6. Pictures and slides of Franklin County buildings and citizens
7. Map of TimsFord Lake
8. Map of Franklin County
9. Poem by Eleanor Barnes Murray
10. Crimson Clover seeds
11. Cotton bolls and seed
12. Pink Dogwood seed
13. Toy 1996 tractor, pictures of other farming equipment and brief history from Russell Mason Tractor Company
14. Pitcher from Hallelujah Pottery
15. Medallion by Patrick Stewart
16. Student essays from 4th graders
17. Tims Ford Marina & Resort-fishing lure
18. Indian arrowhead
19. Jeweler's hammer
20. Brochures from the Franklin County Jail Museum
21. Newspaper about the Franklin County Jail Museum's Centennial Celebration
22. Badges and patches from the sheriff's department
23. 1996 list of law-enforcement personnel
24. Franklin County employee handbook
25. Nissan announcement
26. Arnold Engineer Development Center newsletter
27. Sewanee brochures
28. Coins, paper money, Susan B. Anthony dollar from SunTrust Bank
29. Picture of black draftees for World War I
30. Purple Heart medal of honor
31. Lynch, Lynch Real Estate brochure
32. World War II commemorative stamps
33. Pewter airplane and flying air patch
34. Pewter hot air balloon
35. Train Tunnel brochure
36. Franklin County Tennessee 200 lapel pin
37. Brochure from the Middle Tennessee Home Health Agency, the first licensed agency in Tennessee
38. Information from the University of Tennessee Space Institute
39. Information from the Daughters of the American Revolution
40. Booklet from the F. C. Historical Society
41. Wildlife article by Wayne Sanders
42. Angel pin
43. Franklin County Courthouse certificate
44. Picture of Franklin County sheriff
45. Poem by Lindsay Long

GIBSON

1. Leadership Class Project package
2. Tennessee History of Medina
3. City of Trenton history and photographs from the *Gazette*
4. Baseball cards
5. St. Jude button
6. History of Skullbone
7. Materials donated by Fred Culp
8. Gibson, Bradford, and Dyer town information
9. Buttons
10. Sesquicentennial coin
11. $2 bill
12. Gibson County history book
13. City of Yorkville and Rutherford information
14. Humboldt package
15. Milan package
16. Coins
17. Kenton package
18. Bank directory and calendar
19. Books about Gibson County
20. T-shirts
21. Flag
22. License plate
23. Burlap Bag depicting Gibson County
24. The *Herald Gazette*
25. *Wall Street Journal*

GILES

1. Letter for the time capsule
2. County box
3. Four Pulaski pins
4. Letter from Rand Hayes
5. Postcard of Giles County Courthouse
6. Postcard of Giles County Courthouse and Square
7. Giles County Community profile and business directory
8. Check for $1 from Tina Dalely
9. Two pens and one pencil from local Tennessee 200 committee
10. 1994 calendar of events for Giles County
11. Giles County map
12. Video of Pulaski
13. Boxes of pens from Pulaski
14. Four Pulaski buttons
15. American City brochure
16. Chamber of Commerce brochure
17. Pulaski phone book

18. Letter from Tennessee 200 Committee
19. "Tennessee Heroes of Our Past" picture
20. Coffee mugs
21. Guide to historic sites of Giles County
22. Quilt square
23. Christmas ornament
24. Boxelder bowl
25. Giles County map
26. *Giles Free Press*, January 4, 1996, and February 23, 1995
27. *Pulaski Citizen*, January 2, 1996
28. Stationery of Giles County
29. Main Street membership card
30. County flag
31. Bodenham Meal sack
32. Giles County Board of Education Teacher Handbook

GRAINGER

1. Grainger County cup
2. Tomato Festival memorabilia
3. 1995–1996 Grainger County school calendar
4. Grainger County area photographs
5. *Grainger County 1796–1996*
6. *Grainger County News*, December 21, 1995
7. *Our Past in Pictures*
8. 1996 Citizens Bank & Trust Company calendar
9. Chamber of Commerce press kit
10. Letter from the county executive
11. 1976 county Bicentennial flag
12. Rutledge High School, 1995 curriculum booklet
13. Photographs of John S. Hill, grandchild of Captain L. E. Cruze Hill; Margaret E. Hill; Mary C. Hill

GREENE

1. *The Big Spring, 1780*
2. *A Walk with the President*
3. *Greeneville, Tennessee, 1783*
4. Andrew Johnson National Historic Site information
5. Greeneville lodging and dining brochure
6. *Backroad History in America's First Frontier*
7. "A Walking Tour" of historic sites brochure
8. *Greeneville, Tennessee: Jewel of the Mountains*
9. Greene County Heritage Trust: Early American Dinner brochure
10. Greeneville Guidebook 1995
11. *The Andrew Johnson Homestead at Greeneville, Tennessee*

12. Video
13. *The Birthplace of Andrew Johnson*
14. Andrew Johnson Memorial Association brochure
15. "An Evening with Andrew Johnson" brochure
16. Accomplishments of Andrew Johnson
17. Chronology of Andrew Johnson
18. *Andrew Johnson: Tennessee's Only Military Governor*
19. "His Faith Never Wavered"—script of President Andrew Johnson
20. Dedication program of the Statue of President Andrew Johnson, 6–22–95
21. *Andrew Johnson: Impeachment and the 17th President*
22. National Park Service news release
23. *Andrew Johnson National Historic Park*
24. Andrew Johnson Indian Peace Medal coin
25. Historical sketch of Mt. Bethel Presbyterian Church, 1780
26. Covenant Church—1959, information
27. Sketch of the History of Timber Ridge Church, 1795
28. The First Presbyterian Church, history
29. *A Brief History of the Negro Churches in the City of Greeneville* by Lottie B. Henry
30. *A Historical Perspective of Beef and Dairy in Greene County*, Mr. Steve Hale
31. *A Brief History of Burley Tobacco in Greene County, Tennessee*, Dr. Phil Hunter
32. *Tusculum: Its Progress and Purposes*, 1927
33. Tusculumnus: Annual Report 1994
34. Tusculum College Bicentennial 1794–1994 yearbook
35. Three Tusculum College photographs
36. Tusculum College Bicentennial, pewter plate
37. Examples of early family records and correspondence: Anthony Moore, 1725; William Smith Moore, 1835; McGaughey Family
38. *The Death of General John Morgan*
39. *A Small Boy's Recollection of the Civil War*
40. *The Diary of Anna E. Snupp 1864 1866*
41. *Bethesda, A Bicentennial History* by Wayne Dobson and Marie Harmon
42. *Davy Crockett* and *Olden Times in Greene County* by Harry Roberts
43. *Historic Green County and Its People*, 1783–1992
44. *Greeneville 100 Year Portrait, 1775–1875* by Richard H. Doughty
45. Picture of the dedication of the statue of Andrew Johnson

46. Copies of information about Greeneville
47. Heritage Trust 20th Anniversary Christmas Dinner brochure
48. Zerox clipping of Greene County Bicentennial flag and Time Capsule Presentation Service
49. A rock from the Big Spring
50. News clipping about the christening of the USS *Greeneville*
51. Brochure about the Post State of Franklin Capitol
52. Brochure about the Dickson-Williams Mansion
53. 1995 Greene County Guidebook
54. News clipping about the Bell Ringing Ceremony
55. Album from the Ottway Six: "Pickin' and Grinnin"
56. News clipping about the Time Capsule Material Presentation Service
57. Seventh Annual Greene County Farm-City Banquet Program
58. Education information—Greeneville city school system, Greene County schools, Extended School Program, Greene County Area Educational Directory
59. *Here Comes Papa*
60. *The Foster Grandparent Program*

GRUNDY

1. Coke product from Tracy City
2. Monteagle wine
3. Cherokee Area Council coffee mug
4. Monteagle Mountain brochure
5. Grundy County Post Veterans issue 1989
6. Grundy County Post Special issue 1992
7. Grundy County Post 1994
8. Grundy County Post 1988 vet appreciation month
9. Beersheba Springs folder
10. Pelham Valley history letter
11. Six postcards of local scenery
12. Grundy County officials picture
13. Letter from the Chamber of Commerce
14. Picture of county executive
15. Ruritan calendar 1996
16. Grundy County tourism brochure
17. South Cumberland State Park brochure

HAMBLEN

1. *Hamblen County, Tennessee*, a pictorial history
2. Letter from County Executive David Purkey

3. Letter from Mayor J. B. Shockley
4. "Discover Tennessee Hamblen County" poster
5. Tennessee poster
6. "Discover Tennessee" brochure
7. Tennessee placemat
8. Mug
9. Cap
10. Tote bag
11. Tennessee reader pin
12. Bookmark
13. Industrial directory
14. Churches of Hamblen County listing
15. Clubs and organizations of Hamblen County listing
16. *Morristown* magazine
17. Map of Morristown
18. Morristown-Hamblen High School East and West annuals and handbooks
19. Berkline Recliner and picture
20. Face mask by Sammie Nicely
21. Melville M. Murrell flying machine patent, before the Wright Brothers
22. Professional Business Association picture
23. Professional Business Association ashtray
24. *Historical Guide to Hamblen County* by Susan Roberts
25. Mahle Piston
26. Rose Center and Council of the Arts brochure and Christmas ornament
27. Machinery prices for Hamblen County
28. Shopper's guide to recycled products
29. GFWC Women's Clubs of Hamblen County
30. Digital picture of Jean Keener
31. *Bell Towers of Morristown*, Stapleton Long
32. Picture of Morristown City Center Opening, December 21, 1995
33. Toyota—TRW wives and bookmark
34. Tennessee Technology Center information, pin, calendar
35. *East Tennessee's Lore of Yesteryear* by Emma Deane Smith Trent
36. Song "Oh Tennessee, My Tennessee," music by Kathy and Gregory Pysh, words by William P. Lawrence
37. "Our Foundation of Strength," article by VADM William P. Lawrence, USN (Ret.)

HAMILTON

1. The *Chattanooga Times*, January 1, 1996
2. The *Chattanooga Free Press*, January 1, 1996
3. Newspaper clippings from the *Chattanooga Free Press*, including top local news stories of 1995 and an article on Carolyn Schaerer,

chairman of the Hamilton County
Bicentennial Committee

4. Pictures of city hall, the courthouse, the
county executive with commissioners,
and the mayor with the city council

5. "Tennessee Bicentennial 1796–1996,
Hamilton County: Historic and Scenic
Gateway," article by John Wilson in the
Chattanooga Free Press

6. Chattanooga phone book, 1996

7. Proclamation from Mayor Gene Roberts
and County Executive Claude Ramsey

8. CARTA shuttle map of downtown
Chattanooga

9. Sheet music and lyrics to "Chattanooga
Choo Choo"

10. 1995 and 1996 Riverbend pins

11. *Family under Fire, A Story of the Civil War*, a
Tennessee 200 project by the Chattanooga
Regional History Museum

12. Key to the city of Chattanooga

13. Chattanooga Gold and Country Club
Centennial Celebration information

14. "Christmas at the Courthouse" ornament

15. Letter from the Hamilton County
Bicentennial Committee

16. Chattanooga Convention and Visitor's
Bureau video

17. National article on Chattanooga from The
Trust for Public Land, 1995 Annual Report

18. Hamilton County Bicentennial school package

19. Porcelain plaque

20. Tourist attractions and museum brochures

21. Incline Railway Centennial pin and brochures

22. "Horsin' around Carousel Carving,"
carving mold and brochure

23. Chattanooga Choo Choo lapel pins and
brochure

24. "Chattanooga Choo Choo Scenic Drive,"
tour guidebook

25. Chattanooga visitor's guide

26. Allied Arts calendar

27. Bicentennial calendar

28. Coca Cola bottle

29. Chattanooga Bakery, Inc., Moon Pie box

30. McKee Foods Corporation Little Debbie
Snacks box

31. History of Chattanooga Medicine Co./
Chattem, Inc.

32. Krystal Company brown bag and box

33. Provident Life and Accident Insurance
Company information

34. Brach & Brock Confections, Inc.—pin,
pencil, box, and bag

35. Olan Mills miniature camera

36. Tennessee Valley Authority information

37. Bi-Lo grocery receipt and shopping bag

38. Hamilton County lapel pin

39. Bicentennial Parade of Flags poster

40. *Chattanooga CityScope* magazine

41. *Chattanooga* magazine

42. Copy of the invitation to the "send-off
ceremony" for the time capsule artifacts

43. Letter from Carolyn Schaerer, Tennessee
200 committee chairman

HANCOCK

1. *Hancock County and Its People, 1989 Volume I*

2. *Hancock County and its People, 1994 Volume II*

3. Quart of moonshine

4. America Online computer disc

5. *Recipes from over Home*—Treadway Volunteer
Fire Department

6. Avon book

7. 1996 calendars—Smith-Turner Drug Store,
Greene Insurance Agency, First Claiborne
Bank, GFWC Hancock Woman's Club

8. Historic Sites and Preservation in Upper
East Tennessee booklet

9. *1994–1995 Hancock County High School
Annual*

10. Telephone directory

11. Sneedville Woman's Club—zip code book
with list of local merchants

12. Sneedville First Baptist Church directory

13. Hancock County High School student
handbook

14. *The Melungeons—The Resurrection of a
Proud People* by N. Brent Kennedy

15. The *Wall Street Journal*, article from
January 4, 1995

16. Registered voters list for Hancock County,
1995

17. 1896 silver dollar

18. Binder containing Hancock County statistical data; county commissioners list; city
aldermen list; county events brochures;
list of attractions; historical society officers list, members list; old jail project
information; Bicentennial Committee officers list, members list; gift of Bicentennial
log house with photograph, proposed
renovation floor plans, January 1, 1996,
newsletter; community organizations
membership listings; *Sneedville Shopper*
paper, January 15, 1996; photographs of
Hancock County and Sneedville

HARDEMAN

1. Listing of Hardeman County officials and
signatures

2. List of Hardeman County Bicentennial
Committee members with summary of
events planned

3. Telephone directory for 1995

4. Bumper sticker—"We're Proud of Hardeman County"

5. Flag of state of Tennessee

6. 1995 Hardeman County area guide

7. Postcards

8. Mug

9. Christmas tree ornament made by Ed Maurer

10. Tennessee pewter necklace

11. Volunteer 200 Day scarf, June 1, 1995

HARDIN

1. *Hardin County Pictorial History*

2. *Understandably Hardin County*

3. 1996 phone book

4. Newspaper

5. "Savannah," a poem by Lisa Thomas

6. Flyers

7. List of county and city officials

8. List of doctors and dentists

9. Copy of the county seal

10. List of county schools

11. Pictures of county sites

12. Article about the Hardin County
Bicentennial flag

13. Replica of an antique pistol made by Parris
Manufacturing Company in Savannah,
Tennessee

14. *Shiloh*, by Albert Dillahunty

15. April 7, 1962, Shiloh Centennial ceremony
program with a 4¢ stamp

16. June 29, 1995, Civil War Commemoration
program with a Jefferson Davis stamp

17. Shiloh National Military Park map, Civil
War Battlefield series

18. Shiloh Park brochure

19. Shiloh scout patch

20. Shiloh coke bottle

21. Stamp cachet for the Shiloh stamp,
Pittsburg Landing cancellation

22. Stamp cachet for the U.S. Grant stamp,
Cherry Mansion cancellation

23. Stamp cachet for the W. T. Sherman
stamp, Pittsburg Landing cancellation

24. Postcards from area sites

25. Baseball hat

26. Afghan
27. County brochures
28. Program from the Hardin County Bicentennial tree planting ceremony
29. Program from the Hardin County time capsule sealing
30. The *Courier* newspaper, March 7, 1996, article about Hardin County High School courses and staff listing
31. 1995–1996 Hardin County High School cheerleaders listing
32. List of Hardin County Bicentennial projects
33. Picture of the Savannah Historic Trail overlook
34. Picture of the Grant Headquarters Monument
35. List of the 1996 River City Kiwanis Club members
36. List of the 1996 Lion's Club members
37. The *Courier*, February 29, 1996, article about the Civil War cannon
38. List of Pickwick United Methodist Church members
39. List of the Hardin County Bicentennial Committee
40. List of Hardin County industries
41. List of Hardin County clubs and civic organizations
42. List of Hardin County churches
43. Saltillo points of interest
44. History of Cherry Mansion

HAWKINS

1. Product samples from the International Playing Card and Label Company
2. Newspapers
3. Holston Army Ammunition Plant information
4. TRW information
5. Holston Electronic Company information
6. Currency and coins
7. *Tennessee Magazine*, Holston Electric Cooperative
8. Phone book
9. Audio cassette
10. Local car dealership materials
11. County map
12. Brochure from Historic Bulls Gap

HAYWOOD

1. Letter from county executive
2. Letter from mayor of Stanton and mayor of Brownsville

3. Photographs of the courthouse, city hall, the library, the Chamber of Commerce, and the Brownsville square
4. Photographs of College Hill Center and the Lincoln Museum
5. Photograph and essay by seventh grader
6. Cotton boll
7. Soybeans
8. Corn
9. Chamber of Commerce directory
10. List of churches
11. List of professionals
12. Elected county and city officials
13. *1995 Brownsville States Graphic*—education special section
14. *1995 Brownsville States Graphic*—Peach Festival special section
15. 1973 Sesquicentennial booklet
16. Haywood County map
17. List of Bicentennial Committee and publicity
18. Lincoln Collection brochure
19. County museum brochure
20. Hatchie Wildlife refuge brochure
21. *Brownsville States Graphic*, "1994 Year in Review"
22. Assorted brochures
23. Carver High School reunion, 1994
24. Haywood County history book, 1989

HENDERSON

1. Lexington T-shirt
2. Henderson County Fair book, 1995
3. Magnetek brochure
4. Magnetek employee list
5. Brochures
6. Sardis button
7. 1957 Panoply plywood
8. Dayco hose and brochure
9. Harding Machine screws and brochure
10. Delavan nozzles and other information
11. Columbus McKinnon Corporation chains
12. 1996 Henderson County historic calendar
13. *Lexington Progress 1884–1946* by W. V. Barry
14. *History of Henderson County* by Tillman Stewart
15. Middlefork community cotton boll
16. Henderson County officials document and photograph
17. Lexington High School seniors list
18. Lexington High School stationery
19. Scotts Hill High School seniors list

20. Montgomery High School seniors list
21. Lexington High School hand fan
22. Photograph of courthouse
23. *Progress* newspaper, Bicentennial articles

HENRY

1. Letter from Mayor John T. Van Dyok III
2. Letter from County Executive Herman Jackson
3. Henry County Sesquicentennial souvenir program
4. "Paris: The American Dream," newspaper brochure from October 1992
5. Friday, December 29, 1995 edition of the *Paris Post-Intelligencer*
6. Program for the October 24, 1994 Governor Ned Ray McWherter Bridge Dedication
7. Brochures:
   Downtown Business Association— businesses and locations
   Paris and Henry County
   The Place To Retire
   Eiffel Tower
   1995 Holiday Happenings
   Bicentennial family history book for Henry County
8. Map: Get a Vision of Paris, Tennessee
9. Paris/Henry County Chamber of Commerce newsletter, December 1995
10. Cookbook: *Recipes from the Crockett Family Tree*, 1994
11. *Pen Sketches: Henry County, Tennessee* by W. O. Inman, 1976
12. Program from the dedication ceremony of the Vernan McGarity National Guard Armory, 1989
13. 1996 New Year's card from Representative Don Ridgeway and family
14. Paris/Henry County Chamber of Commerce visitor's guide, 1995
15. Paris, Tennessee, Eiffel Tower tie pin
16. Six photographs of the court square with listing of business name, purpose, and owner
17. Girl Scout tin including the Paris Junior Troop 163 with photo, four patches, and one pin
18. Agenda for the county commission meeting February 20, 1996, and minutes for January 16, 1996
19. County seals
20. Pocket calendar

HICKMAN

1. Grapevine wreath
2. Deer antlers used in deer hunting
3. Pre-1850 Hickman County map
4. Hickman County video—"Land of Optimism and Opportunity"
5. Flashlight from Meriwether Lewis Electric Cooperative
6. The *Tennessee Magazine*, November 1995, December 1995, January 1996
7. Breece's Cafe menu
8. Recyclable litter bag
9. Plastic phone book cover
10. Centerville phone book, November 1994–1995
11. *A Patchwork History of Hickman County, 1807–1984*
12. *Spence's History of Hickman County, Tennessee* by Edward and Olgia Dotson
13. Letter from the county executive
14. Hickman County map
15. Tennessee Valley Authority and Distributors of TVA bag
16. Middle Tennessee Community Date for Centerville 1995
17. Hickman County profile
18. Employee list of the Meriwether Lewis Electric Cooperative, 1995
19. Member handbook for Meriwether Lewis Electric Cooperative
20. Brochure—"This is the Generation of Electricity"
21. Booklet—"Universal Fasteners, Inc. The First 100 Years, 1895–1995"
22. *Hickman County History, 1807–1993*
23. Levi's blue jeans
24. Photograph of Meriwether Lewis Electric Cooperative
25. Armstrong's Home Style Tennessee Turnovers bag from Armstrong Pie Company
26. Grocery store newspaper coupon sections for Piggly Wiggly, Jay's Foods, and Foodland
27. *Hickman County Times*, January 2 and 8, 1996

HOUSTON

1. Key to city
2. Tennessee 200 mug
3. Pencils
4. Paper clip
5. Erin Rotary Club—banner, membership list, letter
6. Houston County census, 1850, 1860, 1870, 1880, 1900
7. *Houston County Review & Erin Review, Vol. 1 & 2*
8. *Roads & Maps of Houston County, Vol. 4*
9. *The News & the Houston County News, Vol. 3*
10. *Newspaper Clipping Collection, Vol. 5*
11. *History of Houston County, 1871–1996*
12. *Stewart Community Center Cookbook*
13. Erin telephone book, January 1995
14. *History of Danville, Tennessee, 1861–1993*
15. Tennessee Ridge Elementary School yearbooks—1991, 1994, 1995
16. Picture of staff and girl's basketball team at Tennessee Ridge Elementary School
17. Tennessee Ridge Elementary School personnel list
18. Tennessee Ridge Elementary School contact list
19. Tennessee Ridge Elementary School student list
20. 1996 calendars
21. Letter from the mayor
22. Houston County High School—1995 Shamrock yearbook
23. Houston County High School newspaper
24. Article for the Tennessee 200 time capsule
25. Erin Elementary School student contact list
26. Erin Elementary School—letter from students
27. Erin Elementary School newsletter
28. Erin Elementary School 1995 yearbook
29. Metal tag, Erin
30. The *Stewart Houston Times* newspaper, December 12, 1995
31. Two Houston County brochures
32. 1995 fact book for Stewart and Houston County
33. Map of Houston County
34. Cee Bee Supermarket—layout of store and calendar
35. County pictures
36. Letter from the county executive
37. Proclamation for National Drinking Water Week and calendar of events
38. Old Wooden Water Pipe—description and picture
39. Houston County Historical Society—membership list and minutes from a meeting
40. Houston County Tennessee 200 Committee meeting minutes
41. Houston County Lion's Club description and membership list
42. Houston County Chamber of Commerce information and membership list
43. Tennessee Ridge Elementary School contact list
44. Houston County Public Library—Open House and Dedication Ceremony program
45. Erin United Methodist Church information

HUMPHREYS

1. *Pictorial History of Humphreys County*
2. *Volume 2—History of Humphreys County*
3. *Explosion in Waverly, Tennessee*
4. Student essays
5. Pictures from Family Fun Day
6. Pictures from Battle of Johnsonville reenactment
7. *Peanut Jubilee* cookbook
8. Humphreys County phone book
9. *Humphreys County Magazine*
10. Brochure on recreational activities
11. Battle of Johnsonville medallion
12. Picture of county commissioners
13. Article—"1995 A Year In Review"
14. Video tape about tourism in the county
15. Humphreys County map
16. Descriptions of three major cities
17. 1995 Waverly United Methodist Church membership directory
18. St. Patrick Irish Picnic and Homecoming brochures and newspaper
19. Coal
20. TVA Johnsonville Fossil Plant—brochures, employee list, newsletter, plant description, 1993 calendar
21. County photographs

JACKSON

1. Jackson County Bicentennial Committee list
2. Jackson County government documents
3. City of Gainesboro government documents
4. Jackson County board of education information
5. Pictures of Jackson County industries and utilities
6. Jackson County Chamber of Commerce material
7. Jackson County newspaper

8. Twin Lakes Telephone Cooperative directory
9. Jackson County agricultural documents
10. Jackson County Bicentennial flag
11. Tennessee's Bicentennial tree—the Yellowwood
12. Jackson County Bicentennial pottery
13. Samples of cloth and textiles used in 1996
14. Jackson County history book
15. *Jennings Creek Community Cookbook*
16. Jackson County Historical Society documents
17. Bible
18. 1996 calendars
19. Freestone pottery
20. Tobacco seed
21. Seed corn

JEFFERSON

1. Holy Bible
2. Copy of Davy Crockett and Polly Findley's marriage bond
3. List of county officials
4. List of industries
5. List of county commissioners
6. List of items placed in the 1992 Jefferson County time capsule
7. List of Jefferson County Bicentennial Committee
8. Letter of endorsement of the Bicentennial Committee from Tom Cooper, Chamber of Commerce
9. Letter from Gary Holiway, county executive
10. Letter from the Bicentennial Committee
11. Print of Jefferson County flag
12. County flag T-shirt
13. Tennessee 200 flyer
14. Press releases from *Standard Banner* newspaper (twelve)
15. Photograph of Bicentennial Committee
16. Copies of photographs in news releases
17. Cookbook from Hills Union Methodist Church
18. Directory of Jefferson County schools
19. *Jefferson County Families 1792–1992*
20. Statistical book of Jefferson County
21. Jefferson County and area telephone book
22. *People and Places of Jefferson County* by E. P. Muncy
23. *Bent Twigs* by Jean Bible
24. *Broken Hearts, Broken Lives* by the Jefferson County Historical Society
25. *Lillies in the Valley* by D. C. Smith

26. *The Battle That History Lost*, by D. C. Smith
27. Heritage of Jefferson County
28. Land Between the Lakes booklet
29. 1990 census
30. *Structures of Faith* by Jefferson County High School art and history students
31. Cloth Yo Yo and description by Juanita Bishop
32. Indian jewelry by Mark Finchum
33. Peach Pit Santa and Pasta Angel by Nettie Cate
34. *Standard Banner* newspaper, June 6, 1995
35. "Heritage and Vision" brochure
36. Jefferson County brochure
37. Hospital brochure
38. Smoky Mountain Travel information
39. Helen Lowe Gallery information
40. Two maps of Jefferson County
41. 1836 map of Jefferson County
42. Map symbols of Tennessee counties
43. 1976 Jefferson City Diamond Jubilee booklet
44. Letter from Jefferson City mayor, Alan Palmieri
45. Tennessee Community Data, Jefferson City
46. Jefferson City Guidebook and Directory 1989–1990
47. Jefferson City, "A Profile 1992"
48. Utilities information
49. Newsletters from the city of Baneberry
50. Letter from city of New Market, recorder, Carolyn Williams
51. List of city of White Pine officials

JOHNSON

1. Pottery plate for the Bicentennial
2. Pottery tile for the Bicentennial
3. Calendar
4. Record of activities for the Bicentennial
5. Letter from the county executive
6. Letter from the mayor
7. Picture of the Bicentennial Pageant
8. Picture of the First Woman of Johnson County
9. Pictures from school children
10. Bicentennial key chain
11. Newspapers
12. Pictures from Neva Elementary School
13. Dirt sample
14. Johnson County lapel pin
15. 1994–1995 Mountain City Elementary School yearbook

16. Mountain City Elementary School description
17. Mountain City Elementary School student/parent handbook
18. Coins
19. Computer disks—Laurel School enrollment 1995–1996
20. Thank you letter to a teacher
21. *A Book of Favorite Recipes, 1995–1996*
22. Picture of quilt
23. Newspaper article of history mural
24. Information on Shady Valley School
25. A star-shaped piece of original Shady Valley stage curtain, circa 1950
26. Pictures from the Cranberry Festival
27. Letter to the county commission
28. Johnson County Bicentennial activity list

KNOX

1. White Lily posters and brochure
2. Flags, banners, and T-shirts from Knox County and Farragut
3. Blount Mansion wood carving and brochures
4. *Past Times* by Stephen V. Ash
5. Haley's Square brochure, photograph of Alex Haley sculpture
6. United Way press kit
7. *Knoxville News Sentinel*, January 1, 1996
8. *A Century of Front Pages*
9. Leadership Knoxville membership directory
10. Pilot Oil Corporation, model truck, fact sheet
11. Travel Centers, Fall 1995 directory
12. East Tennessee Historical Society brochures
13. First Families of Tennessee program information
14. Coffee mugs
15. Media microphone cover
16. Old courthouse replica
17. City-county government letters
18. *Two Centuries of Knox County, Tennessee, 1792–1992*
19. Farragut 2004 plan, brochures, reports, maps
20. Museums of Knoxville brochures
21. County letterhead, envelope
22. Seal of Farragut County
23. Letter from Mayor Eddy Ford
24. Lapel pin
25. Knox visitor's guide
26. Teacher's resource manual

27. *Historic Knoxville and Knox County* by Russ Manning and Sondra Jamieson
28. Boomsday 1995 T-shirt
29. WATE-TV 6 banner
30. WIVK-FM 107.7 T-shirt
31. Flag from the town of Farragut
32. Flag from Knox County
33. 1791 flag
34. WBIR-TV 10 T-shirt
35. *Ossoli Circle, 1961–1986*
36. *Ossoli Juniors*
37. Letter from the *Knoxville News Sentinel* newspaper
38. Knoxville Bicentennial coin
39. Knoxville lapel pins
40. Parking discount tokens
41. Magnet from Action 10 News
42. *Tennessee Ancestors*, December 1995
43. *The Journal of East Tennessee History*
44. Personal Security Awareness Guide, June 1995
45. Proclamation by Tom Schumpert, county executive
46. Litter bag
47. Bijou Theatre Center brochure
48. Farragut Folklife Museum, 1995 Fall newsletter
49. Farragut newspaper, February 22, 1995
50. Farragut 1995 annual report
51. *Farragut Tennessee* magazine 1995–1996 edition
52. *Sevier's Vision* newsletter, Winter 1996
53. John Sevier lapel pin
54. Knox County sites and organizations brochures
55. Central Business Improvement District brochure and 1995 annual report
56. Letter from Mayor Victor Ashe
57. McClung Museum brochure
58. Colonel David Henley family tree
59. Library Development Review 1994–1995
60. *City Wide* newsletter, January 1996
61. Downtown organization brochures
62. Trolley route
63. UTK library record 1994–1995
64. Chamber of Commerce letter from the president
65. Chamber of Commerce brochures and 1995 membership directory
66. Colonel David Henley Association material
67. Knoxville Sports Corporation press kit
68. Knoxville Fire Department brochures and litter bag
69. Downtown Knoxville maps
70. Urban Area Transportation booklet
71. Knox County Metropolitan Planning Commission newsletter, July–September 1995; 1995 directory, description, photographs
72. Beck Cultural Center information
73. Confederate Cemetery information
74. African-American Appalachian Arts, Inc.
75. Letter from the Knox county executive
76. WBIR-TV 10 letter
77. *Tennessee 200—A Celebration of 200 Years of the University* by Betsy Creekmore

LAKE

1. Bargery Farms Corporation information
2. *Daily Guidepost*, 1987
3. *Memories of the 1937 flood*
4. *The Stories They Tell*
5. Essay by Scarlett Algee
6. Farm packet
7. Football team pictures
8. Recreation packet
9. The Tiptonville Woman's Club packet
10. Postcards
11. *Leaves of Gold*
12. *History of Lake County*
13. The *Lakeview Times*
14. "A Loving Community Called Phillippy"
15. Lake County historical packet
16. Letters from county officials
17. Letters from Bicentennial Committee
18. Bible
19. Business cards
20. Churches of Lake County listing

LAUDERDALE

1. City and community area maps
2. Community sheet
4. Fort Pillow brochure
5. Ripley Parks and Recreation brochure
6. Chamber of Commerce brochure
7. Halls community profile
8. Tennessee Wine brochure
9. Baptist Memorial Hospital brochure
10. Stationery and business card from county executive's office
11. List of county commissioners
12. Volunteer 200 Day souvenirs
13. Lauderdale County Council of Arts brochures
14. Lauderdale County phone book
15. Halls First Methodist Music Program souvenir
16. List of Lauderdale county commissioner's committees
17. The *Lauderdale County Enterprise*
18. The *Lauderdale Voice*
19. Information from the Bank of Ripley, Bank of Halls, Lauderdale County Bank of Halls, Gates Banking and Trust, Farmers Union Bank
20. News release from Governor Sundquist's office announcing new prison
21. The *Commercial Appeal*—news release of new prison
22. Volunteer 200 Day photographs
23. Lauderdale County Information booklet
24. *Lauderdale County from Earliest Times*
25. Photographs of Lauderdale County
26. *Visions of Lauderdale County, Past and Present* by Clarice Haynes Hellums and Kara Haynes McCauley
27. Description of Henning United Methodist Church
28. Tomato seeds

LAWRENCE

1. Pictorial history book
2. Brochures on county, industry, and downtown
3. Current pictures
4. Telephone book
5. Annual events and Main Street, Lawrenceburg
6. Current pictures and prices of houses and cars
7. Current officials, artists, schools, population
8. Acts creating county and county seat
9. District maps
10. Arts, poetry, and essays by students
11. Education information for Lawrence County
12. Environment concerns and solutions
13. Bicentennial events and committee members
14. Iron ore sample
15. Cotton boll
16. Coonskin cap
17. Civil War miniballs
18. Arrowhead
19. Tintype picture
20. Lawrence County flag
21. Item from Homecoming 1986
22. Vaughan and Leoma music books
23. Letter from mayor

24. Letter from county executive
25. 1976 U.S. Bicentennial information
26. Amish toothpick holder
27. Fishing tackle
28. Volunteer 200 Day bandanna
29. Letter explaining the significance of each item chosen for the time capsule
30. "Year in Review"
31. Currency and coins
32. Gas credit card

LEWIS

1. Lewis County picture history book
2. Historical papers
3. Slides
4. Phone book
5. Copies of items of historical interest
6. Letter from mayor
7. Letter from county executive
8. Tennessee 200 mug
9. Tennessee 200 pin
10. Volkssport medal
11. German 1896 newspaper copy
12. Cemetery records book
13. Lewis County Chamber of Commerce 1994 Edition book
14. *History of Lewis County*
15. Artwork by Bill Logan
16. *Lewis County Herald*
17. *Traditional Cooking in Howenwald, Tennessee* cookbook
18. Musgrave Pencil Company pencil
19. Tennessee Technological Institute pen
20. Packaging for Armstrong's Home Style Turnover

LINCOLN

1. *Lincoln County* newspaper
2. Coffee mug
3. Personal checkbook of Norma L. Bagley
4. Reprint copy of the old *Bluestocking Cookbook*
5. 1994 and 1995 program of "200 Tennessee Road"
6. Fifty pictures of "200 Tennessee Road"
7. A property from the production of "200 Tennessee Road," the campaign ribbon inscribed "Old Hickory, the Nation's Hero and the People's Friend"
8. T-shirt used to publicize "200 Tennessee Road"
9. List of all productions of Carriage House Players

10. Carriage House Players program of the play *A Midsummer Might's Dream*
11. Carriage House Players program of *Anne of Green Gables*
12. Tennessee automobile license plate of William F. Shouse
13. Uncirculated $1 and $2 bills in Christmas gift envelopes
14. Pictures of businesses on the public square
15. Pictures of a reproduction of the *Lincoln County Banner* and members of this executive board.
16. Wire samples by Copperweld company, pamphlet, paper placemat
17. "In the Beginning," a historical pamphlet by the Marshes
18. A cap, an emblem, and brochures from Amana
19. A cup, a cap, and sample product bags from Eagle Snacks
20. A Lee luggage tag and article about the closing of the plant
21. Christmas tree ornament by the Fayetteville Main Street
22. Pictures showing aerial view of the public square
23. *Pictorial History of Lincoln County* by Pat Lindquist
24. Lincoln County Fair catalog
25. A cup, a narrative, and pictures from C.L.E.A.N. Inc.
26. Pictures of the executive board
27. Chamber of Commerce booklet promoting Fayetteville and Lincoln County
28. The first meeting minutes of Lincoln County's oldest industry, Elk Yarn Mills
29. List of industries with statistics
30. An iris, magazine, and brochure from W & W Ornamental Iron
31. City directory
32. Telephone directory
33. Paper showing organization of county government and a current county budget
34. Paper showing organization of city government and a current budget
35. Reprint of a 1904 historical booklet
36. Automobile "vanity" license plate noting the Lincoln County High School Falcons
37. Information about health facilities
38. 1995 Lincoln County High School annual
39. Brochure from Lincoln County Museum
40. Brochure of "Fayetteville . . . Host of Christmas Past"

41. Shopping guide
42. Report by Stanley Lyon regarding agriculture
43. Materials about Lincoln County's oldest residences
44. Credit cards
45. Booklets from Homecoming '86
46. Samples of local utility bills
47. *Elk Valley Times*, year-end review
48. Student essays
49. 1996 canceled stamped envelope
50. Portable ash tray

LOUDON

1. Three newspaper articles on the Loudon County Tennessee 200 project, 1995
2. Walking tour brochure on Historic Loudon, Tennessee, 1993
3. *Loudon County Living*, 1995–96
4. Manuscript on the Battle of Loudon, 1993
5. Article on Tellico Village, 1994
6. Photograph of the Loudon County Tennessee 200 Committee, 1995
7. Photograph of the Loudon Cumberland Presbyterian Church, circa 1883
8. Photograph of the Loudon County Courthouse, circa 1871
9. Photograph of the Loudon County Museum/Carmichael Inn, circa 1810
10. *Beloved Landmarks of Loudon County, Tennessee*, 1962
11. Rough draft of histories and photographs on Loudon County structures to be used in the new edition of *Beloved Landmarks of Loudon County*, 1995
12. Three essays on "Why I Am Proud to Live in Loudon County," 1995
13. Two articles on the Loudon County Museum/Carmichael Inn
14. History on the relocation and restoration of the Loudon County Museum/Carmichael Inn
15. Brochure on the Loudon County Museum/Carmichael Inn

MACON

1. *History of Macon County, Tennessee* by Harold G. Blankenship
2. *Early Story of Red Boiling Springs, Tennessee* by Vernon Roddy
3. Pamphlet—"Red Boiling Springs, The Traditional Lives" by Jim Bellar

4. Photo album
5. County map
6. Map of the City of Lafayette
7. Pamphlet—"Macon County" by Macon County Chamber of Commerce
8. North Central directory
9. 1995–1996 Macon County budget
10. Community data for Lafayette and Red Boiling Springs
11. Agricultural statistics
12. *Macon County Times*
13. *Macon County Chronicle*
14. Letter from the city of Lafayette/Macon County
15. Letter from the city of Red Boiling Springs
16. Tennessee 200 county committee members
17. Bicentennial brick sales list
18. Volunteer 200 Day volunteer list
19. Church histories and data
20. 1995–1996 Macon County Teacher Handbook
21. *1995 Progressor*
22. *The Doctor from Bugtussle* by Wendell W. Wilson, M.D.
23. *1995 Hilltop*
24. Macon County High School student folder
25. *With Second Army: Somewhere in Tennessee* by Gene H. Sloan
26. *Macon County My Home* by Danny Patterson
27. Homecoming '86 programs
28. Program for Macon County Sesquicentennial
29. Macon County fair catalog
30. Grocery advertisements
31. Civic organization information
32. "The History of the Blind Wolf Pipe" pamphlet from the Macon County Historical Society
33. Lafayette College catalog, 1904–1905
34. Citizen's Bank annual report
35. Macon Bank and Trust Company annual report
36. Macon County General Hospital annual report
37. North Central Telephone Cooperative annual report
38. Tri-County Electrical Membership Cooperation annual report
39. Sassafras walking cane by Willard Walton
40. White oak basket by Jonas Sewell
41. Twist of Macon County chewing tobacco
42. Sulphur water sample from Red Boiling Springs
43. Sample of White Lightning—bootleg whiskey
44. *Macon County Cemetery Book I & II* by Macon County Historical Society

MADISON

1. *Jackson & Madison County, A Pictorial History*
2. Film "Quality of Life in Jackson, Tennessee" and brochure
3. Jackson/Madison County map
4. *History of Jackson-Madison County General Hospital*
5. Journal to Excellence, guide and brochure from Jackson Utility Division
6. City/county education bulletin
7. Madison County budget
8. City of Jackson budget
9. Key to the county
10. Keys to the city
11. Brochures on West Tennessee Agricultural Experiment Station
12. Brochure and history of airport
13. Heart Center brochure
14. West Tennessee Healthcare, Inc., brochure
15. Two issues of the *Grapevine* newspaper
16. *Medical Center News*
17. Hospital annual report
18. Jackson State Community College brochure
19. Lambeth University brochure
20. Union University brochure
21. Jackson Incentives and Taxes brochure
22. Chamber of Commerce directory
23. Booklets on Jackson
24. Convention and Visitor's Bureau information
25. West Tennessee Journal, February 1996
26. Jackson Symphony Orchestra information

MARION

1. *Jasper Journal*, March 30, 1994, and November 28, 1995
2. *South Pittsburg Hustler*, February 26, 1995, and November 9, 1995
3. Pencil
4. Coal
5. Handle from Sequachee Handle Factory
6. Arrowhead
7. Purple and white football thrown at MCHS games
8. 1995 annual from Whitwell Middle School
9. 1995 annual from Whitwell High School
10. 1992 annual from South Pittsburg High School
11. Lodge Manufacturing Company skillet
12. Church bulletins from area cities
13. South Pittsburg High School sports calendar
14. Various South Pittsburg High School pictures
15. MCHS State Champ article
16. JMS Middle School student stories on a computer disc
17. Compact disc of rock-n-roll music
18. Bessie Smith—first day of issue stamp cover
19. Country Music—first day of issue stamp cover
20. Elvis Presley record and program for stamp issue
21. Micky Mantle comic
22. Marion County history
23. A penny
24. Citizens State Bank business cards
25. Family histories
26. *History of South Pittsburg, Kimball, and Whitwell*
27. 1996 Whitwell Middle School calendar
28. Letter from mayor
29. Letter from county executive
30. Pom-poms
31. Student essays
32. Pictures of Marion County
33. Elvis stamp
34. Invitation of SPES Open House
35. Fireworks
36. Small footballs and basketballs
37. *Dream Catcher* by Jamie Kay Rector
38. Book by Whitwell teachers
39. Marion County brochures
40. South Pittsburg postcards
41. South Pittsburg brochures
42. Kimball brochure
43. Picture of Marion County Bicentennial Committee
44. Article from groundbreaking for the town of Kimball
45. Community date for 1995—Jasper, Whitwell, South Pittsburg

MARSHALL

1. Information on Hog Viking Days
2. Tourist information
3. Olympic pins
4. Audio recording from the Fossils

5. Metal sign from Lewisburg
6. Walker Die Casting, Inc., information
7. Owners manual from Dole Refrigerator Company
8. Industry information
9. Sundrop bottle
10. Cosmolab samples
11. Photographs of county flag
12. Marshall County Historic Quarterly (four)
13. *Lewisburg Tribune*, November 30, 1995
14. *Lewisburg Gazette*
15. Instructions on pencil making
16. Pieces of pencil-making process
17. Pencils and erasers from Moon Creative Products
18. Photographs
19. Business cards
20. Two horseshoes
21. Golf ball from Saddle Creek Golf Club
22. Saddle Creek Gold Club golf-score card

MAURY

1. Hampshire brochure
2. Picture of Co-commissioner Whiteside
3. Santa Fe—Benton Lodge #111 history
4. Theta Community Club history
5. *Theta Volunteer Fire Department and Community Center Cookbook*
6. Theta FCE Club history
7. *Memories of Theta School Days*
8. Water Valley Community Club history
9. *Water Valley Homemakers Club Cookbook*
10. Spring Hill brochure
11. Reenactment of Battle of Spring Hill—schedule, guide, map
12. *Car Country News Editions*, October 2 and 30, 1995, and January 1, 1996
13. Spring Hill Library information
14. Spring Hill print by Tommy Thompson
15. Town of Spring Hill directory and business services
16. Town of Spring Hill employee list and application
17. Postcards of area historic sites
18. Policeman's patch and memorabilia
19. Directory of the First United Methodist Church in Mt. Pleasant
20. Bigby Grey's flag handout
21. City of Mt. Pleasant gold seal
22. Map of Mt. Pleasant
23. Mt. Pleasant brochure
24. *History of Hunter Meetinghouse and its Cemetery Records*, 1983

25. History of the Mt. Pleasant Lion's Club
26. Mt. Pleasant, Maury Phosphate Museum information
27. 1995 and 1996 historical calendar
28. Mt. Pleasant city-promotion brochure
29. Mt. Pleasant City Hall print—Bicentennial project, by Mildred Hartsfield
30. Profile of Mt. Pleasant
31. *Mt. Pleasant Record*, May 26, 1988
32. *Mt. Pleasant, Tennessee*
33. Rattle & Snap brochure
34. *Tennessee Historical Quarterly*, Spring 1970
35. *Tennessee Historical Quarterly*, Summer 1994
36. *Let the Drums Roll* by Marsie Lightfoot, USA Bicentennial project of the Maury County Historical Society, 1976
37. James K. Polk Home brochure
38. James K. Polk Memorial Association program of benefit dinner/dance
39. "Walking with History on West Seventh Street, Columbia, Tennessee"
40. Columbia Lion's Club packet
41. Columbia Academy brochure
42. Columbia Historic District, West Sixth Street and Mayes Place information
43. Ritco, Inc., business card
44. Tennessee Southern Railroad and Tennessee Central Railroad *Museum Excursion Train* flyer
45. Bishop's brochure
46. Legend's brochure
47. The Ole Lamplighter brochure
48. Sam Hill's brochure
49. Vito's brochure
50. Graymere Country Club brochure
51. Ramada brochure
52. Richland Inn brochure
53. Jane Knox Chapter of the Daughters of the American Revolution—history, membership list
54. Yearbook, history of the Tenassee Chapter of the Daughters of the American Revolution
55. History of the Thomas McKissick Chapter of the Daughters of the American Revolution
56. Kings Daughters School history
57. Annie White Circle of King's Daughters—history, ancestor chart
58. Lelia Anderson Circle of King's Daughters—history, membership list
59. Margaret Yarbrough Circle of King's Daughters—history
60. Virginia Mai Kittrell Circle of King's Daughters—history

61. American Association of University Women, Columbia Branch—history, membership
62. The Thursday Literary Club—handbook, history, Homecoming '86 project
63. Volunteer Garden Club—history, officers
64. Brick from Central High School, 1915–1993
65. Canvas bag of downtown pride, Columbia
66. Pictures of downtown Columbia
67. Various newspaper articles
68. Outline of Tennessee 200 suggested committees
69. Proposed banner by Chance Church of Maury County to be hung in the Maury County Museum
70. The proposed pageant script
71. Fax from *Southern Living* magazine about the proposed pageant
72. List of clubs and organizations to contact for the Maury County time capsule
73. Maury County introductory guide
74. Maury County map
75. Columbia map
76. Maury County Chapter AARP—history, charter, bylaws
77. Alpha Delta Kappa—Maury County Beta Alpha Chapter Cookbook
78. Antebellum trial guide
79. Packet from the Association for the Preservation of Tennessee Antiquities
80. Antique shopping guide to Maury County
81. "Accents and Antiques," handout
82. Arts Guild of Maury County brochure and performance schedule
83. American Legion Auxiliary of Herbert Griffin, Unit 19, Newspaper articles from the *Daily Herald*, January 22, 1995, February 19, 1995 and March 26, 1995, regarding their seventy-fifth anniversary
84. American Legion Hill Gordon Post 170—membership, officers, the *Daily Herald*, February 7, 1993
85. Boy Scouts—the *Daily Herald* supplement
86. Maury County Business and Professional Women's Organization listing
87. Maury County unit of the American Cancer Society—local history
88. Caves of Maury County listing
89. *Centennial Celebration—A Historical Sketch of Maury County*, July 4, 1876, by W. S. Fleming
90. Chamber of Commerce brochure
91. Clean Community—history, flyer, brochure
92. *Churches of Maury County* by Tenassee DAR and Nell Woodard

93. Columbia State Community College—course offerings, the Emeritus Program
94. Cosmopolitan Club—history, project
95. Duck River Orchards brochure
96. Education Resource Guide
97. *Look Who's Cooking What* cookbook
98. "Exploring Maury County Through 3rd Grade Eyes" brochure
99. The *Daily Herald*, January 28, 1996, Fact Guide 1996 of Maury County
100. Maury County Family and Community Education—history
101. 1995 yearbook of Maury County FCE
102. Activities for Maury County—FCE
103. Maury County Girl Scout Association—history, sticker
104. Henry Horton State Park brochure
105. Health Services in Maury County booklet and Hospice brochure
106. "Bed & breakfast of Historic Maury County," and "Locust Hill and Oak Springs Inn & Gallery" brochures
107. Maury County Historic Benefit Ball—history
108. Historic Maury County, Antebellum Homes Capital of Tennessee—site descriptions and brochure
109. Maury County Historical Society—membership, officers, Preservation Park plaque
110. Maury County Kennel Club flyer
111. Mule Day 1996 brochure
112. Mule Day 1995—the *Daily Herald*, March 29, 1995
113. Monsanto Ponds brochure
114. Natchez Trace Corridor visitor service guide
115. October 1995 Maury County phone book
116. "Presidential Pathways," handout
117. James K. Polk Ancestral Home and association—history
118. Rose Society of Maury County—history
119. Southern Steam booklet
120. Tombigbee Chapter, Sons of the American revolution—history, officers, membership
121. United Daughters of the Confederacy, Captain James Madison Sparkman Chapter—handbook, history
122. United Way of Maury County, Inc.—history
123. Vietnam Veterans Chapter 128—history
124. "Visions"—1994 and 1996
125. Maury County wood craftsmen "Past and Present" brochure
126. Mule Day T-shirt, pin, belt buckle
127. Sterling Marlin coin

128. James K. Polk postage stamp and program
129. 175th Anniversary coin of the City of Columbia
130. Civil War Reenactment program
131. Walking Tour program
132. Information for the Bicentennial brick program
133. Historic Downtown program
134. Majestic Middle Tennessee tour program and book
135. *Hither and Yon, Vol. I & II* by Jill Garrett
136. History of phosphate industry in Maury County
137. History of the Saturn Corporation
138. Maury County flag
139. Letter from County Executive Ed Harlan
140. Maury County brochure
141. Tennessee 200 pin
142. Columbia Main Street Corporation annual report
143. Three Pewter ornaments
144. *Maury County Remembers World War II*, Part One and Part Two, by Maury County Historical Society
145. Drawing of Spring Hill

MCMINN

1. Letter from Bicentennial Committee Chairman Steve Holt
2. McMinn County fact sheet
3. *McMinn County Pictorial History*
4. Brochures of county attractions
5. Bible
6. Map of McMinn County
7. High School annual
8. FYI guide to McMinn County
9. List of industries in McMinn County
10. McMinn County phone book
11. Mayfield Plastic jug and pieces
12. *Then and Now . . .*
13. Map of Tennessee Overhill
14. Photographs
15. Church listing
16. Socks
17. Guide booklet for the county
18. Narrative of DPA newspaper
19. TWC letter
20. Middle-East Tennessee Fair information
21. Bowater paper
22. Local hospital information
23. Interior Views calendar
24. "My Commitment to America"—speech by Brett Benson Allmon; biography
25. 1959 General Journal

MCNAIRY

1. Letters and essays from Talented Academic Creative Students from all McNairy County schools
2. Silver belt buckle, sheriff's badge, autograph from Buford Pusser—from Buford Pusser Museum
3. Photographs and history of Buford Pusser
4. McNairy County map
5. McNairy County service directory
6. News clippings of Bicentennial activities

MEIGS

1. County museum birdhouse replica
2. Student essays
3. Letter from the county executive
4. *Bob Tales from Howard Holler*
5. Community data
6. County brochures
7. Shaw Industries brochure
8. County map
9. Newspaper articles
10. County pictures
11. School brochure
12. Senior Citizens brochure
13. Historical Society brochure
14. Property deeds
15. County court, commission, and trustee records

MONROE

1. Letter from Bicentennial Committee
2. *Pictorial History of Monroe County, Tennessee*
3. Photographs
4. Coker Creek Gold
5. Slide of Bald River Falls
6. Cherokee pottery fragment
7. Musket ball from Fort Loudon
8. Origami crane and silk scarf
9. Letter from the mayor of Sweetwater
10. Letters from school children
11. Brochures
12. Monroe County Industrial Directory
13. 1994 Monroe County financial statement

MONTGOMERY

1. List and photograph of county commissioners
2. Letter from Robert E. Thompson, county executive

3. Industrial list—products and employees
4. Brochures for the Academy for Academic Excellence
5. Photographs of three children from the Academy for Academic Excellence
6. Time capsule thoughts from the Academy for Academic Excellence
7. Letter from the Clarksville Montgomery County Public Library
8. Clarksville Montgomery County Public Library 1995 employee and board of trustees list
9. News articles about the library's renovation
10. *History of Clarksville Montgomery County Public Library* by Timothy W. Pulley
11. Letter from the Clarksville-Montgomery County Museum
12. Photograph of the Clarksville-Montgomery County Museum renovations
13. *Historical Clarksville—The Bicentennial Story 1784–1984* by Charles M. Waters
14. Letter from Clarksville-Montgomery Seniors Association
15. Photograph of Ms. Senior Clarksville
16. Ad donating a minivan
17. Article regarding Senior Games
18. History of the United States Army, Fifth Special Forces Group, Fort Campbell, Kentucky
19. Coins from the 101st Airborne Division "Air Assault"
20. Coins from the Fifth Special Forces Group Airborne
21. Coins from the 160th Special Operation Aviation Regiment
22. Letter and photograph from Mayor Don Trotter
23. Photograph of city council
24. *Worship Along the Warioto* by Eleanor S. Williams
25. Letter from Austin Peay University president
26. Fact booklet from Austin Peay University
27. 1995–1997 undergraduate bulletin from Austin Peay University
28. The *Alumnus* magazine from Austin Peay University
29. "Monday's Memo" from Austin Peay University
30. Men's and women's basketball media guide 1995–1996, Austin Peay University
31. Letter from Clarksville Area Chamber of Commerce director

32. Economic Development Council brochure
33. Clarksville Area Chamber of Commerce 1995 map
34. *A Child's History of Clarksville and Montgomery County, Tennessee* by Eleanor S. Williams
35. *Cabins to Castles* by Eleanor S. Williams
36. *Nineteenth Century Heritage Clarksville, Tennessee* by Eleanor S. Williams
37. *Homes and Happenings* by Eleanor S. Williams
38. Letter from Main Street Clarksville, Inc., director Paula Thacker
39. Packet from Main Street Clarksville, Inc., including newsletter, downtown directory, ruler, postcards
40. *Clarksville, Tennessee, Magazine*, 1995
41. Letter from Clarksville-Montgomery county school, David Baker, director of schools
42. Brochure on the "A+—An Award-Winning Educational System"
43. Letter, list, and photograph from the Montgomery County Bicentennial Committee
44. Photograph of the Bicentennial Committee on Volunteer 200 Day, June 1, 1995
45. Photograph of the Montgomery County quilter's
46. Newspaper article regarding the progress of the local Tennessee 200 committee
47. Photograph of the Clarksville Train Station, Montgomery County's Bicentennial project
48. Volunteer 200 Day program
49. Scraper used on the Clarksville Train Station on Volunteer 200 Day
50. Original brick from the Clarksville Train Station's chimney

MOORE

1. Jack Daniel's Beer bottle
2. Bicentennial commemorative Jack Daniel's bottle
3. Information on the Farris Creek lodge #509
4. State of Tennessee land surveyor license for Joseph E. Hope
5. Various business cards and pictures
6. Various church membership books and information
7. University of Tennessee information on cattle
8. Lynchburg information packet

9. Various essays and pictures by local school children
10. Menus from local restaurants
11. Motlow State College information
12. Historical prints of various local sites
13. Farmers Bank calendar, 1996
14. Jack Daniel Country cookbooks
15. Area phone books

MORGAN

1. Picture negatives
2. Obed map
3. Frozen Head State Park map
4. Newspapers
5. Deer Lodge materials
6. *Centennial Book 1884–1984*, Deer Lodge
7. Various county school rosters
8. Examples of weavings from Tennford Weaving Company
9. Rugby brochure
10. County pictures
11. Brushy Mountain State Penitentiary
12. Coalfield letter
13. Family history
14. Letter from county officials
15. Letter from senior citizen
16. Genealogical Society information
17. Historical Society information
18. Sunbright High School football and T-shirt

OBION

1. 277 color slides depicting life in Obion County
2. Goodyear miniature tire
3. Goodyear newsletter
4. Women's shorts from Gurien Finishing Company
5. Bicentennial afghan
6. Models of farm equipment—tractor, cotton picker, grain drill, mulch tiller
7. Pewter medallion of Obion County Courthouse
8. Derringer, 44 cal., made for Dixie Gun Works in Italy
9. Dixie Gun Works pin
10. Coca-Cola bottle, mid-twentieth century
11. 1990 aerial view of Union City
12. *A Concise History of Obion County* by Rebel C. Forrester
13. Letter from County Executive Norris Cranford

14. Letter from Union City mayor, Terry Hailey
15. Letter from county school superintendent, Vinson Thompson
16. Letter from the executive director of the Obion County Industrial Development Corporation
17. *Obion County Pictorial History* by Threlkeld
18. *Obion County Family History, Volume I & II*
19. *Glory and Tears* by Forrester
20. *Now Let's Go Back* by Dietzel
21. *I Had A Real Good Time* by Brice
22. *Obion County Cemetery Records, Volume I & II*
23. *Writer's Ink*, 1995 annual collection
24. *Dixie Gun Works Car Museum*
25. Cookbook—*Obion County Recipes*, 1995, Bicentennial Committee
26. 1996 calendar by the Obion County Bicentennial Committee
27. Obion County Data booklet
28. Map of Obion County and principal towns
29. Reelfoot Lake information
30. *Union City Daily Messenger*, November 29, 1995, and January 1, 1996
31. Sabin Photoshow brochure
32. Turnpike Levee Green brochure
33. Obion County School system brochure
34. Union City School System brochure
35. Obion County Museum brochure
36. Dixie Gun Works brochure
37. Ken-Tenn Youth Orchestra brochure
38. Masquerade Theater brochure
39. Tennessee State Parks brochure
40. Letters from Cultural Groups and Activities in Obion County
41. Letter from the Obion County Chamber of Commerce directors
42. Drawing of the Obion County Courthouse
43. Card advertising Robin Wood's sled for truckpull
44. Telephone book
45. WENK AM Radio mug
46. Cotton boll
47. Recycling bag

OVERTON

1. Livingston regional hospital brochure
2. Livingston phone book
3. Overton annual
4. Overton County School System brochure
5. Ticket for a Rotary Club benefit
6. Tourism brochure for Livingston

7. Allons Elementary School basketball schedule
8. Family Center brochure
9. Rotary Club meeting minutes
10. The Cuddle Club brochure
11. Church bulletin
12. Academy brochure
13. *Livingston Enterprise*, November 8, 1995
14. *Overton County News*, October 18 and November 8, 1995
15. Overton County School directory, November 15, 1995

PERRY

1. Sculpture and letter by Ellen McGowan
2. *Perry County Family History*
3. South Central Tennessee Development District information
4. Data profile of Perry County
5. Mr. Elbert T. Marvin's 100th birthday
6. *Buffalo River Review*, stories and picture
7. History and picture of the Perry County flag
8. History of Perry County basketball
9. Perry County Bicentennial T-shirt
10. Weaving by Nancy Longfield
11. Letter from Robert McGowan

PICKETT

1. Bobcats State Champs basketball
2. Dale Hollow Lake T-shirt
3. "Reflections of the Past" postcard
4. Holly Creek Resort brochure
5. Dale Hollow postcard
6. Byrdstown tourism brochure
7. Sunset Marina and Resort brochure
8. Byrdstown Community data sheet
9. Cordell Hull birthplace postcard
10. Historic Byrdstown brochure
11. Pickett County business directory

POLK

1. Area telephone directory
2. *The Old Homeplace*
3. First issue of the Polk County Historical and Genealogical Society Quarterly
4. Polk County High School annual
5. Benton Elementary School annual
6. South Polk High School annual
7. Ocoee River Whitewater Olympics Package
8. Copper Basin package (postcards, Ducktown museum calendar)

9. Churches in Action Association report
10. Letter from students
11. Tennessee community report
12. Slides of county scenes
13. U.S. Mint proof set
14. 125th edition of *Polk County News*
15. "Tennessee and the Olympics" video
16. Ocoee Kayakers jersey
17. Letter from County Executive Firestone

PUTNAM

1. Civic clubs directory
2. Putnam County data sheet
3. Chamber of Commerce board of directors list
4. Teledyne stillman brochure
5. *Homeland of Cookeville* magazine
6. Metcam Mic brochure
7. Fibercal information
8. *Where To Retire* magazine
9. Tennessee Technology University folder with various information
10. *Industry Week* magazine
11. Suburban Tool Company brochure
12. Letters to industry leaders for Chamber of Commerce
13. Adams Industry catalog
14. Letter to industry leaders with Dixie Dock
15. Letter to industry leaders with Baron industry information
16. Information from Norwalk Woods Products, Inc.
17. Image Technology, Inc., brochure
18. Picture of Preferred Pallets employees
19. *Tennessee Treasures* cookbook for Putnam County
20. Local Bicentennial Committee information and picture
21. 1995 Cookeville phone book
22. Burgess Falls brochure
23. Center Hill Lake map
24. Putnam County School brochure
25. Tennessee Technology University catalog and marketing brochure
26. Center for Manufacturing Research/ Tennessee Technology Institute information
27. *Cookeville's Finest* magazine
28. Totco Applied Heating brochure
29. Letter for Aquatech, Inc., and pictures
30. The Duriron Company brochure and letter
31. Snow Flare Corn Stove, Inc., information
32. Monterey brochure
33. Chamber of Commerce newsletter

34. Leasing information for the county
35. Chamber of Commerce magazine
36. Putnam County brochure
37. Algood brochure
38. Tourism brochure
39. Cookeville/Putnam County map
40. "Bill Bilyeu for Sheriff" card with written review of his career
41. Letters from citizens
42. Picture of the Pyle family
43. Newspaper article requesting time capsule artifacts

RHEA

1. List of the Rhea County Bicentennial Committee
2. County facts and pictures
3. Huben Industries information
4. The *Herald News*, December 31, 1995
5. Dayton Garden Club, 1995–1996 listing
6. Materials from the county executive
7. Pictures of areas in Rhea County
8. *The Source, Rhea County's Guide Book*
9. Rhea Tool and Dye Company information
10. County maps
11. Scopes Trial information
12. Eagle Scout information
13. June Griffin information
14. The Citizens for Decency on Taxation
15. Bryan College catalog
16. Kiwanis Club information
17. Spring City Elementary School annual
18. County History book
19. Church-school book
20. Lazyboy pen
21. Depot tile
22. Frazier Elementary School annual
23. Rhea County High School annual
24. Curly Fox's harmonica and picture
25. Third grader's rendition of Watts Bar Dam
26. Dayton Centennial Celebration
27. Pictures from Grayville School

ROANE

1. *Roane County News*, February 27 and 28 1995
2. Collection of pictures
3. Brass key to Harriman
4. Brochures
5. Carbon fiber sample
6. Pictures, information, product samples, video profiles from Oak Ridge Nail Lab
7. *Two Years of Harriman Tennessee*

8. *Souvenir Edition—One Year of Harriman Tennessee*
9. Picture of the Roane County Bicentennial Committee
10. Stained glass iris
11. Roane County flag
12. City of Kingston banner
13. Roane County map
14. Foreign language Bible
15. Holy Bible
16. Self-guided tours of pre-Civil War
17. Video recording of Roane County on compact disc
18. Essay by Jamee L. Casteel
19. Roane County press kit
20. Harriman 1995 and 1996 calendar
21. Roane County phone book May 1995
22. Roane Choral Society letter, picture, program

ROBERTSON

1. Letter from County Executive Roy Apple
2. Copy of courthouse note card with a note from the Time Capsule Committee
3. County and city maps
4. Twist of tobacco from the World's Finest Dark Fired Tobacco Market
5. Springfield souvenir pewter spoon
6. Booklet compiled by election commission office
7. County operating budget for the fiscal year ending June 30, 1996
8. Map of school districts with current student distribution
9. Picture and list for the Robertson County Bicentennial Committee
10. List of Robertson County Bicentennial events
11. News releases regarding Bicentennial events
12. Script of theater play *Making Hands* by Mark Edens
13. Three essays by elementary school students
14. T-shirt featuring the courthouse clock
15. *Robertson County Fact Book—Bicentennial Edition*
16. Community data sheet
17. *Our Community*
18. City of Springfield Social and Economic Indicators
19. June 1995 telephone book
20. Invitation to Robertson County Family YMCA Groundbreaking, June 29, 1995, and souvenir

21. Souvenir pin from the July 1995 Tennessee-Kentucky Theshermen Show
22. Medal commemorating the 150th anniversary of Austin and Bell Funeral Home
23. *Robertson County Times*, January 10, 1996
24. *Bargain Browser*, January 2, 1996
25. Magazine celebrating opening of North Crest Medical Center
26. *Robertson County Distilleries* pamphlet
27. *Robertson County's Heritage of Homes*
28. *The Bell Witch of Tennessee* by Charles Bailey Bell
29. *Robertson County Historical Society Cookbook*
30. Robertson County commemorative afghan

RUTHERFORD

1. Middle Tennessee State University music department brochure
2. *MTSU* magazine
3. MTSU fact card
4. Miller Trust Fund material
5. MTSU graduation program, December 1995
6. MTSU various articles
7. MTSU Graduate Catalog, 1995–1997
8. MTSU bulletin from the Office of Information Technology
9. MTSU undergraduate catalog
10. MTSU bulletin about Teacher Education Programs
11. MTSU Graduate Student Handbook
12. Picture of the Murfreesboro mayor and city council
13. County information mat
14. County resource and site guide
15. County executive and commissioners list
16. Purchasing committee meeting minutes
17. 1995 Rutherford County budget
18. County phone book
19. *Heart of Tennessee* by Terry Weeks
20. *Rutherford County Magazine*
21. Brochure for Bicentennial brick program
22. Brochure on purchase of official coins
23. Bicentennial coin
24. Various articles from the *Daily News Journal*
25. Program from the Tennessee State Championship Horse Show, Tennessee Walking Horses
26. Brochures featuring Rutherford County horses
27. Pictures of stallions in Rutherford County
28. Menus from the City Cafe
29. Southeast Baptist Church bulletin

30. Opening program for the Center for the Arts
31. Nissan—slides, brochures, Job I truck from 1983
32. Postcard and brochure from the Sam Davis Home in Smyrna
33. Map of LaVergne
34. LaVergne Church of Christ bulletin
35. January 1996 meeting minutes from a public hearing in LaVergne
36. Item from Eagleville city council
37. Item from Eagleville mayor
38. Eagleville churches listing
39. Eagleville business cards
40. Item from Eagleville colonial home
41. Rutherford Agricultural Co-op annual report
42. Seales Funeral Home article
43. "Rutherford County Tennessee Teachers in Hall of Fame," article
44. "Gordon celebrates 35 years as pastor of First Baptist Church," article
45. "Allen Chapel Church listed on National Register of Historic Places," article
46. "Hancock, World War II Veteran," article
47. "OHS outfielder Joe McHenry signs with Minnesota twins," article
48. State Farm Insurance Company key chain and memorabilia
49. "Preservation of Bradley Academy," article
50. Article about James D. "Red" Berry, World War II veteran
51. Wooden token for Smyrna, eighty years
52. County commission meeting
53. Inspection report for December 1995
54. Rutherford County budget, July 1995–June 30, 1996
55. Tennessee Valley Pioneer Power Tractor Club information
56. Essays from 7th graders
57. Postal rates and fees
58. LaVergne phone book, January 1995
59. TDS Telecom—phone rates, employee list
60. Articles about library, *Nashville Banner*, December 7, 1994, and the *Rutherford County Tennessean*, August 19,1992
61. Cookbook—LaVergne Public Library
62. LaVergne Public Library statistics
63. LaVergne High School press kit
64. 1995 yearbook for Roy L. Waldron School
65. Sports jersey from Roy L. Waldron School
66. Student handbook from Roy L. Waldron School
67. LaVergne Primary School—certificate of accreditation
68. LaVergne Primary School—picture of the Cook Travel Indians, the *Rutherford Courier*, July 7, 1994
69. Various newspaper articles regarding LaVergne Primary School
70. Story by Dallas Dwenger
71. Drawings by Miss Wilcox's class
72. Drawings by Mrs. Davis's class
73. Original concept drawing by Kem Hinton of the Tennessee Bicentennial Capitol Mall

SCOTT

1. Oneida High School material
2. Newspaper clippings
3. H. T. Hackney packet
4. 21st Century Schools information
5. Scott County registered voters list
6. Picture of Almeda Strunk
7. Picture of Haylee Moody
8. Picture of James Rondal Moody III
9. Picture of James, Vanessa, and Haylee Moody
10. Letter from Almeda Strunk
11. Wedding and shower invitation for Vanessa M. Strunk
12. Certificate of birth for Almeda Louise Strunk
13. Certificate of birth for Roger Lecil Strunk
14. Certificate of birth for Vanessa Michelle Strunk
15. Roger Lecil Strunk DD214
16. *Tennessee Technology Center*
17. Christmas Parade history
18. Oneida High School pictures
19. Hotel/Motel Restaurant Guide
20. Scott County Fair Association directors listing
21. Scott County churches listing
22. Industrial Directory for Scott County
23. Listing of directors of Scott County Chamber of Commerce
24. List of Scott County Bicentennial Committee
25. List of Industrial Development Board of Directors
26. Newspaper article—"Adventure Awaits Big South Fork"
27. Newspaper article regarding the Tennessee 200 grant
28. Newspaper article—"Tourism Week Proclaimed"
29. 1995 winners of Fairest of Fair listing
30. Chamber raises $12,000 article
31. County flag contest winner
32. Item from BSFRA officers
33. Bicentennial art
34. Big South Fork brochure
35. Flooring from Hartco Flooring company
36. Two letters from Howard H. Baker Jr.
37. Item from Senator Howard H. Baker
38. Newspaper article—"Enterprise Community 8.2 million"
39. Scott County brochure
40. Pictures of the Memorial Wall
41. "Tricentennial"—a poem by Hattie Bushman
42. A writing about Scott County—by Hattie Bushman
43. Picture of New Oneida High/Middle School
44. Picture of 1992 football champs—Oneida High School
45. Letter from Betty C. Cecil
46. Tabloid of Oneida High School
47. Courthouse print #100
48. Listing of Scott County Election Commission
49. *Independent Herald*, June 17, 1976

SEQUATCHIE

1. Sequatchie Valley postcard
2. Article on Dunlap land for local park, *Chattanooga Free Press*, May 15, 1995
3. Remembrances of Sequatchie Valley, four drawings by Carson Camp
4. The Cupola bulletin
5. Flyer of "Coke Ovens," a local bluegrass festival
6. *Running Water Historical News*, Vol. 1, No. 11, June 1995
7. The *Dunlap Tribune* one hundredth anniversary issue, 1989
8. Griffith Elementary yearbook 1995
9. Sequatchie Valley Historical Association announcements
10. Ewtonville Baptist Church bulletin
11. Dunlap United Methodist Church directory
12. Dunlap United Methodist Church bulletin
13. Dunlap United Methodist Church brochure
14. Dunlap United Methodist Church postcard
15. First Baptist Church 1994 calendar
16. Sequatchie County High School annual 1995
17. Tennessee Association for Family and Community Education 1996 yearbook
18. Sequatchie County Middle School yearbook 1995

19. Dunlap Church of God bulletin
20. First Baptist Church bulletin
21. First Baptist Church directory
22. 1995 Valley Garden Club directory
23. Citizen's Tri-County Bank stationery, card, passbook, and brochure
24. 1996 tax form
25. Bledsoe Telephone Cooperative phone book, October 1995
26. Map of Dunlap
27. Community data sheet
28. Recycle bag
29. Coloring book
30. Sequatchie County Bank passbook, account slip, data sheet, and 1995 calendar
31. Two pencils
32. Three pens
33. Key to the city of Dunlap
34. Citizens Tri-County Bank 1996 calendar
35. Adult Basis Education brochure
36. Sequatchie County Public Library brochure
37. Dunlap Coke Ovens Park brochure
38. The *Dunlap Tribune*, March 7, 1996

SEVIER

1. Letter from Sevier County Executive Larry Waters
2. Sevier County Courthouse ornament
3. *Sevier County, Tennessee and Its Heritage*
4. The *Mountain Press*, "Progress: Recollection," Sunday Edition, February 26, 1995
5. *Tennessee Star Journal*, December 29, 1995–January 5, 1996
6. Smoky Mountain Historical Society Journals
7. "Pittman Community Center, A Mountain Mission," by the Pittman Community Center Alumni Association
8. *Memories of a Country Esquire* by Conley Huskey
9. Letter from Gatlinburg Mayor Fred McMahan and City Manager Cindy Ogle
10. List of Gatlinburg city officials, 1996
11. "Gatlinburg Vacation Guide 1996"
12. "Wish You Were Here" cassette tape, Gary Chapman
13. Photographs of people and places in Gatlinburg
14. Proclamation from Chuck Bradley, mayor of Gatlinburg, 1995
15. Gatlinburg logo pin
16. Gatlinburg Chamber of Commerce logo pin

17. Gatlinburg Fiftieth Anniversary pin
18. Commemorative goblet from Gatlinburg's Fiftieth Anniversary
19. Books about the Great Smoky Mountains National Park, *Exploring the Smokies, The Black Bear, Naturalists' Guide to the Smokies*
20. Pigeon Forge information packet
21. *Reunion at the River, Official History of Pigeon Forge, Tennessee, 1783–1930*
22. Dolly Parton cassette tape, "Something Special," and autographed photograph
23. Black bear made at Pigeon Forge Pottery
24. Bag of corn meal from the Old Mill in colorful tin
25. Letter from the mayor of Sevierville, Bryan Atchley
26. Sevierville Visitors Guide 1996
27. 1995 Sevierville Community Guide from the Chamber of Commerce
28. Sevierville "Then and Now," Bicentennial calendar
29. Sevierville Bicentennial coin, logo pin, and postcard
30. The New Cherokee Corporation, textile samples
31. Sevierville Downtown Association flyer
32. Sevier County Heritage Museum grand opening brochure and picture
33. *The Story of Kodak, Tennessee,* by Freda O'Dell Hodges
34. Henry's Cross Roads Methodist Church coffee mug
35. Selected articles from the Kodak Cookbook
36. Postal slip
37. Note from Seymour postmistress, Brenda Kirby
38. *Tri-County News,* March 14, 1995, regarding the opening of the new Seymour Post Office
39. *Tri-County News,* January 9, 1996
40. New Testament Bible
41. Letter from Superintendent of Schools Jack Parton
42. Letter from Patsy Bradford, Tennessee 200 coordinator, with photographs, quilt square, and cookbook

SHELBY

1. Germantown Area Chamber of Commerce booklet
2. Germantown Performing Arts Center information

3. Germantown 150th commemorative brass coin
4. Germantown Symphony Orchestra booklet
5. City of Germantown 1996 calendar
6. Millington International Goat Days frisbee, button, cap
7. Collierville Town flag with explanation
8. Edward F. Williams III business card
9. Program for Swearing In Ceremony for W. W. Herenton
10. Houston Middle School essays and letter from teacher, Shirley Bryant
11. Badge for County Mayor James Rout
12. Germantown Community Theater, 1995–1996 season
13. Germantown Area Business Location map
14. *A Brief Historical Survey of Germantown, Tennessee*, compiled by Dr. J. Miller Darnell
15. City of Germantown gold key pin
16. Pictures of Bicentennial teams—Memphis and Shelby County Bicentennial Commission, Bicentennial volunteers, Tennessee 200, Volunteer 200
17. Firefighters of Tennessee brochure
18. "Through the Years"—Bicentennial calendar
19. Volunteer 200—project event summaries
20. Restoration of the Memphis wharf, Tennessee Bicentennial 1796–1996 project overview
21. The "Main Street Trolley" issue of *Downtowner Magazine*, Vol. 3, No. 4, May 1993
22. The Memphis Main Street Trolley Renovation Project information sheet concerning fund-raising efforts
23. Proclamation by Mayor Herenton, marking the start of the Main Street Trolley Company Project
24. Commemorative gold coins for the Memphis Main Street Trolley Company, 1992–1993
25. Commemorative $25 Memphis Main Street Trolley Company stock certificate
26. St. Jude's Children's Research Hospital commemorative silver spoon
27. St. Jude's Children's Research Hospital fact folder and fact sheet
28. St. Jude's Children's Research Hospital paperweight commemorating the ALSAC Thirty-seventh National Convention, Patient Care Center Dedication, October 7, 1994

29. The University of Tennessee, Memphis, prospectus
30. The *Record* newsletter from the University of Tennessee at Memphis, for the Health Science Center
31. The South Central Bell white pages cover page featuring the University of Tennessee at Memphis
32. Paper on Development of Sickle Cell Center in Memphis signed by Alfred P. Kraus, M.D.
33. Promotional folder from the Pyramid in Memphis
34. The Peabody Hotel—"The Legend of the Ducks"
35. Duck feather from the Peabody Hotel
36. Peabody Hotel brochure
37. History of the First Presbyterian Church
38. Audio tape—"A Slice of Southern Music"
39. Beale Street postcard
40. Memphis Music and Heritage Festival 1995 information
41. Map of downtown Memphis and pictures
42. Media coverage about the Center for Southern Folklore
43. Poster from the Center for Southern Folklore
44. Guide to Memphis Music and Heritage Festival, July 1995
45. Collection on Memphis Cultural History
46. Elvis Presley compact disc set of two— "The Top 10 Hits"
47. Elvis Presley commemorative stamp on envelope
48. "Official Guidebook" to Graceland, home of Elvis Presley
49. Opera Memphis—score for opera *Different Fields*
50. Booklet—"Celebrating 40 Sensational Years With 5 Sensational Shows," with letter from Ching about *Different Fields*
51. Flyer—"The Best of Memphis," January 25–31
52. *Downtowner Magazine*, "Two Mayors, One Vision," January 1996
53. *Memphis Magazine*, "Best and Worst of Memphis," December 1995–January 1996
54. Menu from Corky's Ribs and BBQ
55. Menu from BB King's Blues Club
56. Menu from Rendevous
57. Collard greens seeds
58. Ferry morse seeds
59. Tennessee Sunshine Hot Pepper Sauce
60. Rendevous paper hat worn by chefs and servers

61. *Mr. Crump of Memphis* by William D. Miller
62. FedEx box

SMITH

1. Picture of Al Gore
2. *Smith County History*
3. Christmas ornament
4. Block with Chamber of Commerce banquet invitation on it
5. Chamber of Commerce sign
6. First Bridge picture copy
7. Hospital invoice for a baby
8. Article on Fred Vantrease
9. World War II veterans from Smith County, list and pictures
10. Tobacco products from Smith County
11. Smith County commissioner meeting minutes
12. Smith County calendar
13. Newspaper article on the riverboat cruise
14. Smith County blanket
15. Item from 1920s Gordonsville High School student
16. Smith County Courthouse pictures
17. Dixona brochure
18. Newspaper article on Oldham's Drugstore
19. Gordonsville Academy picture
20. Newspaper article about a bridge
21. Smith County program for the time capsule collection event
22. Smith County brochures
23. Memorial brochure
24. Smith County phone book
25. Picture of the Smith County flag
26. Bicentennial print brochure
27. Picture of Sharon Wyatt
28. Wages for Middle Tennessee
29. Mini ball from the Civil War
30. Women's club picture
31. Memorial Hospital folder
32. History of Chestnut Mound
33. Early picture of Carthage
34. Elementary School records
35. Quilted flags—Tennessee flag and Smith County Bicentennial flag
36. Cap from the tobacco warehouse
37. *A Dash of Hope and Care Cookbook*
38. Landcaster family history
39. Vice President coffee mug
40. NADA trade-in guide
41. *Carthage United Methodist Church Cookbook*
42. Two team flags for Smith County
43. Letter and picture of William Young Jr.
44. Truck brochure

STEWART

1. Essays from students—Dover Elementary School and North Stewart Elementary School
2. Newspaper articles
3. Scenes from Cumberland City
4. Scenes from Indian Mound
5. Scenes from Bumpus Mills
6. Scenes from Big Rock
7. Scenes from Dover
8. Photograph of Cumberland Fossil plant
9. Photograph of Cumberland Ferry
10. Photograph of Stewart County War Memorial
11. Scenes from Fort Donelson National Battlefield
12. Photographs of the Surrender House and Rice House, historical houses
13. Photograph from 1870 of the Stewart County Courthouse
14. Photograph from 1995 of the courthouse
15. Photograph of Stewart County schools
16. Photograph of Cumberland City councilmen and mayor
17. Photograph of Dover councilmen and mayor
18. Photograph of Stewart County Tennessee 200 Committee: Carlon Sills, Rick Joiner, Rebecca Byrd, Bryan Watson, Jimmy Scurlock, Jim Myers
19. Bicentennial flag
20. Various county photographs

SULLIVAN

1. Historic sites of Sullivan County—Bristol, Kingsport, Blountville
2. 1995–1996 senior class picture and class roster of Sullivan East patriots, Sullivan Central Cougars, Tennessee High Vikings, Dobyns Bennett Indians, Northeast State Technical Community College, Kingsport Design School
3. Information from Holston Valley Medical Center and the Bristol Regional Medical Center
4. Information from Sullivan County industries: AFG, Quebecor, Raytheon, General Shale, Eastman Chemical, Kingsport Power, Meade
5. Entertainment materials: Troublesome Hollow Band, Bristol International Raceway, First Night, Fun-Fest, Bristol Birthplace of Music Radio

6. Information from the Sullivan County airport
7. Information from car dealerships: Oldsmobile, Ford, Isuzu, Chevrolet
8. Fashions—J.C. Penney, Sears
9. Food—Skoby's Restaurant, Pals, Market Basket, Food City, White's, Kroger, Oakwood
10. *Home Magazine*-listings of Tri-cities
11. Tri City Bank—information about checking, savings, and certificates of deposit
12. Farm Bureau Life Insurance proposal
13. Stamps
14. City of Kingsport annual report
15. Sullivan County budget report
16. City of Bristol mayors
17. Kingsport guide
18. Sullivan County calendar of events
19. Kingsport directory
20. Meadow Conference Center information
21. Brass medallion of Bristol
22. Bristol newcomer guide
23. Guide of data
24. "Kingsport Tomorrow" annual report
25. Kingsport downtown report
26. Healthy Means Drug Free information
27. Kingsport Bicentennial events listing
28. Tennessee 200 license plate
29. Newspaper articles
30. Hat
31. Mug
32. Key chains

SUMNER

1. Tourism brochures and history of tourism promotion efforts
2. County map
3. Gallatin Chamber of Commerce executive director business card
4. Kroger advertisement showing 1996 food prices
5. The *News Examiner*, January 3 and 15, 1996
6. Christmas 1995 Open House and Trolley Stops sheet and pictures
7. Article in American Association of Retired Persons newsletter concerning problems facing the aged and terminally ill patients
8. List of people whose letters to the editor of the *News Examiner* were printed in 1995
9. Daughters of the American Revolution 1995 yearbook and "Good Citizenship" essay award winner listing

10. Article on the twelfth annual Main Street Festival
11. *History of Civil District #1* by Betty Chenault, 1906
12. Pictures of Gallatin Senior Citizen activities
13. Pictures of the 1995 Main Street Festival
14. Pictures of the presentation of the Sumner County Bicentennial flag
15. World Day of Prayer program
16. Sumner County board of education information
17. Main Street Festival T-shirt
18. Program for the First Methodist Church production of *Godspell*
19. Pictures and a bookmark from the Sumner County Library
20. Patches from the Gallatin Fire and Police Departments
21. Sample of burley tobacco and a history of the RC Owen Tobacco Company
22. Items from the Sumner Regional Medical Center
23. Letter from the Gallatin Ministerial Association
24. Church bulletins and directories from local churches
25. Gallatin Chamber of Commerce newsletter, membership card, and "Get It Here" shop at home campaign information
26. Articles about Gallatin events
27. Sumner County agriculture statistics data sheet
28. "I Love Gallatin" button
29. Autographed picture of local singing group, Smokey and the Impossibles
30. Gallatin Industrial Center information sheet
31. Gallatin Chamber of Commerce brochure and business directory
32. Gallatin High School cap
33. Volunteer State Community College information booklet
34. Leadership Sumner brochure
35. Regional Air Show program, October 21, 1995
36. 1996 Community Events Calendar for Goodlettsville
37. Hendersonville Vision 2000 long-range plan and window decal
38. Hendersonville design review manual
39. Hendersonville Chamber of Commerce business directory, key chain, and pin
40. Bradford-Berry House Quilt Show booklet

41. "I Love Hendersonville" bumper sticker
42. Industrial recruitment packet
43. Patches from the Hendersonville Fire and Police Departments, Leisure Services, and ASA
44. Hendersonville postcard
45. Hendersonville Community Development pin
46. Hendersonville basketball pin
47. Hendersonville city charter
48. Tennessee Bicentennial Week proclamation
49. Hendersonville Long Range Planning Ordinance
50. Letter from the mayor of Hendersonville, Hank Thompson
51. Hendersonville newcomer's packet
52. Hendersonville Parks Department cap
53. Hendersonville-Worth Softball Classic T-shirt and parking permit
54. 1995 Hendersonville Twenty-fifth Anniversary T-shirt
55. Proclamation making Tsuru, Japan, Hendersonville's sister city
56. Hendersonville paperweight
57. Hendersonville Bicentennial calendar
58. Hendersonville parks information
59. Hendersonville school information
60. History of the Hendersonville Chamber of Commerce
61. Hendersonville flag
62. Conway Twitty Softball Classic tag
63. "Progress in '95," newspaper article on Portland
64. City of Portland information booklet
65. Portland data sheets
66. 1995 Portland Chamber of Commerce banquet program, brochure, and newsletters
67. Portland City Parks and Recreation booklet
68. Leadership Sumner brochure
69. 1995 guide to Portland
70. Cartoon map of Portland
71. Packet from Clyde Riggs Elementary School—pictures, newspaper clippings, 1878 map of Fountain Head
72. Bicentennial calendar
73. Sumner County Bicentennial button
74. Tennessee 200 merchandise price list
75. *News Examiner*, February 1, 1995, article about Miss Ellen Wemyss
76. Pictures of the Summer County Bicentennial Committee Co-chairs Randy Cline and Tracy Carman with U.S. Postmaster General Marvin Runyon

77. Pictures of Sumner County Bicentennial Committee
78. Brief history of Westmoreland
79. Newspaper clippings showing city and Chamber of Commerce events in Westmoreland
80. Article highlighting life of statesman Mayo Wix
81. *Westmoreland Journal*, January 11, 1996
82. Westmoreland Chamber of Commerce newsletters and program of 1995 banquet
83. Westmoreland map
84. Letter from Ned McWherter to the Westmoreland Chamber of Commerce
85. Women's Suffrage Commemorative Stamp
86. Key to the city of White House
87. "I Love White House" button
88. "Shop White House First" key chain
89. White House Chamber of Commerce bumper sticker, newsletter, and executive director business card
90. White House map
91. White House Library brochures
92. City of White House stationery
93. Copy of the official White House seal
94. White House newsletters
95. Pictures of Mayor Billy Hobbs and the 1995 White House employee Christmas breakfast
96. White House parks and recreation brochure
97. White House community data sheet
98. White House Realtor booklet
99. Article about the Homecoming '86 project to build a replica of the White House Inn to use as a city library

TIPTON

1. Miniature cotton bale
2. Charms Candy suckers
3. County budget
4. County commission meeting minutes from May 8, 1995
5. 911 map
6. Baptist Memorial Hospital—Tipton information
7. Tipton County churches listing
8. *Covington/Tipton County* magazine
9. Chamber report on Tipton County
10. Schedule for Dyersburg State and Tennessee Technology Center
11. Covington Court Square postcards
12. Tipton County map
13. *Parks and Recreation* magazine
14. Tipton County ceramic plates

15. Covington Downtown Merchants shopping bag
16. Volunteer 200 Day T-shirt
17. 4-H ribbon
18. Brighton Honor Roll ribbon
19. Brighton Elementary School brochure
20. Bozo's Bar-B-Que menu
21. Park Day 5 K tile
22. Chamber of Commerce tile
23. *True Tales of Tipton*
24. *Tipton County, Tennessee; A Place of Memories—A People Moving Forward*
25. Cotton throw blanket
26. Newspaper inserts and articles
27. Local newspaper from February 21, 1996

TROUSDALE

1. Tobacco history of Middle Tennessee
2. *Tobacco Market News* for 1995
3. Large tobacco twists
4. Trousdale patch
5. Hartsville button
6. Homecoming '86 belt buckle
7. Item from Tennessee High School football game
8. Flyer for Trousdale County State Champs 1990–1993
9. Tennessee Secondary School Athletic Association Hall of Fame
10. Championship card
11. Trousdale County football jersey
12. *Trousdale, A Constitutional County* by J. C. McMurtry
13. "Dickens on the Square" button
14. Keep America Beautiful Trousdale litter bag
15. Homecoming '86 license plate
16. Article proposing the development of Taylor Landing
17. Article on Glamorous Grannies
18. Note cards with drawings of local historic buildings
19. Calendar of events list for the Chamber of Commerce
20. Flyer of Thunderbolt picture
21. Six issues of the Trousdale County Historical Society newsletter
22. Hartsville data sheet
23. Trousdale tourism brochure
24. Trousdale phone book
25. Trousdale County Courthouse postcard
26. Article on immigration
27. Picture of blacksmith shop
28. Picture of 1922 championship football team

29. List of receipts
30. Historic article on depot
31. Tobacco calendar
32. Picture of gazebo
33. Picture of old rock house and articles
34. Picture of winter of 1940
35. Article on Mongol's Gap
36. Article on first bank
37. Article on Branch Perkins
38. Article on largest motor
39. Article on flood in 1926
40. Article on first church
41. Article on vidette
42. Picture of Ms. Tennessee Sr.
43. Article on tobacco farm museum

UNICOI

1. Letter from county executive
2. Drawings and pictures of city halls
3. *The Center Cookbook* from the Clinchfield Senior Center and I.D. key chain
4. Unicoi County incorporation documents
5. Town seal
6. Listing of churches and church bulletins
7. Unicoi County Public Library bar-coded library card
8. Model of the Clinchfield Railroad Depot
9. Rock samples found in Unicoi County: Unquote, feldspar, quartz, and Sequoia cone; seeds
10. *Erwin Record* newspaper
11. Chamber of Commerce 1994 Christmas ornament
12. Chamber of Commerce brochure, 1996 calendar, and relocation packet
13. Pictures of the two county courthouses engraved on bells
14. Steel ball bearings made by Hoover and N & N Roller and Ball
15. Desk tray of polystyrene made by AB Plastics, Inc.
16. Gold card materials from the Incentive for Achievement program of Nuclear Fuel Services—brochure, badge
17. Apple Festival refrigerator magnet, quilted piece forming the logo of the Unaka Piecemakers
18. T-shirt from the Monday Club sold at the Apple Festival
19. Economic Development Board brochure
20. Unicoi Bicentennial flag
21. Pictures of the Unicoi County Heritage Museum

22. *Information Resource Guide to the Unicoi County Public Schools*
23. County pictures

UNION

1. Union County tax roll
2. *Our Union County Heritage, Volume I*
3. *Our Union County Families*
4. *Union County Faces of War*
5. *From Hearth and Hoe*
6. *Rain Crow: Part One*
7. *Rain Crow: Part Two*
8. *To Loys Cross Roads*
9. *Pathways*, Vol. 12, September 1993
10. School annuals 1993–1995
11. Union County map
12. Union County budget
13. Minutes from county commission
14. Union County teachers list, 1995–1996
15. The History of Hickory Valley Baptist Church, 1845–1995
16. Newspaper articles
17. Groundbreaking ceremony notes for new high school
18. Community Lecture Series Program announcement and attendees
19. Volunteer 200 Day list of participants
20. List of Tennessee 200 Committee
21. List of purchasers of display cases for museum
22. Spiderman comic book
23. Photographs of Roy Acuff, Chet Atkins, Kenny Chesney
24. Admission tickets to 1995 Business on Display
25. Membership meeting minutes for Union County Business and Professional Association
26. Proposed changes to Constitution and By-laws of Union County Business and Professional Association
27. 1995 Business on Display schedule of exhibitors
28. Promotional flyers for *Union County Faces of War* and *Our Union County Families*
29. Letter from Matthew John Heath
30. Luttrell School photograph 1925–1926
31. East Tennessee Development District newsletter, June 1995
32. 1996 Home Federal Savings Bank calendar
33. Ailordale Baptist Church photographs and history
34. Metal box containing pocket knife, coins, tape, and news clipping
35. Knoxville/Union County phone book
36. Union County Church directory
37. Millers Chapel Methodist Church history and bulletin
38. Northern Association of Baptists meeting minutes
39. Tennessee Teachers Association newsletter
40. Retired Teachers bulletin
41. Program from Museum of Appalachia Homecoming 1995
42. Museum of Appalachia map
43. Poem—"Ancestors"
44. Program from Tennessee State Museum
45. Program from Fallen Water Festival
46. Tennessee 200 meeting agendas
47. Union County Chapter from Goodspeed's History
48. Program from Luttrell Elementary School ball game
49. Horace Maynard High School Class of 1953 list
50. Invitation from Governor Don Sundquist
51. Biographical sketches of Hurle McClain and James Parker
52. Names on 1830 Union County census
53. *Decision Magazine*
54. Menu from Gangsters restaurant
55. Letter from County Executive Roy Carter
56. Bicentennial brick brochure
57. Rodin Exhibit brochure

VAN BUREN

1. County statistics and information
2. Bottle of wine made by county commissioner David Cocke
3. Legislative gavel
4. Machine parts
5. Photographs of historic buildings
6. Information on annual events
7. Information from Fall Creek Falls State Park
8. Artwork and writings of local school children
9. Letter from the mayor of Spencer
10. Letter from State Representative Rhinehart
11. Letter from county commissioner David Cocke
12. History of Townsend Factory
13. School projects from elementary and high school students
14. History and parts from local industries Camcar/Tektron
15. Van Buren County/Spencer Chamber of Commerce brochures
16. Photographs of areas in the county
17. County historic document 1996
18. Booklet on Van Buren County's plans for the Bicentennial
19. Information on city of Spencer
20. Annual Mountain Homecoming information
21. *The History of Van Buren County, Tennessee: The Early Canebreakers, 1840–1940* by Landon Daryle Medley, 1987

WARREN

1. Wooden car made from local wood
2. Pictures of bike ride and county flag
3. Cumberland Caverns brochure
4. Fair program
5. Warren County guidebook
6. Warren County license plate
7. Various seeds from local nurseries
8. Tennessee Airport Directory 1996
9. County flag
10. McMinville flag
11. Chamber of Commerce map
12. Historic McMinville directory
13. Historic Walking Tour guide
14. Picture of library
15. Two phone books
16. *Sharing Our Best Cookbook*
17. Warren County profile
18. Warren County calendar
19. Fifty historic people activities
20. Warren County T-shirt
21. *Southern Standard* newspaper
22. Nursery industry literature
23. *History of the Black House*
24. *McMinville at a Milestone*
25. WTRZ—news tapes
26. Community Library brochure
27. Rotary Club brochure
28. List of Tennessee 200 Committee
29. "Guide to Nursery Capital" brochure
30. McMinville guidebook
31. Warren County tourism brochure
32. First Presbyterian Church brochure
33. Chamber of Commerce membership directory
34. Historic map
35. Winter storm report for WAKI
36. Picture of county flag
37. List of some items in the time capsule
38. WTRZ local news

39. Tennessee Technology Center brochure
40. Warren County government list
41. Letter from county executive

WASHINGTON

1. Knob Creek historic map
2. Harris-Tarkett, Inc., pen
3. Daniel Boone gavel #448
4. *Historic Association Speeches*
5. Historic Jonesborough brochure and reading material
6. Chamber of Commerce paperweight
7. Letter from mayor of Johnson City
8. Letter from county executive
9. Information from Johnson City
10. East Tennessee State University Quillen College of Medicine books
11. *Greater Johnson City*
12. Bicentennial Commission members
13. Chamber of Commerce brochure
14. ECD information packet
15. County information packet
16. VA material
17. Johnson City 125th Anniversary material
18. Letter from the mayor of Johnson City
19. Phone book from Johnson City
20. Tennessee 200 Washington County T-shirt
21. Two golf balls
22. Two ETSU paperweights
23. *Jonesborough—The First Century of Tennessee's First Town* by Paul M. Fink
24. *A University's Story, 1911–1980* by Frank B. Williams Jr.
25. ETSU booklet—"Nobody Goes Through Life Alone"
26. ETSU/Terry Waite lecture-series poster
27. Scissors
28. ETSU cap
29. Lapel pin—ETSU 1911–1986
30. ETSU Christmas card from Roy and Ann Nicks
31. ETSU statistics card
32. ETSU pictures
33. Letter from ETSU President Roy S. Nicks
34. ETSU fact sheet
35. *Johnson City Press*, December 8, 1995, "ETSU golfers No. 1" article
36. ETSU literature
37. The *Business Journal* magazine, "Annual Report 1996" excerpt about ETSU
38. Turning Toward 2011—A report by the commission on the future of ETSU
39. *ETSU Today* magazine, Spring and Fall 1995

40. *Business Journal* magazine, June 1994, "Salute to ETSU"
41. Drawings of buildings at ETSU

WAYNE

1. Miniature cowboy boot
2. Flag flown over the courthouse on January 1, 1996
3. Picture of Wayne County Commission, 1996
4. Clifton High School annual
5. Waynesboro Middle School annual
6. Fifth grade essays on Haley's Comet from 1985
7. Collinwood Elementary School annual
8. Collinwood High School annual
9. Wayne County High School annual
10. Wayne County history book 1817–1995
11. Various letters from individuals
12. Wayne County Recycling Program cup
13. Brass valve by Lincoln Brass Works
14. Various patches from the Department of Correction and CCA
15. Junior Beta Club list of organizational charter members
16. Drawings by Daisy Troop 261 of what the world looks like in 1996
17. Wayne County Litter Program ruler
18. Letter of welcome from Wayne County Tourism
19. Holy Bible

WEAKLEY

1. Chamber of Commerce county profile
2. County map
3. 1996 phone book
4. County flag
5. County History book by Jenny Vaughn
6. County Agriculture Extension Office report on Weakley County agriculture
7. *Dresden Enterprise*, January 21, 1987, and January 25, 1995
8. *Weakley County Press*, June 28, 1973; December 3, 1985; January 29, 1987
9. *Our Town* magazine, May and October 1995
10. The *Pacer*, December 7, 1995
11. Thunderbolt Broadcasting—broadcast history, bumper stickers, 1995–1996 sports handbook
12. Dresden Community profile
13. Iris Festival coaster
14. Dresden Homecoming '86 belt buckle
15. Dresden Rotary Club bulletin, flag, history

16. Gleason Community profile
17. Brick from Boral Brick made from Ball Clay mined in Weakley County
18. Mike Snider cassette tape
19. Greenfield community profile
20. Lapel pin
21. Martin community profile
22. Key to the city lapel pin, Martin
23. Soybean Festival lapel pin
24. City of Martin lapel pin
25. Martin Police Department pen
26. Industrial Board video
27. City of Martin letter opener
28. Sharon community profile
29. Wooden key to the city of Sharon
30. University of Tennessee at Martin key chain, coaster, license plate, banner/flag, scarf

WHITE

1. Sparta/White County Chamber of Commerce directory
2. List of elected officials
3. List of county boards and members
4. County budget
5. Sparta/White County map
6. Sparta/White County brochure
7. Sparta flag
8. White County flag
9. Chamber of Commerce industrial recruiting book
10. Virgin Falls picture and information
11. Scott's Gulf—"Save the Gulf" campaign information
12. Cart's (Citizens for the Arts) Preserve the Oldham's Theater for a Fine Arts Center
13. *White County Pictorial*, book by First National Bank
14. *History of White County*
15. *Horizon's* 1995
16. Pictures of the county
17. *History of White County Churches*
18. 1995–1996 Sparta/White County phone book
19. Area wage and benefit survey
20. 1995 White County Fair book
21. "Chamber of Commerce 100 Years of Service," by the *Expositor*
22. Kornpone Day Festival history and pictures
23. Cancer Society information and Christmas card
24. Old courthouse ornament
25. Auto Tour brochure
26. Rock House brochure

27. Introducing the Church of Christ and Central Church of Christ bulletin
28. New International Version, Holy Bible
29. *Expositor, Pride '89* Edition
30. *The Guide*, January 1995
31. "White County Remembers"—a tribute to White County veterans, *Expositor*, December 7, 1995
32. *Expositor*—January 2, 4, 11, 15, 18, 22, 1996
33. *It Happened in White County*
34. Pictorial history and family trees
35. Sparta/White County, member of the month
36. *Field Trips into White County History*

WILLIAMSON

1. Letter from Robert Ring, county executive
2. Directory of Williamson county officials
3. Civic organizations listing
4. Williamson County industrial manufacturers listing
5. List of Williamson County politicians
6. School board members
7. Agricultural information
8. Williamson County Bicentennial flag
9. Williamson County Bicentennial volunteers list
10. "Walnut Grove Celebrates Bicentennial"
11. Bicentennial scarf
12. *Tennessee Antebellum Trail Guidebook*
13. Williamson Recycles brochure
14. Visitor's guide
15. Chamber of Commerce membership brochure
16. Chamber of Commerce membership directory
17. Chamber Chat Newsletter
18. Chamber Perspective Newsletter
19. "Williamson County, Tennessee"—A Tale of Three Cities brochure
20. Williamson County Board of Education information packet
21. June 30, 1996 Williamson County budget
22. "Where You Live" coloring book
23. Arts Council brochure
24. Voter registration form
25. Williamson County map
26. *National Register Properties of Williamson County, Tennessee*
27. BellSouth phone book
28. Six pictures of the Franklin High School band
29. Williamson County zoning map
30. "Important Farm Land in Williamson County"

31. Reenactment of the Battle of Franklin paperweight
32. Main Street Christmas ornament
33. Williamson County Bicentennial events listing
34. Letter from Jerry Sharber, mayor of Franklin
35. Item from board of Mayor Jerry Sharber and alderman
36. June 1996 budget for Franklin
37. Zoning map for Franklin
38. Franklin Special School District packet
39. Franklin Special School District budget
40. Franklin sites brochures
41. Letter from State Representative Mike Williams
42. Christmas card featuring the Heritage Foundation office
43. Set of Marvin Stalnaker prints
44. Postcards
45. Belt buckle made by Doyle Neeley, and instructions on making a belt buckle
46. Franklin coffee mug
47. Williamson County Resource Guide
48. Williamson County magazine
49. Letter from the mayor of Brentwood
50. Brentwood community information
51. Brentwood annual budget
52. Brentwood Civitan Youth, Inc.
53. *Brentwood Journal* article
54. *Oodles of Noodles* article
55. Funnoodle sample
56. City of Brentwood Citizen's Update
57. Brentwood Chamber of Commerce information packet
58. *Historic Brentwood*
59. Picture of Brentwood High band
60. Brentwood magazine
61. City of Brentwood Activity Book
62. *Granny White and Her Pumpkins*
63. *Brentwood Journal*, "Year End Review"
64. Map of Brentwood
65. Zoning map of Brentwood
66. Brentwood site brochures
67. Brentwood license plate
68. Brentwood ruler
69. City of Brentwood coffee mug
70. Brentwood pins
71. Letter and information from the mayor of Thompson Station
72. Thompson Station ordinance
73. The Depot at Thompson Station brochure
74. City profile of Fairview
75. City charter of Fairview
76. "Miss Bowie's Treasured Forest" article

77. Fairview budget
78. Payroll for Fairview
79. Fairview pictures
80. Cultured marble
81. Doll dress
82. France box
83. *Fairview Observer*, "Year in Review"
84. The *Williamson Leader*
85. *Our Voices, 1995 Williamson County Literary Review*, Cool Springs Press

WILSON

1. *History of Wilson County*
2. *In a Place Called Watertown, Somewhere in Tennessee*
3. *West Wilson County neighbors*
4. *Our Home* magazine
5. Chamber annual report
6. County history paper
7. Bicentennial letter
8. Two letters from the mayor
9. *Leadership Wilson* paper
10. Wilson County meeting minutes
11. Cumberland University President's 1000 Club paperweight
12. City of Lebanon Sesquicentennial coin
13. Castle Heights Military Academy medal
14. Post office box door from Watertown
15. Limestone rock from Wilson County
16. Cedars of Lebanon State Park cedar box, pens, block, brochure
17. Castle Heights Military Main Building Christmas ornament
18. Cumberland University—catalog, brochure, flag, patch
19. Wilson County plates
20. Lebanon T-shirt
21. Wilson County tourism bag
22. United States Mint proof set, 1995
23. City and county maps of Watertown, Mt. Juliet, Lebanon
24. "Damn Pigeons" hat
25. Brochures from Watertown, Wilson, Mt. Juliet, antiques district
26. Watertown Bed & Breakfast postcard
27. "Fakes and Hooker" hat
28. Hartmann Luggage key chain
29. Wilson County Fair pin
30. Mt. Juliet Chamber of Commerce pin
31. Lebanon Chamber of Commerce director pin
32. University Medical Center Physicians guide
33. *Lebanon Democrat, Wilson World*, and *Mt. Juliet* newspapers

ML

214

ACKNOWLEDGMENTS

The ideal condition
Would be, I admit, that men should be right by instinct;
But since we are all likely to go astray,
The reasonable thing is to learn from those who can teach.

Sophocles

I am most grateful to the following individuals who helped provide information, materials, assistance, guidance, and encouragement during my journey to assemble this book:

Liz Altobel, F. Lynne Bachleda, Craig Baird, Jennifer M. Bartlett, Cindy Bean, Kay Beasley, Ann Betts, Gary Bozeman, John Bridges, Andrea Burroughs, Robert Cameron, Virginia Campbell, Elizabeth Carden, Dennis Carmichael, Julie Christie, Jon Coddington, Edward Cole, David Craig, James Crutchfield, Janice Cunningham, P. Casey Daley, Larry Daughtrey, Jed DeKalb, James R. Dixey, Don Doyle, Sandra Duncan, Joe Edwards, Michael Emrick, James M. Evans, Nick Fielder, Kenneth Fieth, Dennis Findley, Mike Fitts, Leonard Folgarait, Gary Follis, Michael Fowler, Sandra Fulton, John Furgess, Jan Galletta, Curt Garrigan, Georgia Gaye, Edwin Gleaves, Bill Goodman, Howard B. Gotlieb, Luanne Grandinetti, David Gregory, Mary Hance, Ron E. Harr, Roy P. Harrover, Robert Lamb Hart, Mary Glenn Hearne, Leigh Hendry, R. D. Herbert, Greta Hinds, Marilyn and T. J. Hinton, Nora and Earl Hinton, Joe Hodgson, James Hoobler, Robin Hood, Donna House, Harriett Howard, George D. Hulsey Jr., Steve Izenour, Lucinda P. Janke, Joanne Jaworski, David A. Johnson, Steve Johnson, Victor Johnson, Frank E. Jones, Laurie Jones, Carol Kaplan, Jim Kennedy, James Kennon Jr., Elaine Kernea, Dhan Kinnick, Christine Kreyling, Bobby Lawrence, Slick Lawson, Gary Layda, Murray Lee, Patricia Ledford, Alan LeQuire, Ruth Letson, David Logsdon, Harold G. Lowe Jr., Barbara J. Marshall, Bert Mathews, Janet D. McCarthy, Bruce McCarty, Karina McDaniels, Dan McGown, Evadine McMahan, Olivia McNair, Shilpa Mehta, Andrew B. Miller, Nancy Ann Min, Marian Moffett, Wayne Moore, David H. Moss, Thurman Mullins, Elizabeth O'Leary, Frank Orr, Wesley Paine, Herb Peck, Dan Pomeroy, Van Pond, Jerry Preston, Fred Prouty, Julia Rather, Joanne Rathman, Ann Reynolds, Lois Riggins-Ezzell, Mary Roskilly, Fred Russell, Cherry L. vonSchmittou, Denise Scott Brown, Rob Simbeck, Brian Smallwood, Jonathan Smith, J. Ritchie Smith Jr., Tom Stanford, Wilma Dykeman Stokely, Charles P. Stripling, Jeanne Sugg, Kim Sulik, Howard Symons, Debi Tate, Paul Tetreault, Jennifer Thomas, George Thompson, David Tirpack, David Todd, Kelly Tolson, Seab A. Tuck III, Virginia Vaughan, Margaret Britton Vaughn, Robert Venturi, Charles Warterfield Jr., Stroud Watson, Mary Bray Wheeler, Bill Whittaker, Dan Whittle, Walter Williams, Ridley Wills II, Daniel Wright

RESOURCES AND MATERIALS

Special information, photographs, maps, and historic documents were obtained through the generosity of the following:

American Antiquarian Society; Craig Baird, photographer; Tony Beazley, photographer; Boston University Library Special Collections; Chromatics Photo Imaging; the *Commercial Appeal*; Cornell University; James Crutchfield; P. Casey Daley, photographer; EDAW, Inc.; Ginn & Company Archives at Columbia University; Bill Goodman, photographer; Ron Harr, photographer; Roy Harrover Architect; Robert Lamb Hart Planners and Architects; Hodgson & Douglas Landscape Architects; Robin Hood, photographer; Kentucky Historical Society; Slick Lawson, photographer; Kiplinger Washington Collection; Gary Layda, photographer; Michael Lewis, photographer; Harold G. Lowe Jr., photographer; Harcourt Brace & Company; Map Sales & Services of Nashville; McCarty-Holsaple-McCarty Architects; Metropolitan Nashville Development and Housing Agency; Metropolitan Nashville Department of Public Works; Metropolitan Nashville Historical Commission; Metropolitan Nashville Photographic Services; Minnesota Capitol Area Architectural and Planning Board; The M.I.T. Press; *Nashville Banner*; Nashville Room, Metropolitan Nashville Public Library; Nathan-Evans-Taylor Architects; Van Pond, photographer; Ross/Fowler, PC, Landscape Architects; Rutledge Hill Press; Brian Smallwood, photographer; the *Tennessean*; Tennessee 200; Tennessee Department of Environment and Conservation; Tennessee State Photographic Services; Tennessee State Library and Archives; Tennessee State Museum; Tuck Hinton Architects; Twin City Photography; United States Department of the Interior; United States Military Academy, West Point; United States Parks & History Association; University of Pennsylvania Architectural Archives; Venturi, Scott Brown & Associates; Charles Warterfield Jr. Architects

CREDITS

There would be no architecture without the faith and courage of the client, without the understanding of those who exert control and authority, without the help and commitment of collaborators. Architecture is never the work of a single person. No architect can create anything valid without the collaboration and spiritual stimulus of all those who have a part in it.

Only by true collaboration between architect, engineer, technicians and builders, only when they all play in harmony, can any given work of architecture be created. The architect is no more than one of the instruments, at most the conductor, in this orchestra of talents and skills. Recognition goes above all to the soloists who have most often shown their skill and ability.

O. M. Ungers

Special thanks to Governors Ned McWherter and Don Sundquist and their cabinets and staffs; Commissioners of Finance and Administration David Manning, Bob Corker, and John Ferguson; State Treasurer Steve Adams; Secretary of State Riley Darnell; Comptroller William Snodgrass; and the Ninety-eighth and Ninety-ninth General Assemblies headed by Lieutenant Governor and Speaker of the Senate John Wilder and Speaker of the House of Representatives Jimmy Naifeh, including Senator Douglas Henry and Representative John Bragg; and to members of the Tennessee State Building Commission.

Special appreciation to Assistant Commissioners Jerry Preston, Bill McDonald, and Larry Kirk; Capital Projects Managers Jim Dixey, Jim Ritchason, Ken Scalf, and Ed Belbusti; and State Architect Mike Fitts.

Thanks also to the members of the Tennessee Bicentennial Commission, chaired by Martha Ingram; the Tennessee 200 board of directors and organization, directed by Kelly Tolson; and to the members of the State Capitol Commission, chaired by Amon Carter Evans, who, through the early encouragement of Planning Executive Jim Hall and many others, endorsed and supported the early vision of the Tennessee Bicentennial Capitol Mall as an appropriate permanent civic gift to honor the state's two-hundredth birthday.

For their ongoing participation, dedication, talent, and hard work as part of the design and construction effort on the Tennessee Bicentennial Capitol Mall, I am particularly indebted to architect-philosopher Jon Coddington; to landscape architects Mike Fowler, David Craig, Joe Hodgson, and Ritchie Smith; to planner David Johnson and architects Charles Warterfield Jr. and Jim Evans; to engineers Dwain Hibdon, John Turner, Ron Hale, Dave Verner, Terry Scholes, David Moss, Thomas Schaeffer, and David Hormby; to Hardaway Construction Corporation of Tennessee, Ray Bell Construction Company, and Gary Follis; and to the entire staff of Tuck Hinton Architects, especially studio director Virginia Campbell, project manager James Kennon Jr., and my partner Seab A. Tuck III.

STATE BUILDING COMMISSION

Ned McWherter, governor (1987–1995); Don Sundquist, governor (1995—); John S. Wilder, lieutenant governor; Jimmy Naifeh, speaker of the House; David Manning, commissioner of Finance and Administration (1991–1995); Bob Corker, commissioner of Finance and Administration (1995–1996); John Ferguson, commissioner of Finance and Administration (1996—); Steve Adams, state treasurer; Riley C. Darnell, secretary of state; William Snodgrass, comptroller of the treasury; Michael A. Fitts, state architect

TENNESSEE BICENTENNIAL COMMISSION AND TENNESSEE 200 BOARD OF DIRECTORS

Governor and Mrs. Don Sundquist, honorary chairmen; Martha R. Ingram, chairman; Dancy Lewallen Jones, vice chairman; Steve Adams, Joan Ashe, Andy Bennett, Johnny Cash, Irby Cooper, Riley Darnell, Winfield Dunn, James H. Epps III, Amon Carter Evans, Joe Fowlkes, John P. Franklin, Pam Garrett, H. Carey Hanlin, Thelma Harper, Joyce Hassell, Douglas Henry, Alfred D. Hill, John M. Jones Sr., Keith Jordan, Kay Leibowitz, Mary Jane McWherter, Jimmy Naifeh, William J. Peeler, Mary Pruitt, Jeanette Rudy, William Snodgrass, Wilma Dykeman Stokely, Jesse H. Turner Jr., Virginia Vaughan, Bill Whitson, John Wilder, Marcelle Wilder

STATE CAPITOL COMMISSION

Amon Carter Evans, chairman; David Manning, commissioner of Finance and Administration (1991–1995); Bob Corker, commissioner of Finance and Administration (1995–1996); John Ferguson, commissioner of Finance and Administration (1996—); Steve Adams, state treasurer; Riley C. Darnell, secretary of state; William Snodgrass, comptroller of the treasury; William Whitson, commissioner of General Services (1987–1995); Larry Haynes, commissioner of General Services (1995—); Douglas Henry, state senator; John Bragg, state representative; Betty Gunter; Robert Corlew; David Dickson

GOVERNOR NED MCWHERTER
1987–1995

Senior Staff
Jim Kennedy, chief of staff and deputy to the governor; Betty Haynes, chief administrative officer; David Welles, legal counsel to the governor; Harlan Matthews, deputy to the governor; Billy Stair, executive assistant for policy and planning; Jim Hall, executive assistant for planning; Carol White, director of planning; Dianne Neal, legal counsel to the governor; David Gregory, director of legislative affairs and chief of staff

Commissioners
Betty Adams, Youth Development; Christine Bradley, Corrections; Charles Cardwell, Revenue; Allan Curtis, Commerce and Insurance; James Davenport, Employment Security; Richard Dawson, Safety; Jimmy Evans, Transportation; Sandra Fulton, Tourism; Talmadge Gilley, Financial Institutions; Bob Grunow, Human Services; Johnny Hayes, Economic Development; Don Holt, Personnel; Joe Huddleston, Revenue; L. H. Ivy, Agriculture; Carl Johnson, Economic Development; Carl Johnson, Transportation; William Jones, Military; Robert Lawson, Safety; J. W. Luna, Environment and Conservation; David Manning, Finance and Administration; W. D. Manning, Veterans Affairs; Elaine McReynolds, Commerce and Insurance; Nancy Ann Min, Human Services; Wayne Qualls, Education; W. Jeff Reynolds, Corrections; Rich Riebling, Economic Development; Evelyn Robertson, Mental Health; Charles Smith, Education; Eric Taylor, Mental Health; H. Russell White, Health; James White, Labor; William Whitson, General Services; Carl Woods, Transportation; Jerry Wyatt, Military

GOVERNOR DON SUNDQUIST
1995—

Senior Staff
Hardy Mays, deputy to the governor and chief of staff; R. Wendell Moore, chief administrative officer; Peaches Simpkins, deputy to the governor and chief of staff; Beth Fortune, director of communications and press secretary; Elizabeth Carden, deputy press secretary; David Locke, assistant to the governor for legislation; Nancy Menke, special assistant to the governor; Ralph Perry, assistant to the governor for strategic planning; Billy Stokes, special assistant to the governor; Dancy L. Jones, deputy to the governor for administration

Commissioners
Al Bodie, Labor; Donal Campbell, Corrections; Marjorie Nell Cardwell, Mental Health and Mental Retardation; Bob Corker, Finance and Administration; Margaret Culpepper, Employment Security; Bill Dunavant, Economic and Community Development; John Ferguson, Finance and Administration; Mike Green, Safety; George Hattaway, Children's Services; Milton Hamilton, Environment and Conservation; Larry Haynes, General Services; Bill Houston, Financial Institutions; Ruth Johnson, Revenue; Susan Richardson-Williams, Personnel; Linda Rudolph, Human Services; Bruce Saltsman, Transportation; Doug Sizemore, Commerce and Insurance; Fred Tucker, Veterans Affairs; John Wade, Tourist Development; Fredia Wadley, Health; Jane Walters, Education; Dan Wheeler, Agriculture; Justin Wilson, Environment and Conservation; Jackie D. Wood, Military

ML

NINETY-EIGHTH GENERAL ASSEMBLY

Senate

John S. Wilder, speaker; Robert Rochelle, speaker pro tempore; Milton Hamilton Jr., deputy speaker; Ray C. Albright, Ben Atchley, Tommy Burks, Stephen I. Cohen, Jerry W. Cooper, Rusty Crowe, Ward Crutchfield, Edward Davis, Gene Elsea, John Ford, C. Coulter Gilbert, J. Ronnie Greer, Thelma M. Harper, Joe M. Haynes, Douglas Henry, Jim Lyne Holcomb, Keith Jordan, Carl O. Koella Jr., James F. Kyle, Thomas F. Leatherwood III, Joe Nip McKnight, Randy McNally, Anna Belle O'Brien, Lou Patten, Curtis S. Person Jr., Carol J. Rice, Kenneth N. Springer, Danny Wallace, Andy Womack, Don Wright

House of Representatives

Jimmy Naifeh, speaker; Lois M. DeBerry, speaker pro tempore; John T. Bragg, deputy speaker; Charles E. Allen Jr., W. Townsend Anderson, Joe Armstrong, John Arriola, Joe W. Bell, H. E. Bittle, Jim Boyer, Henri E. Brooks, Tommie F. Brown, Frank Buck, Dan R. Byrd, Clint Callicott, John Chiles, Carol J. Chummey, Richard R. Clark, David L. Coffey, Ralph Cole, Ronnie Cole, William H. Collier, Floyd Crain, Jerry Cross, Eugene E. Davidson, Ronnie Davis, Roscoe Dixon, Maria Peroulas Draper, Shirley Powell Duer, Dennis Ferguson, Richard A. Fisher, Joe F. Fowlkes, Tim Garrett, Ken Givens, Doug Gunnels, Ed Haley, Jere Hargrove, Beth Halteman Harwell, Joyce Barnett Hassell, Tommy Haun, Tommy Head, Roy Herron, I. V. Hillis, Larry C. Huskey, Douglas S. Jackson, Gary R. Johnson, Rufus E. Jones, Ulysses Jones Jr., Tim Joyce, Joe Kent, Michael L. Kernell, Matthew Kisber, Peggy Steed Knight, Doyle Lewis Jr., Mike J. Liles, Harold M. Love, Bill H. McAfee, Stephen K. McDaniel, Robert S. McKee, Ken Meyer, Larry J. Miller, Monty E. Mires, Calvin M. Moore, J. B. Napier, Gary Odom, Mae Stamey Owenby, Paul E. Phelan, Clarence Pete Phillips, Phillip E. Pinion, Mary Pruitt, Bill Purcell, Ronald L. Ramsey, Shelby A. Rhinehart, Don Ridgeway, Billy Rigsby, Randy Rinks, Wayne A. Ritchie, Robb Robinson, Charles M. Severance, David A. Shirley, Randy Stamps, Harold E. Stockburger, Arnold A. Stulce, Bretran Thompson, Harry J. Tindell, Brenda Kaye Turner, Larry Turner, Richard S. Venable, Page Walley, Ben West Jr., Keith Westmoreland, Zane C. Whitson Jr., Karen R. Williams, Micheal R. Williams, L. Mike Williams, John Mark Windle, Leslie Winningham, Mayo Wix, Bobby G. Wood

NINETY-NINTH GENERAL ASSEMBLY

Senate

John S. Wilder, speaker; Robert Rochelle, speaker pro tempore; Milton H. Hamilton Jr., deputy speaker; Ben Atchley, Tommy Burks, Robert E. Carter, Stephen I. Cohen, Jerry W. Cooper, Rusty Crowe, War Crutchfield, Roscoe Dixon, Gene Elsea, John Ford, David Fowler, C. Coulter Gilbert, Thelma M. Harper, Tommy G. Haun, Joe M. Haynes, Douglas Henry, Jim Lyne Holcomb, Keith Jordan, Carl O. Koella Jr., James F. Kyle, Thomas F. Leatherwood III, Randy McNally, Jeff Miller, Anna Belle O'Brien, Curtis S. Person Jr., Carol J. Rice, Kenneth N. Springer, Danny Wallace, Andy Womack, Don Wright

House of Representatives

Jimmy Naifeh, speaker; Lois M. DeBerry, speaker pro tempore; John T. Bragg, deputy speaker; Joe Armstrong, John Arriola, Mae Beavers, Joe W. Bell, Donald R. Bird, H. E. Bittle, Kathryn I. Bowers, Jim Boyer, Henri E. Brooks, Tommie F. Brown, Frank Buck, Tim Burchett, Dan R. Byrd, Clint Callicott, Bruce E. Cantrell, Carol J. Chummey, William C. Clabough, David L. Coffey, Ralph Cole, Ronnie Cole, Jerry Cross, Charles Curtiss, Eugene E. Davidson, Ronnie Davis, John J. DeBerry Jr., Shirley Powell Duer, Bill Dunn, Mary Ann Eckles, Craig Fitzhugh, Stancil Ford, Joe F. Fowlkes, Tim Garrett, Ken Givens, Doug Gummels, Ed Haley, Jere Hargrove, Beth Halteman Harwell, Joyce Barnett Hassell, Tommy Head, Roy Herron, Bobby Gene Hicks, Larry C. Huskey, Douglas S. Jackson, Sherry Jones, Ulysses Jones Jr., Tim Joyce, Joe Kent, Michael L. Kernell, Howard T. Kerr, Matthew Kisber, Edith Taylor Langster, Doyle Lewis Jr., Bill H. McAfee, Stephen K. McDaniel, Michael R. McDonald, Robert S. McKee, Kim McMillan, Larry J. Miller, J. B. Napier, J. Chris Newton, Gary Odom, Robert D. Patton, James L. Peach Sr., Paul E. Phelan, Clarence Pete Phillips, Phillip E. Pinion, Mary Pruitt, Bill Purcell, Ronald L. Ramsey, Shelby A. Rhinehart, L. Don Ridgeway, Billy Rigsby, Randy Rinks, Wayne A. Ritchie, Dennis Edward Roach, Robb Robinson, Jack Sharp, David A. Shirley, Randy Stamps, Arnold A. Stulce, Harry J. Tindell, Joe Towns Jr., Brenda Kaye Turner, Larry Turner, Richard S. Venable, Page Walley, Ben West Jr., Keith Westmoreland, John M. White, Zane C. Whitson Jr., Micheal R. Williams, L. Mike Williams, John Mark Windle, Leslie Winningham, Bobby G. Wood

DEPARTMENT OF FINANCE AND ADMINISTRATION CAPITAL PROJECTS MANAGEMENT

Jerry Preston, assistant to the commissioner; Bill McDonald, assistant commissioner; Larry Kirk, assistant commissioner; James R. Dixey, director of construction; Jim Ritchason, project manager; Ken Scalf, project manager; Edward Belbusti, project manager; Hugh Gaston, project manager; Tom Robinson, director of architectural services; Charles Garrett, director of facilities management; Jeff Fields, construction representative; Fount Smothers, director of planning; Howard Symons, assistant to director of planning

DEPARTMENT OF ENVIRONMENT AND CONSERVATION

J.W. Luna, commissioner (1991–1995); Don Dills, commissioner (1995–1996); Justin P. Wilson, commissioner (1996–1997); Milton Hamilton, commissioner (1997——); William B. Whitson, chairman, Conservation Commission; Edward Cole, assistant commissioner; Gerald Kinney, assistant commissioner; Delton Truitt, assistant commissioner; Walter Butler, assistant commissioner; Ollie Keller, assistant commissioner; Bill Boswell, park management administrator; Jack Gilpin, conservation planner; Terry Bonham, planning director; Dan Webber, museum chief curator; David Tirpak, map specialist; Thurman Mullins, park manager and head ranger; and rangers: Angela Beverly, Jim Brannon, Jeff Buchanan, Joey Clark, Christopher Cole, Steve Hall, Vicki Loveday, Ross Pahnke, Steve Talley, Steve Ward, Keith Wimberly, Theda Young

DEPARTMENT OF GENERAL SERVICES

William B. Whitson, commissioner (1987–1995); Larry N. Haynes, commissioner (1995——); Dennis Johnson, assistant commissioner; James Baker, area administrator; Ed Lenfalt, facility manager; Bill Tolbert, horticultural manager

DEPARTMENT OF TOURIST DEVELOPMENT

Sandra F. Fulton, commissioner (1987–1995); John A. Wade, commissioner (1995——); Patricia Ledford, deputy commissioner

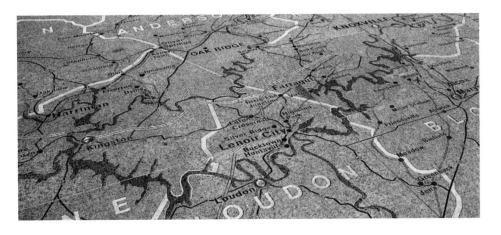

State Museum; F. Lynne Bachleda, history researcher and writer; Duane Wilson, theater designer; Hydrodramatics, fountain consultant; Cold Springs Granite Company; Verdin Carillon Company; Intrepid Enterprises, stone masons; Susan Tudor, graphic designer; Paul Tetreault, signage consultant

The following organizations also deserve recognition for their assistance in the design of the Tennessee Bicentennial Capitol Mall:

Chattanooga Urban Design Center, Country Music Foundation, CSX Transportation, Minnesota Capitol Area Planning Commission, Metropolitan Nashville City Council, Metropolitan Nashville Davidson County Farmers' Market, Metropolitan Nashville Davidson County: Office of the Mayor, City Council, Historical Commission, Development and Housing Agency, Planning and Commission, Public Works, Public Library, Nashville Opera Company, Nashville Room at the Metropolitan Nashville Public Library, the Nashville Symphony, Pennsylvania Avenue Development Corporation, Tennessee Building Commission, Tennessee State Government Departments: Environment and Conservation, Finance and Administration, General Services, Tourist Development, Transportation, Tennessee Repertory Theatre Company, Tennessee State Library and Archives, Tennessee State Museum, Urban Marketing Collaborative of Toronto, University of Tennessee College of Architecture and Planning

Tuck Hinton Architects
Seab A. Tuck III, principal in charge of Farmers' Market; Kem G. Hinton, principal in charge of Bicentennial Mall; Virginia C. Campbell, studio director; James Kennon Jr., project manager; Kent McLaughlin, project manager; George Thomas Bauer, project manager; Margaret Longmire Butler, project manager; Jonathan Smith, David Baird, Mary Roskilly, David Joffe, Laurie V. Jones, James Nickle, Van Pond, Charles Miller, Kara Babin, Joe Ellis, Andrew Gosselin, Walter Kiskaddon, Brian Smallwood, James Lowen, Tina Hall, Barbara Marshall, Loren Parquette, Amanda Lightman-Jones, Shawn Hollingsworth, Jill Hammond, Joan Durand, Bo Sundius, Philip Ashby, Jon Maass

Ross/Fowler, PC
Michael F. Fowler, principal in charge; Charles Ross, principal; David Craig, project manager; Ben Pethel, David Bailey, John Russell, Patricia Harrison, JoLena Wiley, Christy Lane

SSOE, Inc.
Gary R. Miner, principal in charge; T. Dwain Hibdon, project manager; David S. Verner, project manager; John T. Turner, project manager; Robert McKinney, project manager; Charles Pickney, Ronald E. Hale, Wesley Dorothy, Barry Burgess, Ary Bowker, Carol Cosby, Ed Dilts, Matt Fell, Amanda McComb, Danielle Rendon, Edward Ringel, Michael Vincent

Charles Warterfield Jr. Architects
Charles Warterfield Jr., principal in charge; Robert Johnson, Neal Downing

Hodgson & Douglas
Joseph M. Hodgson, principal in charge; S. Georgia Harrison, Robert Crowell

EMC Structural Engineers
Terry P. Scholes, principal in charge; Daniel K. Borsos, engineer; Gerry Holt

Barge, Waggoner, Sumner & Cannon, Inc.
Harold C. Fulghum, principal in charge; David H. Moss, project manager; Michael W. Morris, James N. Gilliam, Wendell H. Talley, David R. Riesland, Rick Dearman

Nathan-Evans-Taylor Architects
James M. Evans, principal in charge; Tim Ogburn, Spencer Law

Stanley D. Lindsey & Associates, Ltd.
Thomas Schaeffer, project manager; David E. Hormby, design engineer; Robert Bovine, engineer; Marvene Bilbrey, Travis Wright

Gresham, Smith and Partners
Everett H. Cowan, principal in charge; Michael Hunkler, project manager; Tony Denami, Al Pramak, Lisa Kennedy, Steve Snoddy, Debra Hightower, Don Davis, Randy Allen

Ritchie Smith Associates
J. Ritchie Smith Jr., principal in charge; Lissa Thompson, Mike Lemm, Barbara Keathley

I. C. Thomasson Associates
William T. Tinnell, project manager; Kenneth R. Carter, Robert L. Coss, C. Robert Gee

Ragan Smith Associates
Bob Nichols, principal in charge; George Welch, project manager; Jim Endsley, Bud Clymer, Mike Fuller

CONTRACTORS

Bicentennial Mall, Capitol Hill, and World War II Memorial
Hardaway Construction Corporation of Tennessee

Amphitheater, Railroad Bridges, and Farmers' Market
Ray Bell Construction Company

Street Improvements
Alman Construction Company, Inc.

Employee Parking Areas
Jones Brothers, Inc.; Rogers Group, Inc.

Demolition
Mid-South Wrecking Company, Inc.

Construction Coordination
Heery International, Inc.

Hardaway Construction Corporation of Tennessee
L. Hall Hardaway Jr., chairman; Billy D. Grover, president; George Griffin, group manager; Jim Stivender, group manager; Ted Davidson, project manager; Richard Sweatman, Randy Davidson, Butch Rose, George Thompson

Bicentennial Mall Subcontractors

ABG Caulking; Cold Spring Granite; Contractors Tile Company, Inc.; DeKalb Concrete; Erie Landmark Company; Florida Steel Corporation; Georgia Fountain Company, Inc.; H & A Steel Erectors; Harvest Corporation; Intrepid Enterprises, Inc.; Jones Stone Company, Inc.; M. D. Flatt, Inc.; Marcorp, Inc.; Nashville Painting; Neenah Foundry Company; Peterson Machinery; Professional Service; Scott Irrigation Systems; Sessions Paving Company; Shaw & Jones Masonry; Thomas Bros. Grass; Tri-State Concrete & Masonry, Inc.; Triple Steel, Inc.; Valley Crest Landscape, Inc.; Wolfe & Travis Electric Company

Capitol Hill Subcontractors

AAA Lawn Industries; ABG Caulking; American Tile, Inc.; B & E Irrigation; Explosives Engineering Services, Inc.; Florida Steel Corporation; H & A Steel Erectors; Marcorp, Inc.; Nashville Painting; Rio Grande Fence Company; Roy T. Goodwin; Sessions Paving Company; The Fountain People; Triple Steel, Inc.; Valdez Concrete Company; WASCO, Inc.; Wolfe & Travis

Ray Bell Construction Company, Inc.

Ray Bell, president; Bruce Nicely, project manager; Bill Akin, Robert Brame, Marshall Sullivan, Don Hassenrick, Enos Thurman, Vince Adams, Roger Dale Sutton, Ken Turner

Amphitheater Subcontractors

ABG Caulking Contractors, Inc.; Allinder Plumbing Company, Inc.; Alman Construction Company, Inc.; Alvin Krantz Painting Company, Inc.; Concrete Form Erectors, Inc.; Enco Materials, Inc.; Florida Steel Corporation; General Steel Construction Company; Greathouse Landscape Company, Inc.; Green Thumb Enterprises, Inc.; Hardware Services of Tennessee, Inc.; Hightech Signs; Liddle Brothers Contractors, Inc.; Meadow's Excavating and Landscaping Company; Metro Ready Mix Concrete; Professional Service Industries, Inc.; R. D. Herbert and Sons Company; Rio Grande Fence Company; Roy T. Goodwin Contractors, Inc.; Scott Irrigation Systems; Shaw and Jones Masonry, Inc.; Stansell Electric Company, Inc.; Tennessee Glass Company; TRC International Ltd.; Tri-State Concrete and Masonry, Inc.; Triple Steel, Inc.; Vulcan Materials; Waste Management of Tennessee

Railroad Bridges and Trestle Subcontractors

ABG Caulking Contractors, Inc.; Allinder Plumbing Company, Inc.; Alman Construction Company, Inc.; Commercial Painting, Inc.; Concrete Form Erectors, Inc.; Florida Steel Corporation; General Steel Construction Company; Goodwin & Wall Contractors, Inc.; Hardware Services of Tennessee; Howze Engineering & Surveying; Long Foundation Drilling Company; Masonry Arts, Inc.; Metro Ready Mix Concrete; Powell Construction Company; Professional Service Industries, Inc.; Queen City, Inc.; R. D. Herbert and Sons Company; Rio Grande Fence Company; Rogers Group; Roy T. Goodwin Contractors, Inc.; Sherman Dixie Concrete, Inc.; Stansell Electric Company, Inc.; Tennessee Glass Company; Tri-State Concrete and Masonry, Inc.; Trinity Industries, Inc.; Triple Steel, Inc.

Farmers' Market Subcontractors

A-1 Signs; ABG Caulking Contractors; Ace Energy Service, Inc.; Acoustical Concepts, Inc.; Allinder Plumbing Company, Inc.; Alman Construction Company, Inc.; Arrow Exterminators, Inc.; Artistic Ironworks, Inc.; Automated Framers of Hendersonville, Inc.; B & E Irrigation; Bolden Pipe Construction Company, Inc.; Concrete Form Erectors, Inc.; Crawford Door Sales of Nashville, Inc.; D. D. S. Painting; Florentine Tile and Terrazzo Company; Florida Steel Corporation; Gary Bridges Company; General Steel Construction Company; Green Thumb Enterprises, Inc.; H & H Associates, Inc.; Jim Johnson Landscaping; Joe Self Concrete Company; JWC Specialties; Leeds Architectural Letters, Inc.; Liddle Brothers Contractors, Inc.; Maynard Fixturecraft, Inc.; Mesa Interior Construction Company; Metro Flooring, Inc.; Metro Ready Mix Concrete; Milleken's Group, Inc.; Mitchell Plumbing, Inc.; Murphy Recreation, Inc.; Nashville Machine Company; Pan American Electric, Inc.; Professional Service Industries, Inc.; Roy T. Goodwin Contractors, Inc.; Section 10 International; Shaw and Jones Masonry, Inc.; Slayden-Harwell Door and Hardware Company; Tennessee Architectural Projects, Inc.; Tennessee Glass Company; Trinity Steel Corporation; Vulcan Materials

Heery International, Inc.

Dale Randels, area manager; Gary Follis, construction manager; Hassan Ahmad, cost analyst; Henry Anderson, cost analyst; Bob Wolf, scheduler

Alman Construction Company, Inc.

Morris Thurman, owner; Tom Hudgins, owner; Wayne Elkins, vice president; Rod Mayberry, vice president; Larry Tucker, superintendent

Mid-South Wrecking Company, Inc.

J. William Sauve, owner; Douglas Williams, project manager

Jones Brothers, Inc.

Larry Dickens, project manager; Ron Savage, superintendent; Dan Paul, foreman; Denny Scott, foreman

Rogers Group, Inc.

Cecil Cook, vice president; Jay Burke, construction manager; Terry Coggins, estimator; Greg Barrass, superintendent; Stan Maynard, foreman; Tommy Maynard, Jimmy Williams, Larry Kendall

RECOGNITION

"Gardens of XXI Century," presented at Thirty-third World Congress International Federation of Landscape Architects, Florence, Italy, 1996

"Award of Excellence," presented by American Institute of Architects, Tennessee Chapter, 1996

"Outstanding Engineering Project Award for 1996," presented by American Society of Civil Engineers Tennessee Section

"Award of Excellence," 1996 National Excellence in Construction Award, presented by Associated Builders and Contractors

"Honor Award," presented by American Society of Landscape Architects Tennessee Chapter, 1997

"Honor Award," Excellence in Development Awards Program, presented by Greater Nashville Regional Council, 1997

"Commissioners Award," presented by Historical Commission of Metropolitan Nashville and Davidson County, 1997

"Honor Award," presented by American Institute of Architects Gulf States Regional Awards Program, 1997

ABBREVIATIONS

The author is grateful to all those who provided material for the illustrations reproduced in this book. The following is a glossary of those individuals and organizations. All other photographs and drawings are by the author or Tuck Hinton Architects except as noted.

AAS	American Antiquarian Society
ABC	American Book Company
AG	Andy Gosselin
BG	Bill Goodman
BS	Brian Smallwood
BUL	Boston University Library
CA	The *Commercial Appeal*
CB	Craig Baird
CU	Cornell University
CW	Charles Warterfield Jr.
DD	Don Doyle
DF	Dennis Findley
DJ	David Johnson
DT	David Todd
EDAW	EDAW, Inc.
FG	Frank Gonzales
GCA	G.C.A. Publishing Co.
GCU	Ginn & Company Archives, Columbia University
GL	Gary Layda
GTB	George Thomas Bauer
H&D	Hodgson & Douglas

HGL	Harold G. Lowe Jr.
JB	John Bridges
JE	Jimmy Ellis
JL	James Lowen
KWC	Kiplinger Washington Collection
MDHA	Metropolitan Development and Housing Agency
ME	Michael Emrick
MHMA	McCarty-Holsaple-McCarty Architects
ML	Michael Lewis
MM	Marian Moffett
NB	*Nashville Banner*
NETA	Nathan-Evans-Taylor Architects
NHC	Nashville Historical Commission
NPL	Nashville Public Library
NPS	Nashville Photographic Services
PAP	Phoenix Aerial Photography
PCD	P. Casey Daley
RC	Robert Cameron
REH	Ron E. Harr
R/F	Ross/Fowler, PC
RH	Robin Hood
RHP	Rutledge Hill Press
RLH	Robert Lamb Hart Planners and Architects
RPH	Roy P. Harrover
SL	Slick Lawson
TB	Tony Beazley

TCP	Twin City Photography
TDEC	Tennessee Department of Environment and Conservation
TDOT	Tennessee Department of Transportation
TDTD	Tennessee Department of Tourism Development
TEH	T. Earl Hinton
TN	The *Tennessean*
TN200	Tennessee 200
TSLA	Tennessee State Library and Archives
TSM	Tennessee State Museum
TSPS	Tennessee State Photographic Services
UPAA	University of Pennsylvania Architectural Archives
USDI	United States Department of the Interior
USMA	United States Military Academy, West Point
USNA	United States National Archives
USPHA	United States Parks and History Association
UTCAP	University of Tennessee College of Architecture and Planning
VP	Van Pond
VSBA	Venturi, Scott Brown & Associates
WL	Westlight
WW	Walter Williams

223

BIBLIOGRAPHY

Adams, George Rollie, and Ralph Jerry Christian. *Nashville, A Pictorial History.* Norfolk: Donning Co., 1988.

Amick, H. C., and L. H. Rollins. *The Geography of Tennessee.* Boston: Ginn and Company, 1937.

Arnow, Harriett Simpson. *Seedtime on the Cumberland.* New York: The MacMillan Co., 1960.

Ayto, John. *Dictionary of Word Origins.* New York: Arcade Publishing, 1990.

Bartlett, Jennifer M., Charles P. Stripling, and Fred M. Prouty. "Historical and Archaeological Investigations of the Site of the Tennessee Bicentennial Mall." Tennessee Department of Environment and Conservation, Division of Archaeology, Nashville, 1995.

Bean, Cindy, ed. *A Capsule in Time, April 27, 1996.* Nashville: Tennessee 200, 1996.

Beasley, Kay. "Nashville Past," *Nashville Banner*, articles 1986–1994.

Brumbaugh, Thomas, Martha I. Strayhorn, and Gary G. Gore. *Architecture of Middle Tennessee.* Nashville: Vanderbilt University Press, 1974.

Cannon, Devereaux D. *Flags of Tennessee.* Gretna, La.: Pelican Publishing Co., 1990.

"Capitol Hill Redevelopment Project." Nashville Housing Authority, Nashville, 1952.

Compton's Pictured Encyclopedia 14, Chicago: F. E. Compton & Company, 1931.

Connelly, John Lawrence, ed. *North Nashville and Germantown.* Nashville: Ambrose Printing Co., 1982.

Crawford, Charles W. *Tennessee Land, History, and Government.* Austin: Steck-Vaughn Co., 1984.

Criswell, Grover C. Jr. *Confederate and Southern States Currency.* 4th ed. Port Clinton, Ohio: BNR Press, 1992.

Crutchfield, James A. *The Tennessee Almanac and Book of Facts, 1989–1990.* Nashville: Rutledge Hill Press, 1988.

Darnell, Riley. *Tennessee Blue Book, 1991–1994*, 1995.

Darnell, Riley. *Tennessee Blue Book, 1995–1996 Bicentennial Edition*, 1996.

Davis, Louise Littleton. *Nashville Tales.* Gretna, La.: Pelican Publishing Co., 1981.

Davis, Louise. "Refugee's Dream," *Nashville Tennessean Magazine*, July 17, 1949.

Dekle, Clayton B. "The Tennessee State Capitol," *Tennessee Historical Quarterly* 25, no. 3 (Fall 1966).

Dinsmoor, William Bell. *The Architecture of Ancient Greece.* New York: W. W. Norton & Co., 1975.

Doyle, Don. *Nashville in the New South.* Knoxville: University of Tennessee Press, 1985.

Dykeman, Wilma. *Tennessee: A History.* New York: W. W. Norton & Company, 1975.

Elston, Trish. "Edwin A. Keeble's Life & Casualty Tower," *Tennessee Architect*, Fall 1987.

Field, Elizabeth S. "Gideon Shryock" *Register of the Kentucky Historical Society* 50. Frankfort: Kentucky Historical Society, 1952.

Fletcher, Banister. *A History of Architecture.* New York: Charles Scribner's Sons, 1975.

Freidel, Frank, and Lonnelle Aikman. *George Washington, Man and Monument.* Washington, D.C.: Washington National Monument Association, 1973.

Gadski, Mary Ellen. "The Tennessee State Capitol: An Architectural History," *Tennessee Historical Quarterly* 47, no. 2 (Summer 1988).

Gilchrist, Agnes Addison. *William Strickland, Architect and Engineer.* Philadelphia: University of Pennsylvania Press, 1950 (reprint edition by DaCapo Press, New York, 1969).

Hamlin, Talbot. *Benjamin Henry Latrobe.* New York: Oxford University Press, 1955.

Hazlehurst, F. Hamilton. *Gardens of Illusion.* Nashville: Vanderbilt University Press, 1980.

Hodgson & Douglas Landscape Architects and Gresham, Smith and Partners. "Capitol Hill Master Plan," Nashville, 1986.

Hoobler, James. *Cities under the Gun.* Nashville: Rutledge Hill Press, 1986.

Horn, Stanley F. *The Hermitage, Home of Old Hickory.* Nashville: Ladies Hermitage Association, 1950.

"Independence Avenue & Constitution Avenue." Special Street Plans Phase I Study, National Capital Planning Commission, Washington, D.C., 1980.

Jackson, Joseph. *Development of American Architecture.* Philadelphia: David McKay, 1926.

Johnson, Leland R. *Engineers on the Twin Rivers.* Nashville: U.S. Army Engineer District, 1978.

Kreyling, Christine, Wesley Paine, Charles Warterfield Jr., and Susan Ford Wiltshire. *Classical Nashville.* Nashville: Vanderbilt University Press, 1996.

Lane, Mills. *Architecture of the Old South: Kentucky and Tennessee*. Savannah, Ga.: Beehive Press, 1993.

Lowry, Bates. *Building a National Image: Architectural Drawings for the American Democracy: 1789–1912*. Washington, D.C.: The National Building Museum, 1985.

Mathews, Robert C. H. IV. "North Nashville: A History of Urban Development." Master's thesis, University of North Carolina, 1976.

Mayernik and Rajkovich in Association with Hammel, Green and Abrahamison, Inc. "Project for the Completion of the Capitol Mall." Saint Paul, Minn., 1988.

McGee, Gentry R. *A History of Tennessee*. New York: American Book Company, 1899.

McRaven, Henry. *Nashville, Athens of the South*. Charleston: Tennessee Book Company by Scheer & Jervis, 1949.

Mendel, Mesick, Cohen, Waite and Hall Architects. "Tennessee State Capitol Historic Structure Report." State of Tennessee, Nashville, 1986.

"Minnesota State Capitol Mall: Minnesota's Front Yard." Partners of Livable Places and the Capitol Area Planning Board, 1990.

"Nashville: Conserving a Heritage." Historical Commission of Metropolitan Nashville, Davidson County, 1977.

Orr, Frank, Elbridge White, and Charles W. Warterfield Jr. "Notable Nashville Architecture 1930–1980." Middle Tennessee Chapter of American Institute of Architects, Nashville, 1989.

Parks, Joseph H., and Stanley J. Folmsbee. *The Story of Tennessee*. Oklahoma City: Harlow Publishing Corporation, 1952.

Patrick, James. *Architecture in Tennessee 1768–1897*. Knoxville: University of Tennessee Press, 1981.

Patrick, James. "The Capitol Commissioners' Competition, 1844–1845." *Tennessee Architect*, Winter, 1984.

"Pennsylvania Avenue." Report of the President's Council on Pennsylvania Avenue, 1964.

Reynolds, Ann. "Nashville's Parthenon as Symbol." Unpublished.

Robert, Charles E. *Nashville and Her Trade*. Nashville: F. L. Davies & Bros., 1870.

Rothrock, Mary U. *Discovering Tennessee*. Kingsport, Tenn.: Kingsport Press, 1951.

Simbeck, Rob. *Tennessee State Symbols*. Nashville: Altheus Press, 1995.

Smith, G. E. Kidder. *A Pictorial History of Architecture in America*. New York: American Heritage Publishing Co., Inc., 1976.

Stritch, Thomas. *The Catholic Church in Tennessee*. Nashville: The Catholic Center, 1987.

Summerville, James. *Southern Epic: Nashville through Two Hundred Years*. Gloucester Point, Va.: Hallmark Publishing Company, Inc., 1996.

Tennessee State Library and Archives, Map Collection.

Tennessee State Museum, Archives Collection.

Thacker, Christopher. *The History of Gardens*. Berkeley: University of California Press, 1979.

Tuck Hinton Architects, Ritchie Smith and Associates, Jon Coddington, David

Johnson, Charles Warterfield Jr., and SSOE, Inc. "State Capitol Area Master Plan: Analysis and Program Document." Nashville, 1992.

Tuck Hinton Architects, Ritchie Smith and Associates, Jon Coddington, David Johnson, Charles Warterfield Jr., and SSOE, Inc. "Tennessee Bicentennial Capitol Mall and State Capitol Master Plan." Nashville, 1993.

Tuck Hinton Architects; Ross/Fowler, PC, Landscape Architects; and SSOE, Inc. "Tennessee Bicentennial Capitol Mall Design Documents." Nashville, 1994.

Tuck Hinton Everton Architects; Hodgson & Douglas Landscape Architects; RTKL, Inc.; and others. "Subarea 9 and Center City Plan Update." Metropolitan Development and Housing Agency, Nashville, 1991.

Venturi, Robert. *Iconography and Electronics Upon A Generic Architecture*. Cambridge: The M.I.T. Press, 1996.

Venturi, Robert, and Denise Scott Brown. *A View from the Campidoglio*. New York: Harper & Row, 1984.

West, Carroll Van. *Tennessee's Historic Landscapes*. Knoxville: University of Tennessee Press, 1995.

White, Robert H. *Tennessee Old and New, Sesquicentennial Edition*. Collection of essays and papers published by Tennessee Historical Commission and Tennessee Historical Society, 1946.

Wiebenson, Dora. *Sources of Greek Revival Architecture*. London: Pennsylvania State University Press, 1969.

INDEX

231

234